DOING TEACHER-RESEARCH: FROM INQUIRY TO UNDERSTANDING

Donald Freeman
School for International Training

A TeacherSource Book

Donald Freeman
Series Editor

Heinle & Heinle Publishers

Pacific Grove • Albany • Bonn • Boston • Cincinnati • Detroit • London
Madrid • Melbourne • Mexico City • New York • Paris
San Francisco • Tokyo • Toronto • Washington

The publication of *Doing Teacher-Research: From Inquiry to Understanding*
was directed by members of the Newbury House ESL/EFL
Team at Heinle & Heinle:

Erik Gundersen, Editorial Director
Jonathan Boggs, Marketing Director
Kristin M. Thalheimer, Senior Production Services Coordinator
Thomas Healy, Developmental Editor
Stanley J. Galek, Vice President and Publisher/ESL

Also participating in the publication of this program were:

Designer: Jessica Robison
Project management and Composition: Imageset
Manufacturing Coordinator: Mary Beth Hennebury
Associate Market Development Director: Mary Sutton
Cover Designer: Ha D. Nguyen

Manufactured in Canada

p. 19 Illustrations used by permission of Glenn Bernhardt © 1996.

p. 93 Figure 5.2 From Teachers' Voices: Exploring Course Design in a Changing Cuuriculum.
Edited by Anne Burns and Susan Hood. Copyright © 1995. Used by permission of NCELTR.

pp. 219-223 'Downsizing: How it feels to be fired' by Steve Lohr, Shelly Kaplan, Tom Scott,
Nancy K. McGuire, Eugene Versluysen, Michael McGinn, Diana Erani, James C. Megas,
Phillip Ruby, and Mary Berne copyright © 1996, The New York Times. Used by permission.

pp. 172-174 Albert Shanker "Where We Stand: An Important Question" reprinted from
The New York Times. Copyright © The American Federation Of Teachers. Used by permission.

p. 225-252 case studies by Maree Nicholson, Margaret Surguy, Maria Vithoulkas,
Athena Frangos, Roger Kennett reprinted by kind permission of Languages In-Service Program
for Teachers (LIPT).

ISBN 0-8384-7900-6

10   9   8   7   6   5

TABLE OF CONTENTS

Thank You

The series editor, authors and publisher would like to thank the following individuals who offered many helpful insights throughout the development of the **TeacherSource** series.

Linda Lonon Blanton	University of New Orleans
Tommie Brasel	New Mexico School for the Deaf
Jill Burton	University of South Australia
Margaret B. Cassidy	Brattleboro Union High School, Vermont
Florence Decker	University of Texas at El Paso
Silvia G. Diaz	Dade County Public Schools, Florida
Margo Downey	Boston University
Alvino Fantini	School for International Training
Sandra Fradd	University of Miami
Jerry Gebhard	Indiana University of Pennsylvania
Fred Genesee	University of California at Davis
Stacy Gildenston	Colorado State University
Jeannette Gordon	Illinois Resource Center
Else Hamayan	Illinois Resource Center
Sarah Hudelson	Arizona State University
Joan Jamieson	Northern Arizona University
Elliot L. Judd	University of Illinois at Chicago
Donald N. Larson	Bethel College, Minnesota (Emeritus)
Numa Markee	University of Illinois at Urbana Champaign
Denise E. Murray	San Jose State University
Meredith Pike-Baky	University of California at Berkeley
Sara L. Sanders	Coastal Carolina University
Lilia Savova	Indiana University of Pennsylvania
Donna Sievers	Garden Grove Unified School District, California
Ruth Spack	Tufts University
Leo van Lier	Monterey Institute of International Studies

To Ann Freeman,
who has shown me that
teaching is about asking questions,
and that in asking questions,
you will learn.

ACKNOWLEDGMENTS

Over the past ten years, I have had the opportunity and the privilege to work with many teachers on the ideas and practices that have become the foundation of this book. My thinking has evolved through our conversations, largely due to the interest and intelligence of these colleagues around the world, from Slovakia, to South Africa, to Brazil, and the United States.

Two groups of teachers have been central to the genesis of this work. In Brazil, the participants and faculty of the Advanced Program for Teachers of English, sponsored in 1995 by Associação Alumni in São Paulo, took many of these ideas forward into their teaching and brought them back to our work together. There I met Wagner Veillard, who generously contributed his research from the program in Chapters 3 and 6. In the United States, I have had the great opportunity, over the past decade, to work on doing teacher-research with graduate teachers-in-training in the Masters of Arts in Teaching Program at the School for International Training. They have shaped my ideas in inestimable ways. To the six—Kristen Fryling, Ann Hoganson, J.D. Klemme, Clare Landers, David Mathes, and Kim Mortimer— excerpts of whose work appears here, many thanks. I also want to recognize the countless interactions and conversations with graduate students and my fellow faculty members that have shaped this book.

My thanks, too, to the friends, colleagues, and mentors who have contributed to the evolution of this book; to Thomas Healy and Erik Gundersen at Heinle and Heinle and to Jessica Robison and Mary Reed at ImageSet Design for helping so skillfully to bring the project to fruition. And, as always, my thanks to Emily, Laura, and Kathleen for putting up with me in the process.

SERIES PREFACE

As I was driving just south of White River Junction, the snow had started falling in earnest. The light was flat, although it was mid-morning, making it almost impossible to distinguish the highway in the gray-white swirling snow. I turned on the radio, partly as a distraction and partly to help me concentrate on the road ahead; the announcer was talking about the snow. "The state highway department advises motorists to use extreme caution and to drive with their headlights on to ensure maximum visibility." He went on, his tone shifting slightly, "Ray Burke, the state highway supervisor, just called to say that one of the plows almost hit a car just south of Exit 6 because the person driving hadn't turned on his lights. He really wants people to put their headlights on because it is very tough to see in this stuff." I checked, almost reflexively, to be sure that my headlights were on, as I drove into the churning snow.

How can information serve those who hear or read it in making sense of their own worlds? How can it enable them to reason about what they do and to take appropriate actions based on that reasoning? My experience with the radio in the snow storm illustrates two different ways of providing the same message: the need to use your headlights when you drive in heavy snow. The first offers dispassionate information; the second tells the same content in a personal, compelling story. The first disguises its point of view; the second explicitly grounds the general information in a particular time and place. Each means of giving information has its role, but I believe the second is ultimately more useful in helping people make sense of what they are doing. When I heard Ray Burke's story about the plow, I made sure my headlights were on.

In what is written about teaching, it is rare to find accounts in which the author's experience and point of view are central. A point of view is not simply an opinion; neither is it a whimsical or impressionistic claim. Rather, a point of view lays out what the author thinks and why; to borrow the phrase from writing teacher Natalie Goldberg, "it sets down the bones." The problem is that much of what is available in professional development in language-teacher education concentrates on telling rather than on point of view. The telling is prescriptive, like the radio announcer's first statement. It is emphasizes what is important to know and do, what is current in theory and research, and therefore what you—as a practicing teacher—should do. But this telling disguises the teller; it hides the point of view that can enable you to make sense of what is told.

The TeacherSource series offers you a point of view on second/foreign language teaching. Each author in this series has had to lay out what she or he believes is central to the topic, and how she or he has come to this understanding. So as a reader, you will find this book has a personality; it is not anonaymous. It comes as a story, not as a directive, and it is meant to create a relationship with you rather than assume your attention. As a practitioner, its point of view can help you in your own work by providing a sounding board for your ideas and a metric for your own thinking. It can suggest courses of action and explain why these make sense to the author. And you can take from it what you will, and do with it what you can. This book will not tell you what to think; it is meant to help you make sense of what you do.

The point of view in **TeacherSource** is built out of three strands: **Teachers' Voices, Frameworks,** and **Investigations.** Each author draws together these strands uniquely, as suits his or her topic and more crucially his or her point of view. All materials in TeacherSource have these three strands. The **Teachers' Voices** are practicing language teachers from various settings who tell about their experience of the topic. The **Frameworks** lay out what the author believes is important to know about his or her topic and its key concepts and issues. These fundamentals define the area of language teaching and learning about which she or he is writing. The **Investigations** are meant to engage you, the reader, in relating the topic to your own teaching, students, and classroom. They are activities which you can do alone or with colleagues, to reflect on teaching and learning and/or try out ideas in practice.

Each strand offers a point of view on the book's topic. The **Teachers' Voices** relate the points of view of various practitioners; the **Frameworks** establish the point of view of the professional community; and the **Investigations** invite you to develop your own point of view, through experience with reference to your setting. Together these strands should serve in making sense of the topic.

This book examines teacher-research as an activity that connects the 'doing' of teaching with the 'questioning' of research. I argue that these two ways of working can — and must — be united if teachers are to become fully recognized as contributors who shape educational policy and define effective classroom practice. In harmonizing the often contrapuntal and even discordant demands of getting the job of teaching done with seeking to better understand how and why learning in classrooms happens as it does, teachers will redefine the territory of their work.

The central notions which form the backbone of this argument originated in several places. Some years ago, at a local meeting of teacher-researchers, a colleague, Catherine Lacey, made the point that good teaching is not enough to recalibrate what counts as knowledge of practice in education. Her comments broke the shell of what I had assumed: namely, that doing a good job as a teacher would be enough to garner professional respect. Simultaneously, as I worked with teachers in different settings on how to do teacher-research, I began to see that, in fact, the practices of research could be adaptable to the demands of teaching. Finally, my own work in teachers' knowledge led me to issues of genre and form, and to thinking closely about how the facts and stories of teaching are usually and naturally told. The confluence of these influences, along with many others, have led to this book, to its presentation of how teacher-research can be done, and to the assertion that teacher-research has a fundamental role in redefining the knowledge-base of teaching.

This book, like all elements of the TeacherSource series, is intended to serve you in understanding your work as a language teacher. It may lead you to thinking about what you do in different ways and/or to taking specific actions in your teaching. Or it may do neither. But we intend, through the variety of points of view presented in this fashion, to offer you access to choices in teaching that you may not have thought of before and thus to help your teaching make more sense.

—Donald Freeman, Series Editor

1

STARTING ANEW

TWO SIDES OF TEACHING

When I started out teaching, doing research was the furthest thing from my mind. I was teaching French in a rural high school. As a first-year teacher my concerns centered on getting through the day, maintaining some semblance of order in my classes, gaining and keeping students' interest, and hopefully teaching them something. I don't think my experience is that different from those of many teachers. In fact, it is probably quite similar (Bullough, 1989). My first five years or so of teaching were pretty much consumed with getting the job done. Gradually, though, I gained a sense of balance and control, of efficiency in what I was doing in the classroom; I began to feel that I knew what I was doing and how to do it.

Several years ensued during which I moved from teaching French in a rural American high school to teaching English as a Foreign Language (EFL) to adults in Asia. Along the way I increased my skills, deepened my understanding of students and different learning environments, and became a more proficient teacher. In the process, the locus of my interests shifted. Because I now felt that I had the basics under control, I became less concerned with getting the job done and more interested in how I was teaching. Questions of method and curriculum became more engaging, while my interest in activities and technique per se waned (Genberg, 1992; Berliner, 1988). To draw an analogy: It was like riding a bicycle. Now that I knew how to balance, brake, and shift the gears smoothly, I became intrigued with how to speed up or slow down, how to navigate different road surfaces such as gravel or dirt, and even how to ride without my hands on the handlebars. With this proficiency, I became interested in where bicycle riding could take me.

But even as my dexterity in teaching increased—and with it my self-confidence as a teacher—my sense of certainty did not. Knowing *how* things work in the classroom is not the same as knowing that they *will* work. I continued to puzzle about why a familiar activity or exercise that had worked so well in the past did not work with a particular class, to speculate why one aspect of the language was difficult for students, or to ask myself why some students seemed to benefit from an activity while others did not. In fact, if I am honest, the list of these unresolved aspects of my work probably increased, rather than decreased, the more I taught. As a teacher I was caught between increasing my proficiency in the classroom and pondering this growing number of uncertainties. So I turned my attention to proficiency, to getting the job done.

Looking back, I realize I did so in large part because competence in teaching is usually defined in terms of action and activity, by doing the job, and not by speculating on the structure, efficacy, or outcomes of those actions. I found, as other teachers often do, that frankly there was little reward in asking questions about my work. I wasn't paid to speculate or to wonder; I was paid to teach. This emphasis on teaching as doing the job of managing students and delivering the content did not mean that the other side of teaching—the wondering and speculating, the doubting and having hunches, the puzzling and questioning—disappeared. Far from it. In my experience, this other side of teaching was simply held in abeyance; it was driven underground.

These two sides of teaching are the heart of this book. As the title indicates, I am writing about "teacher-research," which I see as the formal union of these two sides of teaching. I see the labels "teaching" and "researching" as tied to the inherent qualities of these processes and not to the individuals who perform them or their social positions. Thus the book is about 'doing teacher-research,' as the title says. "Doing" is about as basic as verbs get in English. It is a verb that is as prosaic and functional as it is ubiquitous and fundamental. All of these are qualities I want to associate with uniting these two sides of teaching. In the following chapters I will examine how these two often contradictory dimensions of teachers' work come together within a common perspective of disciplined inquiry. Like any union, however, the synergy is more than the respective parts. The activity of teaching—indeed the whole notion of the teacher's work—is changed when the process of research is introduced. Likewise, research and the researcher's work are changed when these functions are undertaken by teachers. Some of these changes are intimate, internal to the teacher, and small scale. Some are broader and more sociopolitical in nature. They are changes that can reposition teachers in relation to those in our society who are seen as creators of knowledge, managers of educational policy, and who direct the ways in which teachers do their jobs.

On the idea of doing, see Chapter 8, p. 180.

In my experience, these larger changes are neither easy nor benign. They can bring teachers in conflict with the ways in which others see their jobs. When I use the term "teacher" here and throughout the book, I refer to those individual adults whose livelihood is based on enabling others to learn specified subject matter in settings that are organized to that end (Pearson, 1989). Concretely, I mean people who are paid to teach particular content to other people, both children and adults, in organizational settings we call "classrooms." Classrooms, whether located in schools or in other organizations, are embedded in values and expectations that help to shape the teaching and learning that go on within them. I want to acknowledge the real pressures that these social contexts of teaching exert on the ways in which teachers' work is organized, how their time is spent, and what is valued and expected of them by administrators, parents, and the larger public community. In most educational systems around the world, and certainly in the United States, this social context does little to recognize or validate teachers who choose to speculate and, in the best sense, to wonder about their work. However, this status-quo can be changed.

On the social context of teachers' work, see Apple 1986 and Sizer 1983.

It is a short step, I believe, from reclaiming the ability to speculate, to puzzle, and to question your work as a teacher to establishing the fact of your expertise and authority for that work. Everyone has an opinion about teaching and schools, based in large part on the fact that they have been students (Lortie, 1975). In public discussions and debates, this social authority of experience can translate into the fact that everyone is an expert on teaching. In these discussions, what can and will distinguish a teacher's view as professional, in the best sense, from others in the school community and those of the public at large, is the fact that it is based not simply on experience but on an articulated, disciplined understanding of that experience. So in a larger sense, being or becoming a teacher-researcher is about repositioning yourself as a teacher in relation to what you are expected to do in your job. This repositioning hinges on articulating your knowledge and understanding of teaching and learning. Here again the terms are potentially confusing. Like separating the dancer from the dance, it is difficult and even counterproductive to separate the function of teaching from the individual who is doing it. For this reason, I use the words "teacher" and "teaching," and "researcher" and "research" or "researching," rather fluidly and often interchangeably. The arguments I make here refer to the processes and functions of teaching and researching; however, I will often do so through the names of people who carry out these functions.

This book is about uniting the two sides of teaching—the doing and the wondering—into one form of practice I am calling **"teacher-research."** The chapters that follow weave together the story of this unification with the skills and techniques for making it happen. The thread of the story of moving from teacher to teacher-researcher is told in Chapters 3 and 6 by a teacher and colleague, Wagner Veillard. His voice presents the larger canvas on which specific skills and techniques are sketched. Most of these skills and techniques derive from conventional social science and, in particular, from qualitative research in education. In entering the classroom they are reshaped by the demands of teaching. This refashioning is subtle but critical because it is what makes teacher-research doable. The techniques and skills for doing teacher-research are hung on a series of theoretical **frameworks** that serve as coathangers on which specific aspects of the work of teacher-research can be displayed and examined closely. As they accumulate, these frameworks provide an overall view of the relations among the various skills so that the cycle of teacher-research can be seen as an integral whole.

Interspersed throughout the text are **investigations,** which are tasks that will anchor what you are reading in your experience. Some of the tasks assume you have students with whom you are presently working as a teacher or intern; others can be done by reflecting on your own experiences as a person, learner, and teacher. The investigations are meant to take you beyond the book into your own thinking and practices as a teacher. They will help you to try out and master particular research skills as well as examine this larger notion of repositioning your work as a teacher from doing to wondering. This is the overall aim of the book: To help you to examine what you do as a teacher, how your work is structured and how you carry it out on a daily basis, why some things you do work or don't work for the learners you teach, and how in large and small ways the work can be done differently and/or better. This aim sits within the larger frame of implications of what it means to reintroduce speculation, puzzlement, and wondering into teaching and to strengthen the intimate connection between these qualities and doing the job.

The structure of the book

See The teacher-research cycle, Chapter 2, p. 33.

The Larger Frame of Implications: Five Propositions about Teacher-Research

For work on positionality, see Fine (1994).

Like any set of values, and the skills that are used to implement them, the thinking and skills of teacher-research spring from a certain point of view. To set the stage for the specifics of the teacher-research process, I want to outline this theoretical terrain in which teaching and research can be united. This larger framework provides a rationale for repositioning the work of the teacher; making it explicit serves a number of purposes. Most immediately this discussion can orient you as the reader to the arguments I will make in this book. I am putting my cards on the table so you can know what to expect; you can learn what I value and what I assume or take for granted. It is a bit like knowing the kind of restaurant you are in so you know what to expect on the menu. More generally, however, I want to make explicit my point of view because I believe that any research and the understandings and statements of facts or findings that result from it serve larger purposes or ends. Research is never neutral; it is not simply a matter of investigating the world and finding what is "true" about it. Rather, it always involves elements of valuing, of assuming certain things and discounting others. By making explicit the assumptions from which I depart, I intend to own the starting point of my argument. Thus you can know what to expect from me as the writer and why to expect it. You can position my arguments within what you believe, and you can act accordingly on the ideas I provide.

On validity in research, see Chapter 7, p. 164.

1.1 *How Do You define "Research"?*

Before you read further, I suggest that you do the following Investigation. The aim is to explore your own thinking and assumptions about research.

Responding . . .

Work by yourself without consulting others. Using index cards or paper to write on, respond to each of the following questions using the prompt. Don't limit yourself; write as many answers as come to mind. The aim is to exhaust your thinking, not to fashion a well-crafted response. Write each answer on a separate card or slip of paper.

- How do you react to the word "research"?
  "When I hear/see the word *research*, I . . ."

- How would you define the word "research"?
  "To me, research means . . ."

Analyzing . . .

After you have completed your responses to the questions, use one of the following procedures to analyze what you have written:

If you are working alone: Set your responses aside and come back to them after you have read the next section on the Five Propositions (pp. 5–16).

If you are working with others: Arrange your responses on a surface where everyone can see them easily. Use a table or the floor if there are a lot of responses. Take one question at a time. Read through all the responses silently. As you read, look for common elements or patterns in what people have written. Also look for "outliers;" these are single or distinctive responses that "lie outside" the common patterns found in the rest of the responses.

When everyone has read the responses, discuss the patterns and outliers you see. You may want to list what you find. Ask yourselves, "Where does the particular pattern come from? Why do we think/believe it? What is its basis in our collective experience?"

Then stand back again from the patterns themselves and look for themes among them. Look at how the outliers may also connect to these same themes.

This process is called "grounded analysis;" it is discussed more fully in Chapter 5, p. 101.

What you have just done in this Investigation is to begin to articulate your individual point of view on what research is before you read mine. By comparing your ideas to those of your peers (if you did so) and to my point of view as you read what follows, you should be able to sharpen your beliefs.

FIVE PROPOSITIONS ABOUT TEACHER-RESEARCH

The following five propositions build a cumulative theoretical position on what teacher-research is and how it can reshape the work of teachers and the knowledge-base of teaching. I call the statements "propositions" for two reasons. First, they provide the foundation in a logical sense of my thinking about teacher-research. Second, they contain the elements of the theory on which this approach to melding the work of the teacher and that of the researcher is based. They are propositions, however, because they are open to argument in the best sense. They outline my thinking, but they must be tested against your experience and beliefs as you read and do what follows.

Proposition 1: To truly make research a central part of teaching, we must redefine research.

Teacher-research is the story of two nouns joined by a hyphen; being a teacher-researcher means working at that hyphen (Fine, 1996). As nouns, the two words may seem somewhat asymmetrical, even logically unequal, parts of a new, composite whole. The "teacher" is a person and "research" is a process. Putting the two together with a hyphen does several things: It creates a person-process, which suggests the agency of the teacher who takes on a process—research—that is different from teaching. Thus in teacher-research, the doer and the doing combine to mutually redefine one another. The hyphen also emphasizes both the connection and the difference between the two elements in this new equation. The connection speaks to the potential; teacher-research means teachers researching teaching. But the hyphen also calls attention to the differences and

Working at
the hyphen
(Fine, 1996)

possible distance between two separate and separable professional roles and processes: One can teach or one can research. To be and do both is to unite roles by undertaking two processes, teaching and researching, that have conventionally been separated and seen as distinct. Thus some writers will talk about teacher-research as "blurring roles" (Boles, 1996) or "spanning boundaries" (Fine, 1996).

While the boundaries between them have begun to blur in some settings, the distinction in territory continues to be part of most teachers' and researchers' experience as well as their perspectives on what they do. This separation between teaching and researching is based on a view that the two communities have very different aims. In the field of education, research is supposed to generate knowledge, while teachers are supposed to implement it. Numerous elements in the social contexts of teaching and research contribute to this assumption. Researchers receive one specialized form of training and teachers receive another. Full-time researchers usually work in one setting while full-time teachers work in another. Researchers contribute to the understanding and knowledge of a professional community, while teachers have a community that is based in large measure on activity, defined by their subject matters, the grade levels or the school settings in which they teach. To generate knowledge that transcends settings it is often assumed, perhaps erroneously, that a researcher can enter a classroom without ever teaching or having taught, can understand what is happening in that environment, can gather information about it, and can understand what goes on there, while the teacher who works in that classroom day-in-and-day-out does not have ready access to the same level of information, nor can he or she articulate the same type of knowledge and understanding.

Issues of time and autonomy shape these respective roles of teacher and researcher in critical ways. Time is an acknowledged central feature of teachers' lives. In their book *Inside/Outside: Teacher Research and Knowledge*, on teacher-research in the Philadelphia public-school system through Project START (Student Teachers as Researching Teachers), Marilyn Cochran-Smith and Susan Lytle (1993) write:

> Time is one of the most critical factors in the formation and maintenance of learning communities for teacher research. Unlike other professions which are organized to support research activities, teaching is a profession in which it is extraordinarily difficult to find enough time to collect data and it is almost impossible to find time to reflect, reread, or share with colleagues. (p. 91)

Like increasing numbers of professionals who practice for the public good, such as social workers, general practitioners, or family doctors, teachers for the most part do not control their own professional schedules in the same ways that researchers, who are often employed by colleges and universities, do. Nor do teachers usually have the same degree of professional autonomy in directing their work. In the case of teaching, it is usually other people who set the curriculum, select the materials, place the students, decide how the job is to be done, and then evaluate it. Most researchers have far greater control over what they do and how they do it than do their colleagues who are teachers. While this is partly a function of the intensification of work in our society generally (Apple,

1986), it seems to be particularly true in education as teachers' work includes a wider and wider range of responsibilities beyond actual classroom teaching.

Ultimately the two roles diverge in their goals. As I have argued, teaching is generally concerned with doing things so others learn. Research is concerned with asking questions, examining phenomena, and documenting understandings for why things happen as they do. It is possible, of course, to overemphasize the divergence between teaching and researching. Indeed, there are people who successfully combine both processes in one professional role. However, it is fair to say that the tide of expectation and the social contexts of work generally run against such integration of roles. This is unfortunate because, although they may differ in terms of the means they employ to do their work and even the ends they aim to achieve, the teacher and the researcher can share the common focus of understanding teaching, learning, and learners within the organized settings of classrooms and schools. James Baumann, a university researcher who returned for a year to teach elementary school, describes the distinction in roles in terms of his "emerging philosophy of teacher research." Baumann (1996) outlines his philosophy in terms of two ethical principles: "the primacy of teaching and students, and the pragmatic constraints of classroom inquiry" which he describes as follows:

On roles and purpose in teacher-research, see Wong (1995) Wilson (1995) and Baumann (1996).

> 1. the primacy of teaching and students . . . means that research can never interfere with or detract from a teacher's primary responsibility to help students learn and grow;

> 2. the pragmatic constraints of classroom inquiry . . . mean that the work demands and realities of full-time teaching affect decisions about the course of classroom inquiry. (p. 30)

Baumann's principles describe the friction inherent in combining the two roles. He is alert to the fact that there are things that one does as a teacher that may shape or even preclude one's role as a researcher, and ethically the *teacher* in teacher-research must take precedence. Certainly, as they contribute to learning, teacher-research efforts will always be ethically valid. However, the ways in which research is carried out in classrooms by teachers will be shaped by their basic responsibility to learners.

It is important also to see beyond this friction to where teaching and researching converge. At their most fundamental, both teaching and researching are concerned with processes of knowing and establishing knowledge. For teachers, these processes focus on the learning of students; the knowledge established in classroom teaching is what the students learn through the teaching-learning process. For teacher-researchers, the processes concentrate on understanding what is going on in classroom teaching and learning, and the knowledge established reflects those understandings. To put the connection simply: Teaching seeks knowledge in students as its end; researching seeks knowledge of teaching-learning processes as a means toward that end.

Taken together, these differences in training, time, autonomy, and goals have tended to distinguish—indeed separate—teaching from researching. They have emphasized the roles of teacher and researcher, and the people who hold those roles, over the processes in which they engage and what those processes may have in common. Working at the hyphen brings together the two activities to emphasize their common focus. However, it also reshapes both activities. For teachers to do research, research must be redefined to make it sensibly and actively a part of teaching. This entails addressing the factors of time and autonomy in the social context of work that shape teachers' professional lives, even as we reconsider our basic definitions of "research." This task of finding the common core is one that teacher-researchers are uniquely positioned to undertake.

Proposition 2: Research can be defined as an orientation toward one's practice. It is a questioning attitude toward the world, leading to inquiry conducted within a disciplined framework.

Like any professional domain, research, like teaching, depends on terminology to define the terrain. This terminology creates a map that highlights certain features of the activity and, of course, also downplays others. This proposition introduces three key words, **orientation, inquiry,** and **discipline,** on which the conception of teacher-research in this book is built. To take the last word first, educator Lee Shulman describes research as drawing on two interrelated meanings of the word "discipline" (Shulman, 1988): **discipline** as a methodical practical undertaking and **discipline** as a field of study. The first, and perhaps more common, meaning of "disciplined framework" captures this idea of a methodical approach to doing things that can be scrutinized and, if need be, repeated by others. This meaning of "discipline" is concerned with how the investigator approaches the question or phenomenon he or she wants to study. Cronbach and Suppes (1969) outline this meaning of discipline in this way:

> Whatever the character of a study, if it is **disciplined** the investigator . . . institutes control at each step of information collection and reasoning to avoid sources of error. . . . If errors cannot be eliminated he [or she] takes them into account by discussing the margin of error in his [or her] conclusions. Thus, the report of a disciplined inquiry has a texture that displays the raw materials entering the argument and the logical processes by which they are compressed and rearranged to make the conclusion credible. (pp. 15–16)

The central notion here is that being disciplined involves both how one examines something and how one reports or makes public what one has found through the investigation. If I tell you that the students in my reading class do not like a certain book, that claim alone is not a disciplined statement. It is an assertion based, perhaps, on my experience and their feedback. But you don't know *how* I know it. If, on the other hand, I tell you that I had the students list the five books they liked best among those we had read in the previous term, and that this particular book was only listed by four out of thirty students, and when it did come up it was listed in fourth or fifth place, I have made a disciplined statement. This second statement is disciplined by the above criteria because it tells you not only *what* I found—that only four out of thirty students report liking the title—but also *how* I found it. So should you wish to repeat— or replicate—the procedure that generated this information, you could do so. As Shulman (1988, p. 5) puts it: "What is important about disciplined inquiry is that its data, arguments, and reasoning be capable of withstanding careful scrutiny by another member of the scientific community." This, then, is Shulman's first meaning of the term "disciplined," that the investigation reflects both *what* is known and *how* it came to be known, and further that the latter may permit others to replicate the *how* in order to verify the *what*.

1.2 MAKING DISCIPLINED STATEMENTS

This Investigation examines what it means to make disciplined—as opposed to intuitive—statements about teaching.

> Think about a class or lesson in which you have recently partici-pated. It may be a class that you taught or it may be one in which you have been a student. Think about something that you know to be true of that class. Write it down as a statement. Write down how you know this statement and on what basis you make it.
>
> Now, using the same statement, outline how someone else could investigate it. What could he or she do to find out whether the state-ment is the case? Draft a set of instructions for how that person could investigate the statement. The instructions can be in the for-mat: First, . . . second, . . . then . . . etc.

Shulman uses the words "scientific community" to link to the second mean-ing of a discipline as a field of study. This is the meaning we refer to when we talk about the academic disciplines of mathematics, philosophy, or linguistics, for example. Here Shulman (1988) connects the two meanings:

> Disciplined inquiry not only refers to *the order, regular, or principled nature of investigation*, it also refers to *the disciplines themselves which serve as the sources for the principles of regularity and canons of evi-dence employed by the investigator.* What distinguishes disciplines from one another is the manner in which they formulate their ques-tions, how they define the content of their domains and organize that content conceptually, and the principles of discovery and verification that constitute the ground rules for creating and testing knowledge in their fields. (emphasis added) (p. 5)

Each discipline has its community, the group of practitioners who accept the rules of its game. What makes a person a chemist or a literary critic is the fact that he or she plays by the rules—which Shulman calls "the principles of regu-larity and canons of evidence"—of the community such that his or her ideas fit within the discipline of that field of inquiry. These paradigms, which Shulman refers to as "principles of regularity and canons of evidence," and I call the rules of the game of particular disciplines, are not static. They, too, shift with time, according to dominant meanings and values.

On different research paradigms, see Neuman (1991); also McLaughlin and Tierney (1993).

In this sense, then, chemistry is basically true for chemists and those who accept the rules of chemistry as a discipline. Disciplines and their communities are closed but permeable systems; you have to believe in their "ground rules for creating and testing knowledge" in order to belong, and by learning to believe

This relates to the discussion of genre; see Chapter 7, p. 150.

you come to belong. The circle works in both directions, however. When you play by the rules of the disciplinary community, you are seen as belonging to that community and you can critique and be critiqued according to its rules. So acting like a member can get you into the community and thinking like a member can help you remain part of it. This takes us back to the two sides of teaching: as doing and as wondering. Are the rules of the community of teaching defined primarily by action and by what members can do? Or are they defined by how members think about what they do—how they puzzle, speculate, and question the actions in which they are engaged and the outcomes of those actions? When you hear a statement such as, "She is a great grammar teacher" or "He works really well with teenagers," is the evidence for these statements based primarily on activity and what these teachers do, or is it found in their approach to their work?

While the dichotomy is, to some degree, overdrawn, it is not entirely a false one. The problem is that teaching is not a discipline. It does not have unified or commonly held "ground rules for creating and testing knowledge," to use Shulman's phrase. In fact, when we speak of people "teaching a discipline" such as math or biology, we are separating the knowledge or content from the activity or the teaching. These traces of activity that teachers accumulate through the doing of teaching are not seen as knowledge; they are referred to as experience. Experience is the only real reference point teachers share: experiences as students that influence their views of teaching, experiences in professional preparation, experience as members of society. This motley and diverse base of experience unites people who teach, but it does not constitute a disciplinary community. Shulman (1988,) argues that education is not a discipline but a field of study, which he defines as "a locus containing phenomena, events, institutions, problems, persons, and processes, which themselves constitute the raw materials for inquiries of many kinds." (p. 5) When researched, education in general and teaching in particular is examined through the lenses of multiple disciplines. When applied to education, these disciplines are themselves modified by the objects of their investigations. Thus we have *educational* psychology, sociology of *education, educational* statistics, and so on. These modifying terms highlight the fact that the discipline is somehow transformed when it is applied to classrooms, schools, teaching, and learning.

Proposition 3: There is, as yet, no publicly recognized "discipline" of teaching. Teachers do not think of themselves as producing knowledge; they think of themselves as using it.

On implementation of policy see Lipsky (1980); on curriculum see Grossman (1990) and Graves (1996).

Teachers are seen—and principally see themselves—as consumers rather than producers of knowledge. Other people write curricula, develop teaching methodologies, create published materials, and make policies and procedures about education that teachers are called upon to implement. But the knowledge always changes in the implementation. When you cook from a recipe, the food you produce is always unique in some way. When teachers use exercises from a textbook, they transform each activity from something that exists in a limbo outside of time and place into the concrete messiness of their classrooms and students. The pristine organization of curriculum, materials, or policies in their received forms is always redefined in smaller or larger ways as these things are enacted in the time and place of particular classrooms by particular people. This fact is not subversive; it is simply true because teaching and learning are human activities. People teach people who are learning, which creates a human environment in which the abstractions of curriculum, materials, and pedagogy are transformed into actual practice. As Earl Stevick (1980) put it, teaching and learning are concerned with "what goes inside and between people." (pp. 4–5)

In the human environments of schools and classrooms, teachers are isolated from one another. As educational sociologist Dan Lortie (1975) said, schools are like "egg crates" in which individual teachers work largely in isolation within their separate rooms with different groups of students, like eggs in the separate sections of their carton (pp. 13–17). Given this structural isolation, it is hardly surprising that a disciplinary community of teaching has not arisen. The knowledge or wisdom of practice that could make up a discipline of teaching resides in individual teachers; it is not shared, exchanged, or communicated as in other disciplines. Teachers learn to talk about what they do, about the techniques and materials they use, about how students are doing, about local school politics, and so on. These conversations center on doing; they refer to information about teaching and learning as embedded in local circumstances and personal experience.

Because teachers' conversations are grounded in local circumstances and experience, they tend to be highly individual and thus do not build a larger shared realm of inquiry. Professional interaction among teachers is usually highly procedural; it tends to focus on classroom issues, students, conditions of work, and so on. On the whole, teachers do not talk about information in terms of principles of regularity or canons of evidence, as other disciplinary communities do. This becomes a major barrier to the creation of a "discipline of teaching." When people hold isolated personal conversations about individual experiences and particular teaching circumstances, they do not build a larger discipline or a professional community to support it. To do so requires a shift of focus. There needs to be an alternative strategy that will build a set of shared assumptions about what constitutes the understandings on which teaching is based. In its political sense, the activity of teacher-research is this alternative strategy. Teacher-research makes public these private conversations and individual intuitions, grounding them in the local circumstances and personal experience of teaching on the one hand, and in the disciplined procedures of inquiry on the other. Thus in a very real sense teacher-research is about the creation of a professional disciplinary community.

There is an instructive parallel to be drawn here with the early days of what we now know as experimental research. Experimental research is the form of inquiry that we usually associate with conventional definitions of science and the production of knowledge. Its assumptions and procedures are at the base of common notions of scientific method: of proving or disproving hypotheses, of research design, of objectively verifiable findings, of validity and generalizability, and so on. However, experimental research has not always been a so-called "solid science." In fact, a disciplinary community of scientific practice had to be created to sponsor and defend this type of work and its approach to knowledge. The process happened in the 1700s, when the British Royal Academy of Sciences

On validity, see Chapter 7, p. 164.

established itself. Charles Bazerman, a teacher and historian of writing, has studied the early written records, or "proceedings," of the Royal Academy to see how what we now take for granted as the "objective nature of science" took hold. Bazerman sees scientific writing as a key to understanding the establishment of science in the public mind, and he wondered how its distinctive genre became established as the norm of communication for the scientific community. In reviewing the records of the first 150 years of meetings of the Royal Academy, Bazerman (1988) noted that the nature of what this community considered to be "science" changed rather dramatically:

On genre, see Chapter 7, p. 150

> Those reported events identified as experiments change in character over the period from 1665–1800. The *definition of experiment moves from any made or done thing, to an intentional investigation, to a test of a theory, to finally a proof of, or evidence for, a claim.* The early definitions seemed to include any disturbance or manipulation of nature, not necessarily focused on demonstration of any preexisting belief, nor even with the intention of discovery. With time, experiments are represented as more clearly investigative, corroborative, and argumentative. (emphasis added) (pp. 65–66)

Thus it seems that experimental science got its start in the same ways that the discipline of teaching might. Experimental science began by simply doing things or, as Bazerman puts it, by "any disturbance or manipulation of nature, not necessarily focused on demonstration of any pre-existing belief, nor even with the intention of discovery." Over a century and a half this definition was refined and made more disciplined. From an experiment as "any made or done thing," the definition evolved through three phases: "an intentional investigation, . . . a test of a theory, . . . a proof of, or evidence for, a claim." Through this process of evolving a definition, the disciplinary community of experimental science was formed. To be a scientist and a member of that community, one had to play by its rules. These rules defined, as Shulman said, the "principles of regularity or canons of evidence" by which the community continues to operate to this day. They defined the procedures that would generate "scientific" knowledge, a definition that was not static but evolving. I wonder if teaching itself may well be in the process of evolving rules of its own game, in the larger sense that Bazerman talks about. Committing to a teacher-research perspective is part of that public repositioning of teaching as it becomes an independent disciplinary community.

If you think about most of our professional meetings in language teaching— or indeed in other types of classroom teaching—they generally show a wide variety of what is valued and worth knowing about teaching. In the best sense, these gatherings of teachers represent a pluralism in both ways of knowing and forms of knowledge. Like the early proceedings of the British Royal Academy, the program books lack the standardization of other disciplines, where the forms of knowledge are much more clearly delineated. I think the multiplicity is due to the fact that there is not yet an established, generally recognized, and accepted form of teaching knowledge. In its absence—perhaps until it develops—we see a variety of accounts that range from demonstrations of techniques, activities, or technologies to discussions of teaching issues and problems, to presentations of individual ways of doing things in the classroom, and so on.

Such multiplicity might be fine, were it not for the fact that teaching is such a central social enterprise and therefore many people outside the classroom try to define what teaching should or shouldn't be. In other words, as teachers we are naive if we think we are somehow insulated from these attempts to define what is important and worth knowing in teaching.

This is the central point in this proposition. Thus far, teachers have left it to others to define the knowledge that forms the official basis of teaching. If they are interested in contributing to that type of knowledge, teachers have generally been asked to change the ways of doing and thinking that serve them as teachers in order to become researchers and to do research. Thus the teacher's interest or concern must be tailored to a question to fit an existing discipline and the rules of its game. In language teaching the so-called "parent" disciplines of psychology and linguistics; their offspring such as second language acquisition research, curriculum development, and teaching methodologies; and the related fields in educational research have shaped the questions asked about language teaching (Stern 1983). These, therefore, have shaped what was thought to be researchable in classrooms, whether by teachers or by researchers; in the broadest sense, these disciplines of psychology and linguistics have circumscribed the questions that are asked about classroom language teaching and learning and the types of data acceptable in response. These disciplinary communities have created the norms and the discourse of research into which teachers have had to fit if they wanted to be recognized in the study of their own practice (Freeman, 1994; van Lier, 1994). Recognition comes at a price; it shapes the concerns that can be pursued and the findings that are accepted.

The alternative is to build an autonomous professional community of teaching to host its own questions and determine, as Shulman phrased it, its own "principles of discovery and verification that constitute the ground rules for creating and testing knowledge." This is the direction that teacher-research represents. In moving from interests and questions that are completely embedded in local circumstances and experience to a larger disciplinary framework of teaching, teacher-research is defining its own territory. Teachers are creating, in their own terms, a new and viable community around the ideas and issues of teaching that are central to their work. At its core, this is a question of power and participation because it means separating from the disciplinary communities that have hosted educational research thus far, and defining new relationships with them. However, it is worth noting that the process has historical roots. It may be little different than the building of a professional community for experimental research through the Royal Academy that Bazerman describes.

1.3 *WHAT DOES THE WORD "SCIENTIFIC" MEAN TO YOU?*

In this Investigation, you gather information about the usual meanings of the word "scientific." The aim is to uncover the deeper ideology that gives power to the term and shapes our use of it.

> If someone says to you "But that isn't *scientific* . . ." what does he or she mean? Where do *your* ideas about what is or isn't scientific come from?

Interview a couple of friends or colleagues. Ask them the same questions and note their responses. It is also interesting to ask these questions of children at various ages, as well as of adults from different backgrounds.

Proposition 4: Inquiry—and not procedure—is the basis of teacher-research.

I believe that to some degree teachers are victims of conventional ideas of science. There is a feeling that systematic procedure, the first meaning of discipline, holds the key to research and being a researcher. However, this leaves the second meaning of discipline, which is larger and ultimately more pervasive and powerful, unchallenged. For teachers, focusing on procedure and not considering the professional disciplinary community that gives meaning and value to that procedure is a risky and disempowering proposition. It can trap teachers in the ways in which their work is conventionally defined and valued. Teachers are not, as I said at the beginning of this chapter, paid to ask questions about what they do; they are paid to *do*. The professional community that hosts their work is founded on the idea of action; it values doing, not asking questions. Therefore, the work is not seen to include building knowledge and understanding about how teaching is done. Simply put, teachers are paid to get students to learn; their job is to teach effectively. They are not paid to understand, document, and generate public knowledge about how students learn and how best to teach them. Out of this basic contradiction arises the imperative of working at the hyphen, of teachers learning to research their teaching and learning with their students in the classroom.

On inquiry, see Chapter 2, p. 34.

Teacher-research redefines these parameters of teachers' work. When teachers start to puzzle about what, how, and why they do as they do and to ask questions and speculate about alternatives, they incorporate the element of inquiry into their work. Inquiry is a state of being engaged in what is going on in the classroom that drives one to better understand what is happening—and can happen—there. This orientation is antithetical to most of the ways in which teachers' work is currently defined, valued, and organized (Freedman, Jackson, and Boles, 1983). In medicine, physics, law, or architecture, for example, being a professional entails being able to apply what is known in the discipline to address new and previously undefined phenomena, contexts, and situations. Practitioners in these fields learn to puzzle and speculate about what lies outside the realm of the known (Schon, 1983). As professionals, they are valued for their abilities to inquire and to apply the known to the new, novel, or unknown. In teaching the process is reversed: Teachers are valued as professionals when they know what to do. In classrooms, teachers usually have to deal with the new, novel, or unknown without adequate time, support, or preparation to investigate it. They often have to act on the unknown in terms of what they do know, so that experience plays a key role in shaping action. The child who is a "slow" reader is dealt with in part based on the teacher's experience with other such learners. Speculating on why that child reads as he does is less a part of the job than getting him to "perform at grade level." As action is rewarded, the psychological space for puzzlement and questioning is diminished.

Teacher-research comes about when teachers start to define inquiry as a routine and expected function of their working lives in classrooms. Doing so, however, means rethinking and restructuring the social organization of teaching and schools. The so-called "egg crate profession" (Lortie, 1975) is not organized to support inquiry or to foster disciplinary communities of teaching among practitioners in schools. So the process of engaging in teacher-research is also a process of changing both the ways in which schools work and what is expected of, and valued in, what teachers do. It is an important step in transforming education from a practice of implementation to a practice devoted to understanding learning.

Proposition 5: Creating a discipline of teaching requires making public one's findings. To do so teacher-researchers need to explore new and different ways of telling what has been learned through their inquiries.

Transforming education and the way in which teaching is viewed involves the wider public sphere. When the inquiries and results of teacher-research remain private, they have little impact on the public domain of teaching or on the ideas or practices of others. Preaching to the choir has little effect on nonbelievers. Creating a discipline of teaching requires public sharing and testing of ideas. It requires, as mentioned in Proposition 2, the ability to present and argue for the results and how they have been arrived at. Public expression of findings is critical; however, it can also be problematic. When teacher-researchers adopt existing ways of making public their ideas and findings, using the current language and genres of scientific debate, for example, they do two things. On the one hand they gain some access to the prestige and power that these forms of talking and writing have in society. Teacher-researchers can be taken seriously if they sound like other researchers. On the other hand, by using these forms of expression teacher-researchers conform to existing canons and disciplines and thus do not develop their own.

1.4 *THE LANGUAGE OF SCIENCE*

This Investigation examines the language we accept as sounding scientific. What are the words or constructions that trigger the sense that we are reading or listening to a scientific account?

> Imagine you are reading a scientific article or listening to someone present a scientific paper. Jot down some of the phrases you would expect to read or hear.

> Interview a couple of friends or colleagues. Ask them to do same activity and note their responses. It is interesting to perform this Investigation with children at various ages.

The power of existing ways of writing and talking scientifically should not be underestimated. Charles Bazerman, a teacher of writing, argues (1988) that "scientific language serves to establish and maintain the authority of science. . . By establishing the special and elevated character of science, scientific communications accrete power to the scientific community" (p. 294). The problem is we tend to forget that so-called scientific ways of writing and talking are first and foremost human: People create them and people give them value. Analyzing the use of language structures like the agentless passive voice ("Studies have shown . . .") and the impersonal third person ("Subjects completed three tasks . . .") common in scientific writing, Bazerman (1988) continues:

> These [language] formulations are a human construction and thus are heir to all the limitations of humanity. [*They*] *do all the social work of being human with no overt means of doing the empirical work which has been considered the work of science.* The appearance of reality projected in scientific texts is itself a social construction. (emphasis added) (pp. 294–295)

On genre, see Chapter 7, p. 150.

Bazerman's observations about scientific writing are certainly true about language more generally. Genres, or language forms that have socially recognized meanings and values, are based on and carry with them social assumptions about and ways of viewing and acting in the world. For teacher-researchers to talk and write like researchers gives them access to research communities; it also constrains them to the issues and ways of thinking that are valued and meaningful to those communities. Therefore, to see teaching in new ways, teacher-researchers will need to create new forms of expression. New understandings will need and compel new forms of expression, new genres, and new forms of public conversation about teaching. There are numerous and emerging examples of this process, as we will see in Chapter 7.

There will, no doubt, continue to be a role for conventional scientific genres in teacher-research. Perhaps the aim should ultimately be one of bilingualism, with teacher-researchers as comfortable in their own language and ways of displaying their understandings as they are in the languages of other disciplinary communities. However, because the language of teacher-research is currently so shrouded by lack of public recognition and thus undervalued, this new genre needs to be explored. Our first job, therefore, must be to discover and strengthen the indigenous ways of telling what teachers come to know about teaching and learning through inquiring into their work as teachers. It is from this position of some strength that teacher-researchers can build an independent disciplinary community that captures what they are capable of seeing (Freeman, 1996). Simply put, my argument is that to tell a different story, we will need different words.

STARTING ANEW

Through these five propositions, I have presented a case that teacher-research can fit into and reshape the larger social sphere of teaching and teachers' work. I have thus positioned myself in relation to the ideas that follow in subsequent chapters about what teacher-research is and ways in which to undertake it. I have begun with this larger argument because I don't believe that you as readers can engage with my ideas and the procedures I present without recognizing that they are animated, as anything, by a point of view. That point of view is as important as the results it may produce. Teacher-research starts with and brings about a shift in the status-quo of teaching and learning; therein lies its joy, its strength, and its challenge. Hugette Ducasse, a Franco-Brazilian teacher-researcher, explains the shift as she started to inquire into her work as a teacher:

Hugette Ducasse

I started from a perfect blank: "Research? Me? I have to do research? On what? Why?" Then I started realizing how wonderful the classroom is as a field for research. The Egyptologist needs a pyramid or an ancient tomb thousands of miles away to carry out his research. But I can do it everyday, the whole year round, right here in my own classroom.

Ducasse's comment suggests the reasoning behind this chapter's title. If you accept the argument that teacher-research is about repositioning teaching and about who generates the primary knowledge on which work in classrooms is based, then doing teacher-research involves starting anew as a teacher. But starting anew doesn't mean abandoning what you know. It means moving away from the perspective of doing and being certain that usually animates our work as teachers to see teaching from a new and different perspective, one of puzzling, questioning, wondering, and not knowing. This is not starting over as a teacher, but starting anew from a different set of assumptions, realizing, as Ducasse says, how wonderful the classroom is as a field for research.

Suggested Readings

Understanding teachers' expertise and how it develops over their careers is a relatively recent area of research in education. David Berliner's 1988 paper, "The development of expertise in pedagogy," (Washington, DC: American Association of Colleges for Teacher Education) is a seminal statement in this area. Victoria Genburg's article, "Patterns and organizing perspectives: a view of expertise," (*Teaching and Teacher Education* 8 [5/6]. pp. 485–496), provides an excellent summary. On the social context of teachers' work, I suggest two authors as ways into this useful literature. Ted Sizer's 1983 book *Horace's Compromise: The Dilemma of the American High School* (Boston: Houghton Mifflin) is a classic and very readable statement of the issues. To follow Sizer's thinking and the reform work that has resulted, see also Sizer's 1992 book *Horace's School: Redesigning the American High School* (Boston: Houghton Mifflin). Michael Apple's *Teachers and Texts: A Political Economy of Class and Gender Relations in Education* (New York: Routledge, 1986) also presents a wide-ranging critical theory perspective on the social context of schooling. Allen Pearson's book, *The Teacher: Theory and Practice in Teacher Education* (New York: Routledge, 1989) is an excellent and clear discussion of the philosophical issues and concepts involved in defining teaching as a practice.

In the notion of teacher-research as work at the hyphen, I have been influenced by Michelle Fine's thinking. Her chapter, "Working the hyphens: Reinventing self and other in qualitative research,"(in *Handbook of Qualitative Research*, edited by N. Denzin and Y. Lincoln. Thousand Oaks, CA: Sage, 1994) is a dense but worthwhile discussion of how the research process often hinges on creating distinctions that are often based on power. In her 1996 book, *Talking Across Boundaries: Participatory Evaluation Research in an Urban Middle School* (New York: City University of New York Press), Fine applies this notion of hyphens as connections and boundaries to teacher-research in schools.

The question of how research supports disciplines in the construction of knowledge is a vast one. Two readings offer a good way into these issues: Chapter 3 in L. Neuman, *Social Research Methods* (Boston: Allyn and Bacon, 1991) provides a good and readable overview. D. McLaughlin and W. Tierney's book *Naming Silenced Lives: Personal Narratives and Processes of Educational Change* (New York: Routledge, 1993) is a fine collection of papers from various perspectives that aim to raise experiences and issues that are "silenced" or not addressed in usual research.

And on how implementation shapes policy and curriculum, Michael Lipsky's book *Street-level Bureaucracy: Dilemmas of the Individual in Public Service* (New York: Russell Sage, 1980) argues that people like police and social workers are actually making policy under the guise of interpreting it as they interact with their clients. Pam Grossman's book *The Making of a Teacher: Teacher Knowledge and Teacher Education* (New York: Teachers College Press, 1990) looks at the same phenomenon in teaching as teachers transform curriculum into what Shulman (1987) has called "pedagogical content knowledge." And Kathleen Graves's edited collection, *Teachers as Course Developers* (New York: Cambridge University Press, 1996), presents six case studies of course development, written by practitioners in ESL/EFL settings, that examine curriculum from the standpoint of implementation.

2

FRAMING THE TEACHER-RESEARCH CYCLE

IT DEPENDS WHERE YOU LOOK

Like many complex phenomena—even the Grand Canyon—teaching and learning look different depending on who you are, where you are standing, and where you are looking. Like the children in the cartoon above, people are naturally drawn to what they *can* see, not necessarily to what there is *to* see. Observations about the world depend on where you look and who you are. In the case of education, because teaching has usually been studied by people who are not teachers or who are not involved in the act of teaching, it has been described in terms that gloss over its messiness and complexity. Philip Jackson, an educational researcher who wrote a seminal study of teaching from a classroom perspective called *Life in Classrooms* (1968), described just such a point of view: "Not only is the classroom a relatively stable physical environment, it also provides a fairly constant social context. Behind the same old desks sit the same old students, in front of the familiar blackboard stands the familiar teacher" (p. 7). To those who teach and learn there, classrooms are at times sta-

Lightfoot's
*The Good High
School* (1983)
is an example of
research that
works to capture
the complexity
of schools as
they are.

ble, constant, and familiar, but they also have a fluid messiness and complexity that is difficult to capture—much less understand and explain.

Two researchers, Rob Halkes and Jon Olson (1984), who pioneered the field of teacher cognition, outline an alternative view of teachers' work which starts to account for this tension between order and complexity. They write:

> Looking from a teacher-thinking perspective at teaching and learning, one is not so much striving for the disclosure of *the* effective teacher, but for the explanation and understanding of teaching processes as they are. After all, it is the teacher's subjective school-related knowledge which determines for the most part what happens in the classroom; whether the teacher can articulate her/his knowledge or not. Instead of reducing the complexities of teaching-learning situations into a few manageable research variables, one tries to find out how teachers cope with these complexities. (p. 1)

For Jackson the challenge is to understand the stable, familiar, regularity of the classroom, while for Halkes and Olson the challenge is to understand how teachers cope with the "complexities" that make up their teaching. This difference in point of view, to which we will return later in the chapter, lies at the heart of teacher-research. Simply put, living teaching and looking at it are two different things. Working at the hyphen of teaching and researching challenges this gap; teacher-researchers have to combine both perspectives as they live and investigate their teaching.

Emic *versus* etic distinction, see Chapter 4, p. 69

Because of the immediacy of teaching, the simultaneity of classrooms and what it means to cope with complexities can quickly melt away when one is not in them. In the following extended description, which captures part of a first-year middle school French class, I want to bring some complexity to life. I do so as an outsider, observing the class, and as an insider to that class, hearing what is going on in other rooms around me. (The sections in italics echo what I hear from other rooms but do not see.) What I have written, based on field notes taken in the class and from talking with the teacher, who is here known as Charles, is a bit like the cartoon. It creates a small hole for you to look at, while the larger landscape of the canyon is only hinted at in the distance.

"Charles"

Four six-digit numbers are written randomly on the board. The class begins as the teacher, Charles, addresses the group of twenty-one seventh graders seated at desks in pairs: "Alors je vous donnerai quelques minutes pour réflechir." [Okay, I'll let you have a few minutes to think about these.] Most kids seem to know implicitly that he is talking about how they will say the numbers in French. They sit quietly, some looking at the board, others involved in their books or looking at the scene in the school parking lot outside the classroom window.

In the silence, through the modular partitions, the sounds of an English class next door can be clearly made out. The teacher is talking about capitalization: "Okay, open your books to page 39 and let's look at capital letters here. Why are capitals important? . . . That's right, they show the beginning of the sentence. Good, now let's look at the exercise." In response to some inaudible student noise, the teacher's voice rises, "Listen up you boys. There's a test on this tomorrow and it's the last one in the quarter and you'd better think about your grades."

Charles rises from where he has been sitting, on the edge of his desk, and speaks to the class: "Mettez-vous avec un partenaire, et vous allez pratiquer comment dire ces numéros. Vous aurez un petit cinq minutes." [Work with a partner and practice saying these numbers. You'll have about five minutes.] The kids fall to work almost immediately. Most pairs are involved as they work through the six digits. A student who is stuck on "924,429" turns to a neighboring pair:

Student 1: "Are you smart in French?"

Student 2: "Yeah . . ."

Student 1: "I know you are." She turns to the other member of the pair.

Student 3: "So after the first number you say 'cent'."

Charles stops the pair work and the student raises her hand to ask about the number she has been struggling with. "How do you say that one. The 924 one . . ." Charles moves across the front of the room and begins to point silently at the numbers. Slowly at first, but then with quick momentum and focus, the class recites: "Neuf cent vingt-quatre milles, quatre cent vingt-neuf." "See, I told ya," says her partner under her breath. Charles continues, reviewing the other numbers. He sets up a rhythm of pointing and student response that pulls the students into the exercise. He then sits at an empty desk and asks for volunteers to try out any of the numbers. There is lively involvement as different kids try out the long numbers; some can handle the numbers fluently, others stumble. Charles gets up now and then to help out by pointing to trouble spots. Generally, though, there is the feeling of the students face-to-face with the numbers.

The volunteering comes to end after about five minutes; both the kids and Charles seem to be satisfied.

In the brief silence, the teacher next door can be heard. "What about the Elizabethan Age? That's number 6. Now that's something I know a little about from my background in English. What's capitalized there? Come on now, follow the rules at the top of the page. It's all laid out for you. . . . That's right, the "E" in Elizabethan and. . . Okay, number 7 . . ."

Charles switches the lesson to a review of verbs. Using stylized gestures, he mimes various verbs as the students call out the French. He cocks one hand to the side of his mouth "Chanter." [Sing] the kids call out. Then, in a fluid transition, he gives the French and the kids do the gestures. Some falter; others look at their neighbors to check. The pace is quick but not oppressive; the students seem involved by it. It seems almost unremarkable that this is the first time, some fifteen minutes into the lesson, that Charles has spoken except to give instructions; all the other French, including corrections, has come from the students.

He switches on the overhead projector, which shows a sheet of fifteen small line drawings of the different verbs. Standing and holding the felt marker in one hand, he looks around at the class. A student asks, "You want us to write them up like last week?" Charles puts down the pen and returns to the empty desk three rows away. By now most of the students are perched on the edges of their chairs, involved, straining to figure out the lesson. A girl next to the projector picks up the marker and writes the first verb. There is discussion as verbs go up in various spellings; most are close but not all are accurate. After eight verbs, as squirming begins to take over, Charles gets up and collects the marker. Without speaking he goes back over what they have done, pointing to mistakes and waiting until the correction surfaces.

From the adjoining classroom the English teacher is announcing the quiz on capital letters for tomorrow: "Now, in the time you have left you can start on your homework. That's on page 38, the passage." She reads, "'This passage contains 28 errors in capitalization. Can you find them?'"

Investigations

2.1 STARTING TO SPECULATE

This Investigation refers you to the previous portrait of Charles's French class. You are asked to imagine two points of view: the first as an observer in the class and the second as Charles, the teacher.

Rereading the French lesson described above, list three to five things you might wonder or have questions about as an observer in the classroom. List them in any form you choose—as questions, phrases, ideas, whatever.

Read through the description again, this time imagining that you are the teacher. Add to your list another three to five things you might speculate on or that might puzzle you in this lesson if you were Charles.

Compare the two lists to see where they overlap and where they diverge. How are the concerns similar or different depending on whether you are an outsider, an observer, or an (imagined) insider, the teacher? Any of these speculations could provide the seeds of an inquiry.

Frameworks

The bed sheet and the kayak

Organizing this fluidity and messiness of speculating, puzzling, and wondering about classroom teaching and learning into a line of inquiry can be daunting. It can feel like trying to fold a bed sheet alone without dirtying it on the ground, or like trying to carry a kayak by yourself for the first time. With the sheet you want to create some order and structure by folding the larger sheet into a smaller, more manageable size so it can be put away, but without dropping the corners or dragging the edges in the dirt. With the kayak, it is a matter of figuring out how to lift up the boat and then balance it on your shoulders, over your head, so you can walk with it. Both tasks depend on structuring the work. To get the job done, you have to decide what you need to control and what you can leave alone or let go. With the sheet, it helps to organize the order—first locate the four corners with one hand while you hold the bunched up sheet with the other, and so on. With the kayak, you need to decide how to interact with the object itself; how much strength to use to lift it and how to find the center of gravity to balance it. Too much power and you will miss the balance point; not enough and you may not find it.

Organizing initial wonderings, speculations, and puzzles into a coherent line of inquiry has many of these same characteristics. In essence, you will need to make some decisions about what to control in your teaching situation and how to control it so that you can research it; by definition you will likewise be deciding what to leave alone. The former will become your hole to look at while the latter will become, temporarily, scenery in the background. This organizing will involve structuring and ordering ideas and thoughts, using energy and perseverance as you seek to clarify ideas and move ahead with the process, and you will need to find the right balance among the many other demands of being a teacher and the methodicalness and discipline of researching in your classroom.

In this chapter I lay out two frameworks that are helpful—indeed are central—in this organizing process. Both frameworks are schematic and visual, so they are like maps of the whole territory of doing teacher-research. They are also big-picture views of the dynamics and processes teacher-research involves. The first framework outlines two basic principles that interact to shape any research inquiry. In grasping these principles you are learning to balance the yin and yang of organization and intervention in research. Like lifting the kayak, this sense of balance is essential to carrying forward a teacher-research project. The second framework is a cycle. It lays out the elements of teacher-research and then connects them to the process of doing the work. Like folding the sheet, it will suggest an order to activity in doing research, and at the same time it should help to hold on to an image of the whole research process.

PRINCIPLES OF CONTROL IN RESEARCH DESIGN: VAN LIER'S TYPOLOGY

Principles of control in research design: How to organize? How to intervene?

Leo van Lier, an educator who has written about the educational research process, suggests an interesting way to think about how researchers organize their relationships and interactions with the environments they are studying. In posing research questions and developing ways to respond to them, van Lier (1988) argues that there are two basic principles at work. The first is the principle of **organization,** which he calls "selectivity." The second is that of **intervention.** Together the two principles outline the kinds of control a researcher can exert in designing an inquiry. In the principle of organization, the researcher is deciding how he or she wants to structure the relationship with the participants and the setting being studied. In the principle of intervention, the researcher is deciding how far he or she wants to intervene and interact with what is happening in that environment as part of the research process.

Figure 2.1: van Lier's typology

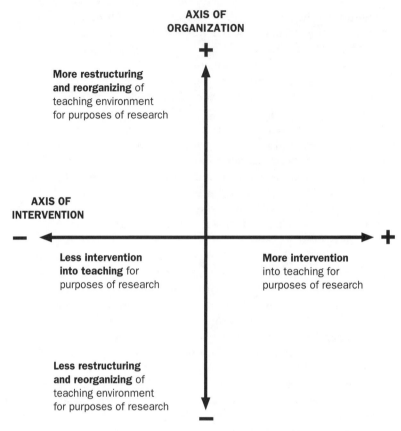

AXIS OF ORGANIZATION

+

**More restructuring
and reorganizing** of
teaching environment
for purposes of research

**AXIS OF
INTERVENTION**

—

**Less intervention
into teaching** for
purposes of research

More intervention
into teaching for
purposes of research

+

**Less restructuring
and reorganizing** of
teaching environment
for purposes of research

—

(after van Lier 1988; p. 57)

Van Lier uses the two principles as axes. The vertical axis of organization runs from greater to lesser structure and researcher-imposed order in the research process, while the horizontal axis of intervention runs from more to less researcher involvement and direct interaction with participants and the research setting.

The following are four vignettes of teacher-researchers organizing their research processes and intervening in their environments. They are intended to describe how organization and intervention might be balanced in each of the four quadrants in Figure 2.1.

Vignette 2A: Maya and using new information to solve a task

For details on the data-gathering techniques mentioned here (in bold), see Appendix C, pp. 201–218.

Maya divides her class of thirty sixth graders into two groups, balancing as far as possible the number, gender, and perceived abilities of students in each group. She then teaches a lesson to the "experimental" group, while the "control" group is out of the room at art class. The lesson, which is on giving spatial directions, includes both easier and more idiomatic ways of expressing the same linguistic functions that the whole class has already studied. The next day Maya gives both groups the same task and she monitors how the students complete it. The task, which is an information-gap activity using a city map, embeds the material Maya taught to the experimental group the previous day into material the whole class has already worked with. She is interested in seeing whether the experimental group will use the extra material in solving the task. She has the experimental and control groups work separately on the task and **audio tapes** each group's work.

Vignette 2B: Joan and emerging literacy

Joan keeps a **teaching journal** on her class of first graders who are learning to read. Using her class as it is, she concentrates in her journaling on the first part of the morning, when the children are involved in free reading and writing. While they are at music in the following period, she is able to spend about 20 minutes looking over the work the students have just done and making notes on what went on during the lesson. She is interested in how various students are progressing in reading, particularly in how their writing and drawings reflect their emerging literacy skills. As she reviews the **students' work,** she actively challenges herself by writing a short **reflective memo** in which she addresses the following question: How am I seeing this student's learning process—as a teacher who needs to intervene and support it or as a researcher who wants to document and understand it? She often writes down her observations in two columns, one titled "teacher" the other titled "researcher." After a month, Joan decides to narrow her research focus by choosing two students who seem to be encountering literacy in very different ways. Every few weeks thereafter she reviews her notes and their work and writes up an **analytical memo** on each of the two students.

Vignette 2C: Vera and what makes "good" conversationalists

Vera has an adult EFL class whose students have diverse interests. In the part of the lesson devoted to conversational activities some students talk quite freely, while others seem less involved. Vera has noticed that the participation varies and seems to depend on the topic and on who is present in class on a given evening. Vera decides to give the whole class a short written **survey** that asks them for some background information (age, job, number of years studying English, use of English professionally and socially) and to rate their interest in various conversation topics. She also asks each student to note the names of the three classmates the student considers the best conversationalists in the class and to explain why. She uses this information to create a **sociogram** of the class.

Vignette 2D: Betty and the comprehensibility of instructions

Betty is concerned with how well her adult beginning-level students understand the instructions she gives for activities. After the first month of class she decides to ask the students which instructional format is easiest to understand. She chooses three formats: (1) oral instructions, (2) oral instructions that a student paraphrases to the group immediately after Betty has given them, and (3) written instructions on the blackboard. She uses each format exclusively for a week and at the end of that week asks her students for **feedback.** After she has used all three formats, she asks the students to rate the formats from one—most preferred—to three, and to say why they prefer the one they rate most highly.

The teachers in each of these vignettes are initiating a teacher-research process. They have each encountered something in their classrooms, among their students, or in what they are doing that triggers some wonder, speculation, or puzzlement. To pursue these lines of inquiry, each makes different decisions about what to control in their situations, how to structure their relationships to what is going on in their classrooms, and when and how much to intervene in the phenomenon they are investigating. Each teacher-researcher's inquiry falls in one of the four quadrants in van Lier's axes of organization and of intervention (Figure 2.1). Within her line of inquiry, each of the four teacher-researchers makes choices about how to gather information or data. To act on these choices, each must control certain aspects of the situation by organizing it in specific ways and/or intervening in the usual flow of teaching to do things differently for purposes of the research. For example, Maya organizes the class into two groups, while Joan decides to gather her data from what the students are already doing in her class. Vera intervenes to do a survey, while Betty structures her teaching into three week-long formats and asks for student feedback on each one.

2.2 *Control in Research Design: How to Organize? How to Intervene?*

This Investigation uses van Lier's typology (Figure 2.1) to examine how the teacher-researchers in the four vignettes balance organization and intervention to control the situation and phenomenon each is investigating.

To do this Investigation take one of two approaches:

1. Reread the four vignettes and describe the research design the teacher-researcher is using. What is she studying and how is she collecting information about it? Then place each vignette in one of the four quadrants on Figure 2.1.

   Explain to yourself—or to colleagues if you are working with others—why you put the vignette in that quadrant. How does the research design reflect the adjacent axes? How does the teacher-researcher reorganize her setting for purposes of her research? How does she intervene with students in the setting she is studying? Then consult Figure 2.2 (p. 27).

2. To reverse the process, begin by looking at Figure 2.2. Then, before reading the narrative that follows it, explain to yourself or your classmates why each vignette is in that particular quadrant. How does the research design reflect the adjacent axes? How does the teacher-researcher reorganize her setting for purposes of her research? How does she intervene with students in the setting she is studying?

Figure 2.2 incorporates the four vignettes into van Lier's typology. Each vignette balances the two axes in some way. The vertical axis of organization focuses on how to structure the research process; the horizontal axis concentrates on how much to intervene in the flow of teaching to carry out the research. The interaction of the axes highlights the range of choices in how each teacher-researcher controls teaching and the classroom setting to carry our her research.

Figure 2.2: van Lier's typology illustrated

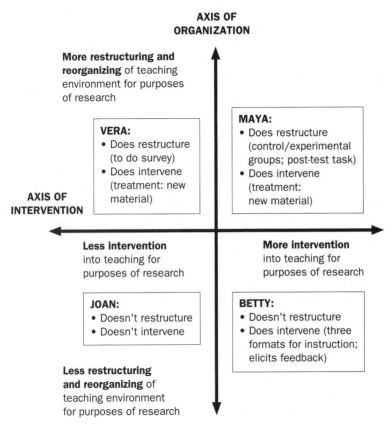

(after van Lier 1988; p. 57)

Maya's vignette (2A) falls in the upper right quadrant, which is "plus restructuring and plus intervention." She wants to examine how a particular intervention—teaching specific additional language—may affect her students' overall ability to do the task of giving directions. Maya adapts a conventional **experimental research design** in which only half the class receives the **"treatment"** of additional instruction for the task. She restructures the situation (the horizontal axis) by subdividing the class into experimental and control groups that are as matched as possible under the circumstances, and she intervenes (the vertical axis) in her normal teaching to give only the experimental group the treatment of the additional language content. She then uses a **"post-test" design** to compare how the two groups do the information-gap activity on how to give directions, which she **audio-tapes.** Maya thus restructures the classroom environment by subdividing the class, and she intervenes in that new structure by presenting additional content to one group. However, given the inherently messy complexity of teaching and classrooms, she cannot create a fully controlled experimental design in which everything about the two groups would be comparable except for the treatment of additional instruction.

On teacher-research as action research, see Stringer (1996), or Kemmis and McTaggart (1995). See Appendix E, the LIPT case studies, for further examples of action-research.

In the lower right quadrant, Betty (2D) engages in a small-scale **action research** project on the clarity of her instructions Unlike Maya, Betty does not restructure the basic flow of her teaching for the purposes of the research process (the vertical axis). She continues to teach the class as usual, however she intervenes (the horizontal axis) by giving instructions to her students in three different formats, using one format a week over a three-week period. Because Betty works with her whole class over the three weeks, there is an inevitable cumulative effect of one format of instructions on the next. She also intervenes by eliciting **feedback** from the students each week and at the end of the three weeks, thus engaging them collectively in the research process. So Betty's research design unfolds over time with a series of ongoing interventions. She asks her students to collectively engage in and respond to how she gives instructions, which is the phenomenon she is investigating. Thus Betty's project illustrates a typical **action-research cycle** in teaching. The teacher-researcher identifies an issue or problem (in Betty's case, the comprehensibility of her instructions), intervenes in the classroom setting to address that problem in some way (Betty tries out the three different formats of giving instructions), and then assesses the impact of the intervention (Betty asks for student feedback).

Contrasting Maya's and Betty's designs, we can see how each controls different dimensions of her classroom setting to accomplish her research. In her research design, Maya intervenes to teach additional content to the experimental group of students. In hers, Betty intervenes in teaching by shifting how she gives instructions each week and by asking for student feedback on each format. But the two designs differ in how the teacher-researchers do or do not restructure their classrooms to carry out their research. Maya divides her class in two groups; Betty carries on as usual in her teaching.

Doing thought experiments

Albert Einstein is supposed to have coined the term **"thought experiment,"** in which you simply think through a situation, research issue, or design using various alternatives and carrying them to their logical conclusions. As a mathematician and physicist Einstein's point was that a great deal of research work is possible using nothing more—or less—than one's own mind. It is an interesting **thought experiment** to mentally convert Betty's action research project on instructions into an experimental design like Maya's, or to convert Maya's study into an action research project like Betty's. What would Maya need to do in order to make her research design like Betty's? What would she need to organize differently and why? And similarly, how would Betty reshape her project to create a design like Maya's?

Figure 2.3: Thought-experiment: Converting action research to an experimental design and vice versa

	MAYA	BETTY
Design	as an **action research design**	as an **experimental design**
Organization	▪ could work with the whole class or could keep the two groups	▪ would need two "matched" groups for comparison
Intervention	▪ would introduce the new material (the intervention) over a specified time period ▪ would document—by audio, video, and/or observation notes—if/how students used the new material in solving the task ▪ could also ask students for their feedback on why they did/didn't use it	▪ would need to establish a standard format of giving instructions (perhaps teacher given oral instructions) for both groups ▪ would then choose one "new" format of instructions as the "treatment" for the "experimental" group over a specified time period ▪ would need to audio or videotape these experimental group sessions

Doing such thought-experiments to convert one research design to another helps to clarify how each design balances organization and intervention. There is no one way to strike this balance; one design is not better or more "scientific" than the other. Rather, teacher-researchers make decisions for the purposes of research, about what to control in their teaching situations and how to control it. These decisions involve two basic principles: organization, whether and how much to restructure the classroom to do the research, and intervention, whether and how much to intervene in the regular course of teaching to carry out the research. Together these two principles embed the notion of disciplined inquiry into the teaching process. If we continue with the other two vignettes, we see how these decisions about organization and intervention differ in the two left-hand quadrants on van Lier's typology (Figure 2.2).

Joan's vignette (2B) falls in the lower left quadrant. She uses what is called a **naturalistic** research design (Lincoln and Guba, 1985); she does not intervene as a researcher in her students' work. Joan does not alter her teaching; she does nothing exceptional during the class, but rather collects her data afterwards through keeping her **teaching journal** and reviewing the **students' work.** She also monitors herself and her own thinking and reactions as part of the research process by doing regular **reflective memos** as she is analyzing her data. She develops **case studies** over time, out of her interest in and attention to what two particular students are doing. She does not affect the organization of her class (vertical axis) by selecting the two students in advance. Instead, she is intrigued

On grounded theory, see Strauss (1987; pp. 5–6; 22–23).

by their differing styles of emerging literacy, on which she then focuses. Joan's approach to her research is what in qualitative research is often called a **grounded approach** (Strauss, 1987) since she is evolving her analysis and her understanding from the data as she collects them, rather than imposing preconceived or **a priori categories** on the data. Anselm Strauss (1987), who pioneered the **grounded theory** in social science research, defines it this way: "Such theory ought to be developed in intimate relationship with data, with researchers fully aware of themselves as instruments for developing that grounded theory. This is true whether they generate the data themselves [as Joan does in the vignette] or ground their theoretical work in data collected by others." (p. 6)

Here is another thought experiment that illustrates the difference between grounded and a priori theory. Let us say, for instance, that Joan decides before beginning her project to focus on two particular first graders, Drew and Sergio. She selects the two students because she knows that they come from very different sociocultural and family-literacy backgrounds. Both of Drew's parents have white collar jobs; he has three older siblings who are close in age, and there appears to be a lot of literacy interaction in English at home. Sergio lives with an aunt who works the night shift at a cannery; he often spends after-school hours with neighbors and friends in the Cape Verdian community, where his home language is a Portuguese Creole. There probably isn't much formal literacy interaction in English in his home life. Joan wants, therefore, to track how these two first graders enter English literacy. She hypothesizes that for Drew the path of literacy in English will be clearer and more direct than for Sergio. Because she speaks Portuguese, Joan also plans to look at how Sergio navigates his way between Portuguese and English in such things as invented spelling as he starts to write.

In this thought experiment Joan brings a number of **articulated assumptions** to shape her research. She assumes, based on both other people's research (e.g., Heath, 1983) and her own experience as a teacher that family literacy interactions in English—such things as the amount and kinds of English-language materials including newspapers, magazines, and books, around the home; reading of bedtime stories; reading aloud; siblings close in age who are reading and doing homework; and so on—will have an impact on Drew's learning. She assumes that Sergio's experience will be different because he does not have the same family literacy interactions in English and, further, that he may have some interference from Portuguese as he learns to read English. Together these assumptions form implicit and explicit ways in which Joan looks at the data from these two children. These **a priori** theories, about family literacy interactions in English for example, and a priori categories, such as Portuguese versus English invented spelling, shape the ways in which she will approach the project and how she will analyze her data.

Bringing a priori understandings to the research process is not a bad thing. It is, arguably, a very human and necessary feature of how people make sense of their worlds, as teacher-researchers and as human beings in general. For instance, on a November morning in New England, if you decide to bring a coat when you go out even though it is warm and sunny, you do so because you assume it may turn cold at some point during the day. You make this prediction based on a number of factors: your own experience, the fact that you have been told it is so, observation and hearing about other people's experiences, and so on. Prediction is based on experience and on making assumptions about the world; it is a feature of being human. It is also a crucial part of the research process. Prediction can be built upon by using a priori understandings to structure the research process (the vertical axis) and/or to guide how the researcher intervenes with what is being studied (the horizontal axis) to collect and analyze the data, as with Maya [2A] or Betty [2D] in the upper or lower right quadrants of Figure 2.2. The researcher can also actively track assumptions and temporarily set them aside, as Joan does when she writes **reflective memos** in her vignette. She thus harnesses prediction so that it works from the data itself to generate grounded categories and theories.

Vera's project [2C], which falls in the upper left quadrant in Figure 2.2, differs from Joan's in one major way. Like Joan, and unlike Betty or Maya, Vera decides not to intervene in her teaching (horizontal axis) to gather data. Rather, she decides to restructure her lesson in a minor way by having the students complete a brief written survey at the close of one class period. The survey is a **structured instrument** through which she gathers information; she would not use it unless she were doing the research. Vera designs the survey based on her a priori assumptions about what may affect the different levels of participation in the class (i.e., choice of discussion topics, fluency and comfort with English, social groupings within the class, etc.). Vera's approach is to leave the class as it is (horizontal axis), but to structure a specific time and instrument to gather information about what is going on. She also uses the survey data to build a **sociogram** of students' perceptions of "good conversation" by asking each of them who he or she sees as the best conversationalists in the class. The sociogram is one way of collecting their views of the social phenomenon of conversation. Alongside the data on topics and student backgrounds and preferences it provides an alternative, "second-order" or participants' view of the phenomenon under study.

For a full discussion of second-order research, see Chapter 4, p. 65.

This typology provides a framework for looking at how the teacher-researcher may structure the research process, along the vertical axis of organization the horizontal axis of intervention. Both axes lay out possible decisions you can make as a teacher-researcher about how much to control the situation you are investigating. As you move up the vertical axis of organization (Figure 2.2) you are deciding to reorganize your teaching situation for purposes of your research. This restructuring can mean a major change in the organization of your teaching, like Maya's dividing students into experimental and control groups [2A], or a minor one, like Vera's [2C] doing the survey at the end of a class. As you move down the vertical axis, you are deciding to leave your teaching situation as it is and not to restructure it for the purposes of your research, like Joan [2B] and Betty [2D]. A second set of decisions interacts with these decisions about organization; they have to do with how and how much to intervene in your teaching as part of the research process. These decisions are represented on the horizontal axis of intervention. They range from not intervening at all, like Joan [2B], to doing something fully different in your teaching for purposes of the research, like Betty [2D] with her three formats of instructions. In contrast, after they decide how to take action to restructure their teaching to pursue their lines of inquiry, Vera and Maya do not intervene in the actual teaching they do.

Figure 2.4: Modified van Lier's typology: Research design and research methods

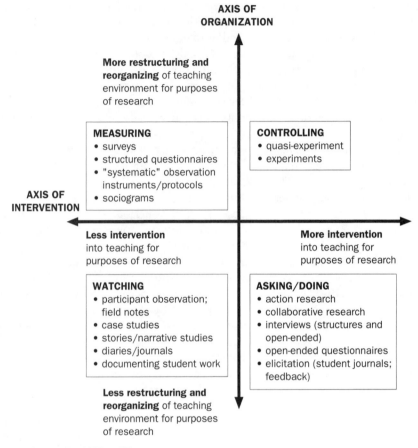

AXIS OF
ORGANIZATION

More restructuring and reorganizing of teaching environment for purposes of research

MEASURING
- surveys
- structured questionnaires
- "systematic" observation instruments/protocols
- sociograms

CONTROLLING
- quasi-experiment
- experiments

AXIS OF
INTERVENTION

Less intervention into teaching for purposes of research

More intervention into teaching for purposes of research

WATCHING
- participant observation; field notes
- case studies
- stories/narrative studies
- diaries/journals
- documenting student work

ASKING/DOING
- action research
- collaborative research
- interviews (structures and open-ended)
- open-ended questionnaires
- elicitation (student journals; feedback)

Less restructuring and reorganizing of teaching environment for purposes of research

(after van Lier 1988; p. 57)

Van Lier describes the principal concerns of the researcher in each quadrant as **controlling** [Maya, 2A]; **asking and doing** [Betty, 2D]; **watching** [Joan, 2B], and **measuring** [Vera, 2C]. One way to think about this display is to say that as a teacher-researcher, when you develop a project you have to ask yourself, "How do I want to structure this project?" and "What role do I want/need to play—both within and outside my teaching—to gather data for it?" Your response can be categorized in terms of one of these four dominant concerns. Figure 2.4 shows how van Lier suggests that various types of research design and approaches to data-gathering map onto this typology. Like the four vignettes, the examples are illustrative and not complete or exhaustive; they do help to clothe the abstraction of the two axes in the particulars of the research process.

This typology helps to lay out the overall landscape of the research process and the researcher's role within it. It frames crucial questions about how you balance control over your teaching situation as you organize your research. If you think about it architecturally, "restructuring" is like adding rooms or putting in new walls in an existing building; "intervening" is like repainting or rewallpapering. When you reorganize your teaching for purposes of your research, you generally add things to what you are doing in the classroom that would not otherwise do. When you intervene in your teaching to accomplish your research, you usually change something within your teaching to do it in another way because of your research. Both restructuring and intervening are about decisions to control—or not control—your work. In a sense, they both capture the idea of possibly doing something differently than you would have done if your sole concern were teaching. This is the work at the hyphen. It is like finding the point of balance in lifting the kayak.

THE ELEMENTS OF THE TEACHER-RESEARCH CYCLE: A GLOSSARY OF TERMS

The elements of the teacher-research cycle

The second framework is meant to help organize the work of doing teacher-research. It is the framework around which the remainder of the book is organized. The framework provides an overview of the teacher-research process; it maps out the specific phases involved and offers a way into the skills associated with each part of the process. The cycle has six basic elements. It is useful to think about the elements individually before putting them in sequence, so I have listed them below in no particular order.

- Understandings
- "Publishing"—making public
- Data collection
- Data analysis
- Question/puzzle
- Inquiry

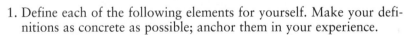

2.3 *DEFINING AND MAPPING THE ELEMENTS OF THE CYCLE*

Investigations

This Investigation is meant to familiarize you with the framework of teacher-research on which this book is based.

1. Define each of the following elements for yourself. Make your definitions as concrete as possible; anchor them in your experience.

   - Understandings
   - "Publishing"—making public
   - Data collection
   - Data analysis
   - Question/puzzle
   - Inquiry

   If you are working with others, define the elements for yourself and then compare your definitions with those of your colleagues. In making the comparison, identify what you all consider essential to the definition of each element.

2. Place the elements in the unlabeled framework in Figure 2.5 (p. 34). As you do so, consider why you put them in the order you do. You will want to think through and/or explain to others, the relationships among the elements.

   Figure 2.6 (p. 38) shows the elements in the labeled framework.

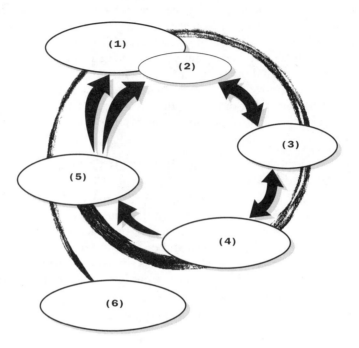

To introduce the elements of the teacher-research cycle in the following dis-cussion, I define each element and then comment on it. The definitions are meant to be a point of departure, while the comments are intended to begin to flesh out some of the complexities and interrelations among the elements in the process.

INQUIRY: Inquiry is speculating about why something is as it is, why it happens or works (or doesn't happen or work) the way it does. It is a state of being engaged in what is going on in the class-room that drives one to better understanding. Inquiry includes both the attitude that spawns this engagement and the energy and activi-ty that put it into action.

Comments: Inquiry is a state of mind that allows you to be unsure, off-balance, intrigued, interested, and wanting to find out more about something in your classroom, your students, what or how you are teaching, or your work as a teacher. If teaching is about knowing, inquiry is about not-knowing. Psychologist and teacher-research advocate Eleanor Duckworth (1987) captured this orientation in a wonderful statement that concludes her essay titled "The virtues of not-knowing": "What you do [as a teacher] about what you don't know is, in the final analysis, what determines what you will ultimately know." (p. 68) Inquiry is motivated by the general sense of "what is going on here?" It unfolds into a **line of inquiry,** a chain of speculation, wonderings, questions or puzzles (see below) that can be transformed into a research plan and design.

QUESTION/PUZZLE: A question or puzzle is the concentration of a line of inquiry into an articulated form. It focuses and specifies the broader inquiry in a form that can be acted upon through investigation.

Comments: In conventional research design, research questions are supposed to drive the research process. In fact, inquiry drives teacher-research. It provides the deep structure of the process of speculation and wonder about teaching and learning, while **research-able questions** become the surface-structure manifestations of inquiry. Not all questions are research questions; some are simply too broad, while others can be better unlocked through teaching alone, as we will discuss later. So I use the hyphen in *research-able* on purpose, to emphasize the "ability" that a question carries in it to be investigated. Research-able questions change; they twist and turn throughout the research process and often redefine themselves in the face of the data or with the insight of retrospection. However, the line of inquiry remains the root out of which these questions grow; it is the backdrop against which they can always be tested.

Dick Allwright (1997) uses the term "puzzle" in his work on exploratory teaching to mean that which sparks the teacher-research process. To me, puzzles and questions grow from the same root, but they are phased differently. As I said, not all questions are research-able; some may exceed the scope of teacher-research in time, resources, and access to data. Further, expressing inquiry is not always sympathetic to the rhetorical structure of questions. Puzzles, on the other hand, are more open-ended rhetorically. They can capture the sense of speculating, wondering, and not-knowing on which teacher-research is based without forcing it into the format of a question. How you make the inquiry specific— whether through questions or puzzles—is less important, however, than the fact that you will need to become clear on your inquiry in concrete, actionable terms. This is what articulating a research-able question or puzzle does: It launches you into action.

For the discussion of teaching versus research-able questions, see Chapter 4, p. 61.

DATA COLLECTION: Data collection is the process of gathering information in a disciplined and systematic way about a puzzle or a research-able question.

Comments: There are two facets reflected in the term *data collection*. There is the issue of **data:** What kinds of information can respond to the question or puzzle? If the inquiry deals with instructions, as Betty's does in the vignette [2D], then class attendance figures are not data. However, if the inquiry deals with in-class conversation activities, as Vera's does [2C], then class attendance may be relevant. For instance, Vera may discover a link between a student who attends class regularly and becomes comfortable with fellow students and class norms that can shed light on her inquiry. Having determined the types of data, the issue is then how to collect them. The point in recognizing **data** and **collection** as separate issues is that they are often confused. People assume that the data and way they are gathered are one and the same. So "student talk," which is data, is confused with audiotaping, which is a means of collection. We will return to this point in Chapter 4.

DATA ANALYSIS: Data analysis involves taking the data apart to see what is there and then putting them together to see how they respond to the question or puzzle under investigation.

Comments: The processes of **disassembling** and **reassembling data,** which form the core of data analysis, are not symmetrical. In a sense, data come prepackaged in assumptions. For instance, we assume data on class attendance will tell us who was or wasn't present in class on a given day. While that is true, these data can also potentially have more or other value, depending on how you analyze them. So taking the data apart to see what is in them is a crucial step that can allow—or push—you away from your assumptions. This step then provides a basis for reassembling the data in different ways to provide new or different information and perspectives on the inquiry.

The following account illustrates this issue of disassembling and reassembling data. In a town in Alaska, I met some teachers at an alternative high school program for students who were "poorly motivated and had discipline problems." These teachers discovered that a large number of their students were sent to the program because of poor attendance and perennial tardiness. Many of these students, it turned out, were poor students of color. Their attendance records did show that they often missed or were late to school, and it was assumed that the problem lay in their lack of interest and motivation. When a couple of teachers began to review the attendance data, to disassemble it, they noticed that many students lived on outlying bus routes, often riding as much as an hour or more to school. The teachers then analyzed, or reassembled, the attendance data by students' home addresses, thus creating a map that showed where the students lived. In this process, they noted a possible **alternative explanation** for these students' tardiness and poor attendance, namely that in bad weather, their buses were often late or did not make it at all. This finding led the teachers to interview some of the students about the possible relation between the late buses, their tardiness or absences, and their attitudes and motivation toward school. The original data on student attendance had been understood in one way to reflect students' lack of motivation. When it was disassembled and reassembled to show the link between geography and student attendance, the data revealed alternative interpretations.

The attendance story: Alternative explanations; see Chapter 7, p. 169.

UNDERSTANDINGS: Understandings are the new—or existing—information, interpretations, insights, and perspectives on the question or puzzle that accumulate through the research process.

Comments: Understandings do not necessarily exhaust a line of inquiry. They do not always answer the question or solve the puzzle. Rather, they are the building blocks of further work. The term "findings" is also used; however, it suggests something more finite and resolved than the teacher-research process usually allows. The understandings that result from the teacher-research process by definition are disciplined, which means that they can show both *what* has been learned and *how* it has been learned. So if the teachers in the previous account wanted to challenge the administration's perception that student tardiness reflected only lack of motivation, they could argue their understanding that transportation difficulties were also a factor. They could support this understanding through the display of the attendance data by geographical location and the student interviews they conducted. Such a discussion puts in play both the understandings and how they were arrived at. It also suggests further research within this line of inquiry. For example, how do transportation problems interact with other factors to affect student attendance? Are there students who somehow overcome the transportation issues, and what factors allow or encourage them to do so?

> "PUBLISHING"—MAKING PUBLIC: Publishing is the point at which teachers voice their understandings and enter into public conversations about them with others beyond the immediate research setting. Publishing may be through discussion, presentations, or advocacy; it may be in print or through other media.

Comment: The idea of publishing used here comes from the work on process writing. In that context, the final phase involves students making public their texts by reading them aloud and/or preparing bound versions that become part of a class library. Becoming authors is a crucial part of the writing process for young learners because it situates them among other literate people. Lucy McCormack Calkins is an elementary school teacher and a teacher-researcher who has studied young children learning to write. Her first book, *Lessons from a Child: On the Teaching and Learning of Writing,* one of the first teacher-research accounts published, gave substantial impetus both to the process writing movement and to teacher-research in general. In a subsequent book, Calkins (1986) quotes a seven-year-old writer-author named Greg who explains the connection between reading and publishing:

> Before I ever wrote a book I used to think there was a big machine and they typed in a title and then the machine went until the book was done. Now I look at a book and know a guy wrote it and it's been his project for a long time. After the guy wrote it, he probably thinks of questions people will ask him and revises it like I do. . . . (p. 224)

The same process happens in teacher-research. When teacher-researchers make their findings public through whatever means, they begin to claim a place in the production of recognized knowledge about teaching and learning. Just as Greg says, they can see themselves as peers within the educational research community. As I said in Chapter 1, research and the generation of knowledge—or publicly recognized understandings—are intimately bound up with power, and making public the understandings gained through teacher-research is a crucial step in asserting such power. The second point that Greg makes is likewise true of teacher-research. Publishing, or making understandings public, moves the research process forward. Presenting your work leads to questions about it, to the urge to revise or extend it, and thus to further work. Because teaching has been an "egg crate profession," the notion of making public what has been private and autonomous classroom practice is not a familiar value for teachers. But if teacher-researchers do not take this last step to make their work public, they risk not achieving the external and public value of teacher-research in influencing educational policy and practice (Freeman, 1996).

Figure 2.6: Teacher-research cycle (labeled)

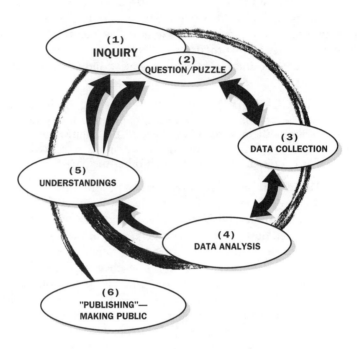

THE TEACHER-RESEARCH CYCLE

Characteristics of the teacher-research cycle

These, then, are the six elements in the complete cycle (Figure 2.6), which serves to organize what you do as you enter into teacher-research. In subsequent chapters we will focus on the phases of the cycle and how the elements in each phase interrelate. I want to make three general observations about the cycle at this point. First, it is a **cycle.** This means that the process has momentum; it feeds itself and carries itself forward. As the seven-year-old author Greg says of writing, "After the guy wrote [the book], he probably thinks of questions people will ask him and revises it. . . ." Similarly, the understandings in most lines of inquiry spawn further questions and puzzles. The end comes when you decide to stop; it rarely comes because you have found an answer.

Second, the cycle can have several **points of entry,** although to do the work completely there is only one starting point. As a teacher you can get hooked at pretty much any point in the process. You may decide to have your students keep learning logs on their progress and this can become the data (**data collection**). You may be looking over some students' written work and begin to speculate about a particular pattern in their mistakes (**data analysis**). You may explain to a colleague why you think a certain activity has been difficult for students at this level (**understanding**), and then wonder if that is always the case (**question/puzzle**). You may hear or read about someone's findings (publishing) and question them from your experience (inquiry), and so on. However, the starting point of the cycle—and the place to which the other five phases ultimately lead back—is inquiry. Inquiry provides the headwaters of the process; it provides the energy to keep it moving.

Third, if you choose, the whole cycle except for publishing can **remain private to the teacher.** Absent making it public, teacher-research need never be known or indeed affect the outside world. But I believe that going public with the understandings that result from teacher-research is critical for two reasons. First, as I have said, making the understandings public gives power to the cycle. Publishing engages the teacher-researcher in the creating of knowledge, which, in turn, can shape policy, practice, and conditions of work as well as improve and deepen understanding of teaching and learning (Kincheloe, 1991). Second, going public is an important way to test one's findings. If teacher-research remains entirely private, it can become solipsistic. Teacher-researchers need to hear others' reactions to their work, to engage in public debate, and to consider various perspectives. Because they stem from research, these discussions are based on information and analysis, not simply on opinion. So while there is a choice about making the work public, there are also consequences of that choice. To go public with the process of teacher-research and the understandings that result from it, helps establish a new professional community. It helps to transform education from a practice of implementation to a practice devoted to understanding learning, and it can strengthen teachers' understandings of what they do by attracting others' informed scrutiny of their work.

In this chapter I have outlined the teacher-research cycle conceptually. The two frameworks presented are meant to provide maps to guide the work at the hyphen. Doing teacher-research requires a special kind of balance in controlling the dimensions and responsibilities of both roles. Like lifting a kayak, it takes a certain amount of strength and energy to restructure your work in the classroom so you can pursue a line of inquiry as you are teaching. It may also demand that you intervene in what you would ordinarily do in teaching for purposes of your research. Understanding teacher-research also requires organization to follow a disciplined sequence from inquiry through data collection and analysis to understanding. Like folding a sheet, the work of teacher-research has its own particular logic and discipline. Finding it in the teacher-research cycle makes the work more doable. But having read these two frameworks, which, as frameworks, are rather abstract, you might well ask what does all this mean in practice? That is the story of the next chapter.

Suggested Readings

There are various approaches to capturing context in doing research. Sara Lawrence-Lightfoot's book, *The Good High School: Portraits in Character and Culture* (New York: Basic Books, 1983), is a pioneering example of what the author calls "portraiture," an approach that works to capture the texture and complexity of teaching and learning. In his article "Tipping the balance," (*Harvard Educational Review* 60 (2) pp. 217–236, 1990) Joseph Cambone applies the procedures of portraiture to write about a teacher working with demanding special-needs students.

There has been a fair amount written about action research as a form of teacher-research. I have found the clearest and most comprehensive account to be Ernest Stringer's book, *Action Research: A Handbook for Practitioners* (Thousand Oaks CA: Sage, 1996). A more classic presentation of action research in education is S. Kemmis and R. McTaggart's *Action Research Planner* (Geelong, Australia: Deakin University Press, 1988).

For more on Leo van Lier's typogology of research methods, see his book *The Classroom and the Language learner* (London: Longman, 1988). Another interesting discussion of this complex territory is L. Neuman's chapter, "The meanings of methodology," (in his book *Social Research Methods*. Boston: Allyn and Bacon, pp. 43–66, 1991). My chapter, "The 'Unstudied problem': Research in teacher learning in language teaching," (in D. Freeman and J. C. Richards (eds). *Teacher Learning in Language Teaching* (New York: Cambridge University Press, pp. 351–378, 1996) outlines approaches to researching teachers' knowledge and perceptions of their work.

3

CARNIVAL RIDES: AN ACCOUNT OF BEGINNING TEACHER-RESEARCH

Wagner Veillard

Wagner Veillard

PREAMBLE:

Dear reader,

It is raining as I write this note to preface this chapter. I am trying to imagine who you are and what you may find as you read this account. As an author, I have to admit that I am excited, and I am also a bit apprehensive. This is the first time I have "gone public" as a teacher-researcher; what you will see here is my first work. To introduce what you will read, I would like to tell you a bit about who I am and what led me to do some teacher-research in my classroom.

I was born in Rio de Janeiro, Brazil, and started learning English at a language school when I was 12. After finishing high school I worked as a chemistry technician until I was awarded a scholarship to attend college in the United States. I graduated with a major in business and then went back to Brazil, where I taught English for five years before returning to the United States to pursue a master's degree in TESOL.

The events in the chapter you are about to read took place several years ago, when I was a middle school English teacher teaching five classes a day at an international school in São Paulo, Brazil. The environment blurred ESL and EFL: The school was in Brazil, but the medium of instruction was English. Therefore, I was using materials prepared for students who were native speakers of English, although more than half of my students did not have English as their first language.

At the time, I was also participating in a teacher development program offered by the School for International Training in partnership with Associação Alumni, a binational center in São Paulo. The program, which lasted the better part of a year, was divided into four modules. There were two intensive modules of course work during school breaks in January and July, which were combined with doing teacher-research on-site from February to June, and then again from August to November. This chapter describes my first work as a teacher-researcher; Chapter 6 recounts my second project.

When I wrote up my first project, I did not think about publishing it. In fact, I did not even have a computer, and the first version of this chapter was handwritten, as you can see from the cover of the report, which I drew. I used the carnival image as a metaphor for my first experience with the discipline of the teacher-research process. I enjoy using metaphors in writing because they help me assemble my ideas within a new perspective. In developing my line of inquiry, I drew on two things that I enjoy tremendously: writing and working with teenagers, especially eighth graders ages 13 and 14 years old.

I hope you enjoy reading this chapter. I also hope that I will read, sometime soon, your accounts of doing teacher-research, and how you felt when you were carrying a kayak by yourself the first time.

Yours,
Wagner Veillard

Investigations

3.1 *SHIFTING ORIENTATIONS: MOVING FROM TEACHER TO TEACHER-RESEARCHER*

This Investigation asks you to examine how Wagner Veillard moves from a teacher's toward a teacher-researcher's orientation over the course of this chapter.

As you read the chapter, make a list of the ways in which the author, Veillard, approaches his teaching *as a teacher* versus *as a teacher-*

researcher. When is he acting as a teacher and when is he acting as a teacher-researcher?

If you are working with peers, do this Investigation alone as you read the chapter and discuss your notes afterward.

ADMISSION TICKET

The school term is over, and I feel like a child in an amusement park. The atmosphere is fascinating: lights, music, movement. I do not know what to try first or where to go next once I make my first choice. A small sign tells me that I am not old enough for certain rides. When I focus my attention on the many rides I am allowed to explore, I get mixed feelings of boredom, anxiety, anticipation, and fear.

The school term is over, and I am fascinated by the possibilities of what one can do with one's data. There are different ways not only of breaking information apart, but also of putting it together. I have learned about instruments, sources, strategies, and the importance of analyzing data before collecting new evidence. I realized how crucial it is to share what you are doing with colleagues so that true collaboration occurs. Somehow overwhelmed by these insights, I really do not know where or how to start my analysis. My only desire is to critique my research procedures. I wish to focus on what I did not do and on what I could have done better. I am anxious to redesign my plan and continue my research with a new group of students when the next term begins in August.

For Veillard's account of his subsequent work, see Chapter 6.

Forced to go back and see what I can say based on the data I have, I feel frustrated. The results are not the ones I would like to present. To make matters worse, there are huge flames in my burning questions; but how did the fire get started? In order to answer this question, we must move on to our first carnival ride.

THE FERRIS WHEEL: THE CONTEXT, THE RESEARCH GROUP, AND MY QUESTIONS

I teach at a Catholic American school in São Paulo, Brazil. Altogether, there were 47 students in my research group: 21 in the first class, and 26 in the second. They were in eighth grade, 13–14 years old, and they had been my students for one semester; they were known as "English 8" classes. The students were in school from 8 A.M. to 3:10 P.M.; the school day was divided into eight periods of 45 minutes each. I saw them every day, either from 12:45 to 1:30 or from 2:25 to 3:10 P.M. The first group came right after lunch, while the second group was the last class of the day. The school used two basic textbooks for this level: one for grammar and one for literature. Besides these, one novel per month was to be assigned as outside reading. Over half of my students were upper-middle-class Brazilians. The non-Brazilians in the group were children of businessmen and diplomats. In most cases, these students attended the school for only two years, because their parents were then transferred out of Brazil. The following table shows the nationalities of the students, in declining frequency, in my research group:

Figure 3.1: Research group: Nationality and number

NATIONALITY	NUMBER	NATIONALITY	NUMBER
Brazilian	27	Mexican	1
Korean	10	Japanese	1
U.S. American	4	Dutch	1
Argentinian	2	Finnish	1
		TOTAL	47

On teaching versus research-able questions, see Chapter 4, p. 61.

Since I really enjoy writing, I decided at the start of the semester that my inquiry would be related to this skill. Aware of my personal bias, however, I started analyzing my own writing. I was intrigued by the steps of the process: what happens from the moment I find an idea worth writing about, to the moment I hand my final version to a reader. I finally stated my research question as:

1. *How can my students assess their own writing?*

As a teacher, my concern was to provide students with whatever tools they needed in order to judge their own writing. I now realize how difficult such an endeavor is, but as I started the term my view of the process was a simple one. These were my supporting questions:

1A. How can I get my students to write more and better?

1B. How can I get them used to rewriting?

1C. How can I provide them with opportunities for self and peer correction so that I, as the teacher, am not the sole evaluator of any specific writing?

On assumptions in the research process, see Chapter 4, p. 53.

Although they were not clearly stated, the following expectations were deeply rooted in my mind:

1. I want my students to see the teacher as a learner/reader in the classroom.

2. I want my students to understand that rewriting is an inevitable step in refining ideas and polishing a writing piece.

3. As I give students the chance of reading one another's work, I hope they will be able to find, and possibly correct, their own mistakes.

4. At some point, I expect students to hand me the final version of an assignment and say, "This is the best I can do, both in terms of what I know and how hard I can work."

As you can clearly see, there are many traps in my expectations. The most dangerous one is the idea that I want students to look at writing in the same way I do. In hoping that they will eventually verbalize a sense of achievement, #4 above, I wonder if I am assuming that they need to say what they have done in order to learn from it. Am I thus looking to be rewarded as the teacher with their statements, even though the students may see their own rewards in the work they do for themselves?

When you are up there on a Ferris wheel seat, you can usually see the entire amusement park, and what lies around it as well. I have tried to give the reader an overall impression of the research project: who my students were, what my initial interest was, and the kind of environment in which we were operating. It is now time to go down so that one can find out what I actually did in the classroom.

THE ROLLER-COASTER OR JOURNALING

In accordance with this ride, I plan to explain very quickly the ups and downs of how I worked with my students and their writing. I chose my journal as the cart for this ride for it is the only piece of evidence on which I can rely to take us from the beginning to the end of this adventure. In looking back at my own work in the first module of the teacher development program, I saw that my reflective writings were the most powerful element in the experience. So, on the very first class, I asked my students to keep journals. I told them that nobody would read their entries unless they agreed. I also told them that I would be keeping a journal myself. To link us together in this common enterprise, I asked them to sign their names on the cover of my journal.

In keeping with Gattegno's ideas on the Silent Way (Gattegno, 1976; Stevick, 1980), my objective was to "learn my students" while "they learned themselves and the language." So I decided that I would ask students to write in their journals in class at least twice a week for a two-month period. The entries might relate to themes that the students would develop further in writing their compositions, but they were not restricted to this focus. Below, I have listed some of topics I assigned in journaling, and my reasons for assigning them:

JOURNAL ENTRY TOPIC	REASON IN ASSIGNING IT For students. . .
Think of guidelines for group work	To come up with their own rules
Write about a book that had an impact on you.	To share titles and popular authors
What makes a good presentation?	To create their own standards for oral presentations
How did you feel when Márcio was lecturing for ten minutes in Finnish?	To experience how Márcio, and other non-Portuguese speakers, might feel when Brazilians used Portuguese in English class activities
Go back to the predictions about the book you chose to read. Were you right?	To develop skills in predicting and guessing as part of reading
Bring a special object to class and describe it	To share something personal, and to improve skills in descriptive writing

Use your journal entries to think about the first four weeks of English class. Write a letter to a friend telling him/her what we did and how you felt about it.	To provide me with student feedback on the first month of the teacher-research project
How do you start your day? Compare your morning routine to that of other classmates, and then to Johnny Tremain's.	To move from their experience into the novel *Johnny Tremain*, to explore similarities and differences
Draw a class map. Go back to the one you drew some time ago. Are you sitting in the same place?	To increase students' awareness of possible social groups and cliques in the class

There were a lot of advantages in asking my students to keep journals. By having them write most of the entries in class, usually for no longer than ten minutes, I had the chance to write in my own journal during class time. Therefore, my field notes referring to students' questions and comments are quite accurate. Once the class was over I sat down, reread my notes, and tried to analyze my students' reactions to the lesson by writing reflective memos to myself. Beyond the research process, this procedure also helped me to prepare materials for the following day. I also used the journals to help my students understand themselves better as individuals and the class as a group. By the end of the first week of school I was using the journal in class almost every day because it had proved to be an excellent tool in preparation for pair work, group tasks, and class discussions. In terms of my research question, I assigned as many different types of journal entries as I could think of so that, later on, my students would have a variety of options to choose from as springboards for composition topics. The journals certainly made my students write more, if I compare their entries to the amount of writing they had done in the previous semester, during which time they wrote only four compositions.

I want to mention three incidents which I think illustrate the students' emerging motivation to write, although I have no way of showing a direct connection between motivation to write and the use of journals in the classroom. In the first case, Márcio, a Finnish boy, continued writing in his journal even after I stopped assigning writing tasks. He kept on making his entries until the last day of class, and offered me his journal as a gift at the end of the semester. In the second, Katia, Patricia and Neuza, in the sixth period class, and Edison, in the eighth period class, got together and transformed a novel they had read during first semester into a play. The play, entitled *The Trojan War*, had sixteen acts, which were more like connected skits. The student actors and actresses interacted with these writers in order to create and refine the dialogues. They plan to start rehearsing next term. Finally, Elizabeth had one of her poems selected by a publisher in the United States to appear in an anthology of works by teenage authors to be published next year.

On anecdotal data, see Appendix C, p. 202.

Despite all the good news, however, there were disadvantages in using the journals. I became too involved in trying to find out how my students were feeling about the writing process, and so there were times when I digressed from my research question. I do not regret what I did, but had I kept a narrower focus, I would have more relevant data. I have since found it difficult to identify the most useful journal entries to code, and the analysis is very time consuming. I was not able to analyze all of my students' journals because I could only work with the journals willingly given to me at the end of the semester. As I had said that they would control their journals, I had to respect my students' privacy. Therefore, I only have six journals, not including my own, to include in the study. When I assigned letters, had them prepare interviews, or organized class discussions, I was able to get a sense of the contents of students' entries without actually reading their journals, because they used their entries as a basis for these activities.

However, when I read the actual journal entries for each day in the six journals I had, I realized that there were many details which I was never aware of. Students were paying more attention to my actions than I could ever have imagined. For instance, Márcio wrote on February 15: "Veillard took notes as he did yesterday." On April 26 he wrote: "I really don't like English now. And Veillard is not Veillard, he's something else, 'regular,' only cares about grammar. Gets angry easily." His entries made me wonder what was I taking for granted in my teaching.

This carnival ride is over.

The Swing Boat: From Writing to Reading

Although I do have samples of students' writing, in particular three drafts of the same composition, I have no basis on which to state that my students became better writers. I realize that I did not have clearly researchable criteria for what "becoming a better writer" meant. In one coding, I counted the number of words in their different drafts. The table below shows two examples:

On a priori data analysis, see Chapter 5, pp. 103–105.

Figure 3.2: Comparing lengths of composition drafts

Student Draft	Michel Number of Words	Euridice Number of Words
#1	77	83
#2	79	86
#3	82	99

What exactly do these data tell me? One might argue that if the number of words increases through the drafting and revising process, students are learning to be more specific and detailed in their descriptions. But someone else might argue that if the number of words decreases, students are learning to be more concise and that, as a result, their writing is more powerful. I realize that data themselves don't tell you the answer. You always have to interpret them in some

On redefining
research
questions,
see Chapter 5,
pp. 91–93.

way. I also tried to analyze the kinds of comments students wrote on one anoth-er's compositions when I gave them the chance to give one another peer feed-back. Unfortunately, I was not able to reduce these comments into categories that made sense to me, partly because I didn't have enough data to make useful comparisons and thus to see the categories.

If I look closely at my data, I am thrown towards the other end of this swing boat. The only question I might be able to answer does not really deal with writ-ing, but rather with reading, a skill that is very much related to writing. My research question would then become:

"What happens when my students choose what they read?"

To explain this shift, let me refresh the reader's memory. My students were required to read one novel per month. According to school rules, the teacher assigned the book, and the whole class read it. Last semester however, I gave my students the opportunity to choose one of the novels they would read, the very first one, so that each student was reading his or her own book. I have outlined the process by which students chose and read their individual books below.

February 7: Homework—"Think of three books you would like to read, but for some reason have not managed to."

February 8: "In groups, share your titles and choose one book you would like to read by February 24. We will all start reading our var-ious books on February 10."

February 9: "Think about a book that had an impact on you. What was it like? What was the story about? Why and when did you read it? Why did it have an impact on you? Would you recommend it? To whom? Remember to bring this book to class tomorrow."

February 10: "Acquaint yourself with the book you brought in. Describe it: the cover, the pictures, the number of pages, table of con-tents, title, author, year of publication. Why did you choose it? When do you plan to read it? What kind of story do you expect?

"Prepare a reading contract and show it to a classmate. For example,

John intends to finish reading *1984* by February 24. If he doesn't, he *will not play on his computer for three days*."

February 13: "Write a brief paragraph about what you have read. Make two predictions based on what you have read so far. Walk around the classroom and share what you wrote with a classmate."

February 14: "Prepare a card according to this model:

Your name is reading *title of your book* by *author of the book you are reading*.

"Tomorrow I will post the cards around the classroom so that every-one knows what everybody else is reading. I want to try and create the feeling of an art gallery by displaying each reader's choice. I will also record all the book titles in my journal."

February 17: Homework—"Continue reading your book. Imagine you are a character in the story. You can be yourself as an extra character, or you can take the place of a character who already exists in the story. What would you change or do differently in the story?"

February 20: "Find a partner and interview each other about your character and the changes you would make."

February 21: "Go back to your predictions about the story (February 13). Were you right?"

February 24: "Retrieve your cards that were posted on February 15. If you are done reading, prepare a drawing that summarizes your book. If you are not done, write a letter to yourself explaining why you have not finished, what the penalty was in your reading contract, and what you can do to finish reading your book."

What can I say based on the evidence I possess? Twenty-six out of 47 students chose to read suspense books. They opted for stories about ghosts, supernatural beings, crimes and detectives, mysteries, or horror books. The table below summarizes the data on how many students read which types of book.

On displaying data, see Chapter 5, pp. 108–119.

Figure 3.3: Students' reading choices

TYPE OF BOOK	NUMBER OF STUDENTS (OUT OF 47) WHO READ THIS TYPE OF BOOK
Suspense	26
Books that have been turned into movies	8
Sports	3
Mythology/Fantasy	2
Science Fiction	1
Other	5

Thirty-five out of 47 students were able to finish reading their books by February 24. It is interesting to look at the 12 students who did not finish reading their chosen books by the agreed-upon deadline. Alone in my office, I laugh at how different our perceptions are. For example, I think I was fair in letting the students decide what and how much they wanted to read by the deadline. But Ayrton justifies not being able to finish his book, writing: "The teacher gave little time." Or there is Rosângela, who, when asked to think about the first four weeks of English class, writes in her letter dated March 12: "Until now we didn't do any reading." In general, students were excited to be able to choose what they were going to read as Benedito put it in his journal: "And what's good, we can choose the next book." Nevertheless, they expressed concerns, such as: "Does it [the book] have to be in English? But what's going to happen if we can choose whatever we want? How can we show that we have read it? Does it have to be a book from the library? How are you going to grade/test us on this book?" This opens up the whole issue of how students perceive what they are doing. Sudeep comes to me at the end of class on February 10 and says: "This class is better than the others, more active. We don't have to write so much." He pauses, "I mean, we do, but it is not the same!" I say, "Hum, that's right. You do write here, but how is it different?" Sudeep replies, "We don't have to copy from a book."

As I have said before, I do not necessarily want to present these as research results, but they do give a flavor of what actually happened.

THE CAROUSEL: HOW THE PARTS (DON'T) FIT TOGETHER

As a child I used to look at the carousel and wonder how it was possible for the horses to move up and down and move around, without getting out of their predetermined places in the circle. Looking at myself as a learner of teacher-research, I believe that my biggest mistake has been trying to make my research work operate like a carousel. In other words, I have attempted to present neat contrasts: writing as a process *versus* writing as a product; oral and written comments in self and peer feedback *versus* number or letter grades; my personal beliefs about learning and teaching *versus* institutional goals. Perhaps I am setting myself up for failure if I take on the task of changing one of these parts and try to keep it from affecting the whole. I see now that is impossible; the parts are interconnected like the carousel horses. On the other hand, the discipline of research, as I understand it, does require structure and regularity, like the spacing of the horses on the carousel. I need some space to figure out this seeming contradiction: How do you separate a part of your teaching from the whole of your work life in order to study it?

Now, I am out of my classroom, in the middle of an exciting ride of the third module in this teacher development program. I am aware that my cart will twist and turn, driven by doubts and insights. Every now and then, I may still grab on to the handle of old beliefs, just for the sake of safety. But I can already picture myself standing in line for the next promising ride, when I will again be back in the classroom, with my students, perhaps to research again.

Working at the hyphen, Chapter 1, pp. 5–8 and Chapter 8, pp. 177–178.

3.2 *THINKING ABOUT RESEARCH DESIGN*

This Investigation asks you to analyze Veillard's account in a particular way, according to the basic questions that drive the process of research design. You may want to familiarize yourself with the Investigation before you read the chapter, or you may want to return to what you have read in order to complete it.

> Respond to the following questions in any order; they provide a framework to move an inquiry toward a planned research project. (I use the terms "you/the reseacher" because the questions can apply equally to reading other people's research.)

- **WHAT?** What is the **inquiry**? What is (are) the **research-able question(s)/puzzle** here? What are the supporting questions/puzzles?

- **WHY?** What is the background or rationale of the research? Why are you/the researcher interested in it? What motivates the work?

- **WHERE?** Where will the research be done? In which particular classroom(s) or site(s)?

- **WHO?** Who will be the participants in your study? What role—if any—will colleagues play in the study?

- **HOW?** What **data** are relevant to the research questions? How do you/the researcher plan to **collect** them? How will you/the researcher **analyze** them?

- **WHEN?** What is the provisional time line or schedule? When and how often will you/the researcher gather data?

- **SO WHAT?** Why will the research matter? To whom might it make a difference? What might you/others understand differently as a result?

Answer these questions, as far as possible, from the information in the chapter. As you do so, also make note of things that you find missing. Which—if any—of these questions does Veillard not address in this account? It can help to do this task in a 7 (rows) x 2 (columns) matrix, in which you list the seven guide question words down the left side, the information you find in this chapter in one column, and things that are missing in the other.

After doing this Investigation, you may want to read Veillard's own comments in Chapter 6, (pp. 143–145), in which he offers a brief critique of the work reported in this chapter.

4

FORMING AN INQUIRY: FROM QUESTIONS TO PLANNING THE PROJECT

One or two months is really too little time to be able to see what is happening in a classroom. I need to go back again and again, to see what is happening . . . whether the things I am finding continue to be there.

Helena Portillo

Teacher-research: Inquiry to Design, Figure #4.1

It is one of life's ironies that sometimes you need to do things that seem complicated in order to arrive at simple insights or understandings. One of the two characters in Edward Albee's one-act play *Zoo Story* captures this idea quite wonderfully when he muses, "Sometimes you have to go a long distance out of your way in order to come a short distance back correctly." This is, in essence, the dilemma of moving from an inquiry to the questions and puzzles that it spawns. As I said in Chapter 2, inquiry drives the teacher-research process, although it may not necessarily be its starting point. It is often only with the passage of time and the commitment of energy to the process that the research-able questions actually distill themselves from the inquiry. To expect otherwise is to misunderstand the research process and perhaps to create unreal expectations for yourself. As one colleague put it, "Teacher-research is a great opportunity for Monday-morning quarterbacking. Once it's over, you recognize what it has been about." This attitude of Monday-morning quarterbacking, or second-guessing how the football game should have been played the day afterwards, is what can propel the teacher-research process into another cycle.

It is important to realize that being clear about your questions is not necessarily where you begin the teacher-research process, but it is usually where you end up. In this chapter we look at the parameters of **inquiry** more closely to see how it can spawn questions, how **teaching questions** and **research-able questions** differ, how research-able questions suggest the **data** that respond to them, and how, on this basis, to **plan** an overall project. This cycle forms the backbone of the teacher-research process; in this chapter we will examine the mechanics of launching yourself into that process.

Figure 4.1: Teacher-research: From inquiry to design

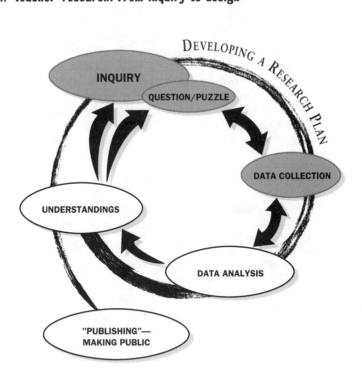

As you can see in Figure 4.1, this chapter focuses on the first part of the teacher-research cycle: How you move through the initial stages of inquiry to identify and elaborate questions, to determine the kinds of data that can respond to those questions, and how you lay out a research plan. However, this first part of the cycle usually stems from what precedes it. It can, and usually does, grow both out of assumptions you bring to the inquiry from your experience, and from understandings that you may have gained through reading or doing other teacher-research. This prior information inevitably shapes the form of the new inquiry. From it grow the preconceptions you may have for why you think things happen as they do in your teaching. An orientation of inquiry and speculation holds these preconceptions up to scrutiny and questioning; an orientation of doing and action generally works simply to reconfirm them.

ASSUMPTIONS, UNDERSTANDINGS, AND DEVELOPING A LINE OF INQUIRY

Kim Mortimer was a beginning teacher-researcher when she wrote the following in a memo. Here she sets out very clearly the intimate connection between the preconceptions she brought into the research process, which she calls her hypotheses, and how she framed her initial inquiry.

Kim Mortimer

Account #4.1: Kim Mortimer, "Adolescents, anxiety, and second language learning"

When I began teaching Spanish to seventh and eighth grade students (ages 12–14) at Marlboro Elementary School, I noticed that they seemed unusually prone to "turning off." While paying attention, listening or reading and comprehending well in English, they would frequently stop listening or reading in Spanish. When I spoke in Spanish for more than a few sentences at a time, they stopped listening and would often speak over me or turn their heads away. They said thing like, "I have no idea what you're saying. What are you talking about?"

In contrast, the fifth and sixth grade students (ages 10–11) were much more willing to listen to or read Spanish, even when it was unfamiliar. They were clearly eager to comprehend the message, often guessing out loud in English about what was being said. When they were wrong, they simply guessed again until they selected the correct meaning. I began to wonder about the cause of this significant difference in behavior between the two age groups. *Why were the older students so much less likely to do the work of comprehension? Did it have to do with how they felt about learning Spanish?* This became my line of **inquiry**:

> How the seventh and eighth grade students felt about learning Spanish, and what effects these feelings had upon their (apparent willingness to engage in) comprehension.

From the beginning I **hypothesized** that the students were "turning off" because of substantial anxiety associated with trying to comprehend an unfamiliar language. I *believed* that the intrapersonal risks involved in interpreting Spanish, trying to respond correctly, were too great. It was safer to refuse to understand at all, to refuse to listen. I *derived this hypothesis* largely from my own experiences in adolescence and with second-language learning and my observations of others. *It seems* a basic human response to react to overwhelming pressure by shutting down and refusing to address any portion of it. *I assumed* that the pressure the seventh and eighth graders were feeling was internal anxiety: that hearing and not understanding Spanish caused them significant (and largely internal) stress, and that this anxiety was outwardly manifested in their refusal to listen or respond. *I also assumed* that by making meaning explicitly clear (usually with much English) at every step of the way, their anxiety would be reduced. *Now I am not sure this was an appropriate assumption.*

In this memo Mortimer elaborates preconceptions from her experiences as a student, as a teacher, and as an individual who holds a certain position in society. These ideas, which she, like any of us, brings to teaching, inevitably shaped her thinking. The teacher-research process, however, pulls her beyond them.

Inquiries, regardless of their nature, do not spring out of thin air; they are rooted both directly and indirectly in who we are, what we believe, and the questions we are socially positioned to ask. For instance, a first-year teacher may well have different questions and perceptions of middle-school boys and classroom discipline from those of a veteran teacher. Or it may be more likely to occur to a gay or lesbian teacher than to a straight teacher to examine how teaching materials represent the lives of gays and lesbians, if they do at all. This fact that inquiry is shaped by the assumptions by which we live our lives suggests two courses of action in embarking on a research project. First, you need to think seriously about what you believe to be true in teaching and learning. These assumptions can provide a solid point of departure for developing a line of inquiry. Second, it is important to review your specific preconceptions about your line of inquiry as it is unfolding. It is worth asking yourself repeatedly, "What am I assuming or taking for granted? How could I be wrong in what I am seeing?" By questioning yourself, your assumptions about teaching and learning generally, and the preconceptions you have about the particular inquiry, you keep yourself slightly off-balance. Being unsure about what you know creates a sense of openness and vulnerability fundamental to good research. You chase down that openness as you organize your inquiry into a research plan, and thus build the discipline of your work.

On what teachers bring to teaching from experience, see Lortie, (1975); see also Bailey et al. (1996).

This principle of challenging yourself to reexamine your assumptions and preconceptions is also central to the notion of validity. Validity has to do with two things. One is procedural. It depends on getting the research process right so the data respond to the research questions, analysis is appropriate to the data, and findings are supported by the analysis. The solidness of this chain depends on controlling the research situation, as we saw in the discussion of van Lier's typology, and on the researcher's skills in carrying out the process. It goes back to Shulman's first meaning of "discipline" as methodicalness. The other side of validity has to do with confidence. Can you, as the researcher, and others who will learn about your work reasonably believe in its results? These two aspects of validity are clearly linked: Solid, disciplined procedures can create confidence in their outcomes. Underlying how procedures are used, however, are the clarity and self-awareness of the researcher, which is why recognizing and articulating your assumptions and preconceptions, as Kim Mortimer did in her memo, is so important. Such insight is the foundation of your work as a teacher-researcher. No amount of good procedure will compensate for being blinded by your own preconceptions.

On validity, see Chapter 7, pp. 164–175.

When talking about research, people often think of validity as synonymous with objectivity. In the conventional view detachment and distance are supposed to come in large part through one person (the researcher) studying others (the teacher and the students). In teacher-research this relationship is recast since the teacher *is* the researcher. Objectivity cannot be located in two separate people, the researcher and the researched (Fine, 1994). Rather, as mentioned in Chapter 1, in teacher-research one person carries out two distinct functions that establish different perspectives on the work he or she is doing. These hyphenated functions of teaching and researching together offer the potential for unique insights into the complexity of classroom teaching and learning. The order and beauty of a landscape seen from afar are quite different from the texture and immediacy of walking through that same countryside. The objectivity of teacher-research is not a function of distance and detachment in a conventional sense. Rather, it hinges on the discipline of how one is involved in both teaching and researching, as mentioned in Chapter 2. In discipline, or the self-aware method-ical control over what you are doing and why, lies the foundation of validity in teacher-research. This foundation begins with keeping track of assumptions that animate the work.

4.1 LOCATING THE INQUIRY

This Investigation begins a series of Investigations throughout this chapter that are aimed at helping you think through a research plan. In this Investigation two alternatives are suggested: (A) using reflective writing, and (B) using video-tape as a prompt.

Alternative (A): Reflective writing

Think about the teaching you have done recently or that you will be doing. Think about the school context, the students, and the content you have been teaching.

Brainstorm the following questions, making notes for yourself as you go along:

- What do you wonder about in your teaching and your students' learning?

- What puzzles you about your students, the content, or the organization of your classroom?

- What aspects of the students' learning do you want to understand better?

- What are some aspects of your teaching situation that intrigue or trouble you? Why?

- What do you know about your teaching or their learning that you are interested in verifying?

Use the **loop-writing process,** outlined in Appendix A (p. 198), to sharpen your inquiry.

Alternative (B): A video prompt

Arrange to have your class, or a portion of it, videotaped. Ideally you would have someone else run the camera as you are teaching. Perhaps a colleague or even a student will do so for you. However, you can also videotape yourself very satisfactorily without help. You need to set up the camera using a wide-angle focus to take in as much of the classroom as possible. Be sure the image catches as many stu-dents as possible. Start the tape recording at the beginning of the les-son and let it run until the tape runs out or the lesson ends.

Review the videotape. Look carefully at what is going on and who is doing what. Think about the following prompts as you watch it:

- What questions do you have about your teaching as you watch your students' learning in this lesson?

- What puzzles you about what you see? What are you unsure of?

- What aspects of the students' learning do you want to better understand?

- Why do you think things are happening as they are on the tape? How would you know? What speculations does this raise about students' learning and/or your teaching?

- What do you know about your teaching or their learning that you are interested in verifying?

Refer to the **video-viewing suggestions** outlined in Appendix A (pp. 198–199) for further ideas of how to work with the videotape.

PURPOSE, TIME, AND OUTCOME

Purpose-
Time-
Outcome

At the beginning of this chapter, Helena Portillo, a Brazilian teacher-researcher, was quoted about time in the research process. Portillo says, "I need to go back again and again, to see what is happening [in my classroom]." Time is at the heart of teacher-research: the time it takes to do the research and, perhaps even more crucially, the time before the research begins. It literally takes time to conceptualize an inquiry, to think about what you take for granted, to look closely at what you assume or hypothesize about a situation or a group of students. Most fundamentally, doing teacher-research is about using your time as a teacher in different ways. The irony is that even planning how to do things differently takes time, which many teachers do not have.

It is useful to put this issue of time in a three-part frame, bracketing it between purpose on one side and outcome on the other. **Purpose** raises basic questions: Why am I interested in this inquiry? Where does it come from in my experience as a teacher (or perhaps as a student, a parent, or a human being)? Why am I asking these questions? Who is this inquiry actually for? Clearly a component of the response to these questions will be personal, as in "I am doing this for me, because I want to know or understand X or Y." There is usually more to it, however. There may be a student or a group of students in your class who indirectly suggest the inquiry to you by who they are or what they are doing. Or it may be circumstances beyond the classroom: a change in the curriculum, the schedule, or the status-quo in general, such as team teaching with a colleague, or using new materials or technologies. Or the impetus may arise out of experience, an intriguing or a nagging issue, or an interest in reexamining something that has become familiar and predictable to try to see it in new ways.

While it has a personal dimension, a particular inquiry's purpose is usually traceable to the situation you are in and the teaching you are doing or have done. This fact grounds the work in your direct experience and in so doing, it introduces the issue of **time.** Unlike colleagues who conduct other forms of research, teacher-researchers always face the challenge of doing at least two things at once. So the idea of doing teacher-research raises the question of how you use your time as a teacher and to what ends. Seen from an external or **etic** point of view, most of the time teachers are primarily engaged in accomplishing purposes set by others, such as finishing the chapter or the unit because it is in

On teachers'
work lives, see
Freedman et al.
(1983).

the curriculum, or monitoring the playground or the lunch room as called for in the labor agreement or job description, and so on. Indeed, for many teachers, the only individually managed time is what are euphemistically called their "planning periods." In this frame, using time for inquiry is difficult; it often goes against the grain of school. But it is not impossible.

Though there is an automatic structure to how teachers spend much of their work time, there is also the space to think differently about what is going on in the classroom. Simply put, it does not have to follow that because time is structured, therefore ways of thinking—and indeed doing things—must be equally structured. While you may have to take attendance at the beginning of the class period, there are many different ways to do so. Calling names off the class roll is only one. Because it is common to our experience, it seems the conventional way to do the job. Too often, the demands of what has to get done in teaching can crowd out creativity and exploration in how those demands are met. I believe it is generally teachers' preconceptions that do most of this crowding. Although inquiring into your work as a teacher does mean using time in somewhat different ways, it also means rethinking the usual and conventional in your work. It can often be harder to push this mental reorientation than to find the time to do the work.

The use of time is closely related to the achievement of **outcomes.** Time in the classroom is generally organized to achieve purposes that are set from the outside, and these achievements are measured in terms of outcomes. Common measures such as test scores, student progress and achievement, and so on are meant to track the accomplishments of teaching, and to a degree they do. However, when purposes are set and outcomes measured by those who are beyond the classroom, the teacher is reduced to an element in an equation. Teacher-research recasts these relationships by overlaying a set of teacher-determined purposes and outcomes on those that already exist in the classroom. This is why doing teacher-research can feel like doing two things at once, and why, therefore, time can become such an issue. The social linguist Mikhail Bahktin wrote that words are hardly empty, that they are "overpopulated with the intentions of others." The same can be said of teachers' time and their classrooms, both of which are formed and populated by other people's intentions. In engaging in an inquiry into your teaching, you reestablish the primacy of your intentions in the classroom. You are setting a purpose—the inquiry and its questions—and aiming for an outcome—the data and their analysis—that will accomplish that purpose and respond to those questions. This process involves carving out time from the fabric of your work life in order to achieve these ends: to think through a line of inquiry to find its research-able questions and to plan the data that will respond to them.

Some ethical
questions

Rethinking how you use your time in the classroom will inevitably raise issues of ethics and responsibility. Jim Baumann, the teacher-researcher cited in Chapter 1, made the point that, of the two jobs, teaching must always take precedence over researching. Put another way, you would not do something as a researcher that directly contradicts or interferes with what you know, or must do, as a teacher. However, drawing that line is not always simple or clear. Because the research process involves reexamining preconceptions and assumptions, you will need to question some of those beliefs. If you only do what you "know" to be right as a teacher, you will be caught in the status-quo. Questioning your assumptions will inevitably mean that you sometimes suspend the known to inquire into the new or unsure. It is always a matter of judgment, and I think the line is basically a personal one. I would not do something that knowingly puts at a disadvantage or otherwise hurts my students or their learning. However, I would also question whether what I believe to be effective is always so. In that space between certainty and questions lies room for a line of inquiry that can open possibilities of new perspectives, understandings, and visions. It also opens the possibility of risk; once you question what you take for granted, you begin to challenge the status quo.

Educational researchers like Baumann have argued the issue of ethics from a number of points of view. Mainly, however, their issues have centered on how a research project might change the norms of the teaching and learning process in a classroom or a school. But since teacher-research is, by definition, a composite undertaking, changing those norms falls under the direct control of one-and-the-same person: the teacher who is researching his or her own teaching. Writing about large-scale educational research projects, Kenneth Howe and Katharine Dougherty (1993, p. 20) outline the following list of caveats for research activities that take place with students in classrooms. The list, which is adopted from the University of Colorado–Boulder School of Education's Policy on Educational Research, is aimed at large, multi-site research undertakings in which researchers come from outside the schools and classrooms they are studying. The scale notwithstanding, these guidelines offer a useful point of departure, particularly when put alongside Baumann's list from Chapter 1 (p. 7). To highlight the contrast in scale, I have annotated each item according to how it relates particularly to teacher-research:

Research activities in classrooms and/or schools will:

1. *Not differ* in any significant ways *from* the *normal* range of
   activities of the classroom, school, or district.

Since teacher-research is embedded in the classroom, this caveat seems a natural one. However, teacher-research may involve challenging what is "normal" or "usual" in the classroom or school in order to better understand or perhaps reshape it. Consider the example of the the teachers who examined problems with school attendance in Chapter 2. If we always live by what is considered "normal," we may trap ourselves in the status quo.

2. *Involve* only *customary* and noncontroversial instructional *goals.*

In general this makes sense. However, again, "customary" and "normal" spring from the same root ("custom" or "norm"), and sometimes the aim of teacher-research is to interrupt what is usual in order to look at it in a different or new way.

3. *Not deny any students educational benefits* they would
   otherwise receive.

This caveat is bedrock to me. Teacher-research should not involve putting students at a disadvantage. However, since you are the teacher, you already have responsibility for what happens in class and you are viewed with that in mind. Teacher-research opens the possibility of examining how to better accomplish the ends for which you are already responsible.

4. *Promise direct benefits* (at least in the form of evaluative information) to the classroom, school, or district.

Because teachers are researching their own work and classrooms, the immediate benefits to students are obvious. Whether those benefits are recognized at the school or district level depends on various factors, many of which are beyond the teacher-researcher's direct control. The publishing phase of the teacher-research cycle, which we look at in Chapter 7, addresses this area.

5. *Incorporate adequate safeguards to protect the privacy* (i.e., anonymity or confidentiality) of all individuals who might be subjects of the research.

While anonymity or confidentiality may be crucial in large-scale work in which researchers visit many schools and classrooms, they are by definition different issues when teachers are researching their own classrooms. There is vulnerability inherent in opening up your own teaching to scrutiny, vulnerability that is mediated by the fact that you are the one who is doing the scrutinizing. It is hard to be anonymous to yourself, and certainly you know who your students are. Issues of anonymity or confidentiality become more central when you "publish" —orally or in writing—your findings. It is important to have agreement from colleagues and your students (or their parents) about what you can and cannot say. These are issues we address more fully in Chapter 7.

6. *Involve only existing data on students* that are, or can be rendered, in ways that are non-identity specific.

Here teacher-research differs from large-scale research studies. By definition, teacher-research involves focusing on information about your students that you might otherwise overlook or not take into account. So "existing data" can mean *data that exist* and can be collected. I do not think it should mean only the data that you now have on record; if it did, what would there be to discover?

Howe and Dougherty's six caveats help to frame ethical issues that need to be considered in researching educational settings. However, they stem from large-scale studies designed by researchers from outside school systems who study schools and classrooms that are not their own. Any teacher-researcher certainly needs to consider these issues. But the scale of work and the locus of control in teacher-research are specific to a classroom and school setting, and the study invariably makes public certain aspects of the teacher-researcher's own work. So some of these caveats do not apply, or they apply differently. The basic assumption—that research should not alter what it finds in classrooms and that it should contribute positively to the setting—is difficult to argue with. But because teaching involves human nature and activity, it is always in flux to some degree. When teachers become their own researchers, they position themselves to inquire into that fluid relationship between teaching and learning, and thus they seek to better understand what is already changing. The questions they ask provide the point of entry of their examination.

4.2 GETTING AT QUESTIONS

This Investigation continues the series on developing a research plan; it focuses on getting at questions.

Reread the notes you made in Investigation 4.1. List three to five questions that spring from your notes. For the time being, don't worry about how you word the questions; just write them in whatever way they come to mind.

If you are working with others, you may want to read aloud the notes you have written for Investigation 4.1. Or, if you are using a videotape, you may want to watch a portion of it together. Then you should first brainstorm questions that the reading or viewing triggers for you. Have someone else write down what you say so that you have a record.

After you have voiced your questions, ask your listener-colleagues to contribute theirs. Do not discuss what you have read or seen. Just gather possible questions. Then change roles and repeat the process.

TEACHING VERSUS RESEARCH-ABLE QUESTIONS

As you approach your line of inquiry, remember that not all questions are equal. Some will pull you toward your role as teacher, while others will pull you toward your work as a researcher. The former we will call "teaching questions," the latter "research-able questions." **Teaching questions** focus on the teacher, on what he or she does and how he or she does it. As questions, they tend to have clear boundaries, and they are sometimes even phrased as yes or no questions. Teaching questions usually carry in them the outlines of their solutions. In other words, "If I (as the teacher) do this, or if this were the case, then the following would be true/happen." **Research-able questions,** in contrast, are open-ended; they capture issues or phenomena without judging how they will be resolved. They are usually focused on others—on students, for instance—and not on the questioner. Rather than solutions or courses of action, they tend to produce understandings, principles, and further questions.

Finding the "fault line" between teaching and research-able questions is a bit like riding a bike; it takes practice, self-monitoring, and awareness to become proficient. Consider these four questions:

1. What kinds of listening activities do my students like?

2. What is the impact of praise on the group dynamics?

3. How much oral correction helps students learn?

4. Why do students take so long to break into small groups for group work?

Each one is legitimate and can lead to understanding teaching and learning more clearly. Beyond the specifics of content, each question differs in its wording, the assumptions it carries, and the outcomes it anticipates. As you read the following analyses, think about this fault line: What makes the difference between teaching and research-able questions?

1. What kinds of listening activities do my students like?

This strikes me as a teaching question. It seeks a concrete list of activities that students like. Thus it serves in teaching this particular group of students. If the question were broadened to consider why students liked particular activities, and how those activities contributed to their listening comprehension, then it would move toward being a research-able question.

Place holders

2. What is the impact of praise on the group dynamics?

In contrast, this has the roots of a research-able question. Although it requires refinement, the question focuses on a phenomenon, praise, and what happens to the class group dynamics because of it. Thus, while it is particular to a group of students, the question carries the seeds of more general issues. This question also includes two words —*praise* and *group dynamics*—that function as **place holders.** They are called place holders because they hold the places of concepts that will be better defined and understood through the research process (Maxwell 1996, pp. 49ff).

Shaped by an assumption

3. How much oral correction helps students learn?

This really sits on the line between a teaching and a research-able question. The key word is *much*, because *how much* suggests a concrete answer about the amount of oral correction. If *much* is taken out of the question, however, it becomes *"How does oral correction help students learn?"* and thus moves toward being a research-able question. However the question still embeds a basic **assumption,** namely that oral correction *does* help students learn. To be more useful for research, the question needs to shed the assumption in its phrasing. By dropping "helps" the question can become *"How do students learn from oral correction?"* There is still a lingering assumption that students learn from oral correction, which can be addressed by recasting the question to *"Do students learn from oral correction and, if so, how?"* Or the question can be broadened as below.

Broaden the question; query the situation

4. Why do students take so long to break into small groups for group work?

This question is rooted in a concrete situation. It starts with a pre-conception from the teacher's point of view, namely that it takes too much time for students to form groups for group work. This pre-conception could push it in the direction of a teaching question that might become *"How can I get students to form their groups more rapidly and efficiently?"* If the question is broadened, however, it becomes research-able. This is done by asking about the concrete situation itself. The two phrases—*"What happens when"* or *"What is going on when"*—shift the focus from the preconception to the situation. Thus the question *"What happens when students are breaking into small groups?"* opens up the concrete situation by seeking to understand it, rather than shutting it down by seeking to resolve it.

Let me summarize this distinction between teaching and research-able questions. **Teaching questions** seek answers to specific problems (#1); they are focused on resolving the particular instance through some course of action (#4). Their power comes from their concrete, active, and rooted quality; they are based in the specifics of a teaching situation (#1, #3, #4). Because they are oriented toward taking action, they often spring directly from assumptions or preconceptions about the situation (#3, #4). This becomes their limitation from a research standpoint. Teaching questions aim at solving teaching problems. In this sense they "cut to the chase," from the question to a solution, without passing through the queries of *why* or the methodical discipline of *how do I know?* **Research-able questions,** on the other hand, are "able to be researched" because they are open-ended and suggest multiple directions and responses. These questions take the phenomenon or the situation as a point of departure (#2) and aim toward a broader understanding that is not context-bound. By using language devices such as place holders (#2) or rephrasing (#3, #4), research-able questions can pull back from the immediacy of the situation to examine it from a more neutral standpoint. As much as possible, they are phrased without assumptions or preconceptions in order to steer the questions toward inquiry and away from specific courses of action.

Teaching versus research-able questions

There is not a one-to-one correspondence between a particular teaching question and its research-able counterpart; rather, it is a matter of focus and emphasis. In Figure 4.2 I have reshaped each of the four questions above into related research-able questions.

Figure 4.2: Recasting teaching questions to be research-able questions

ORIGINAL QUESTION	RESEARCH-ABLE COUNTERPARTS	COMMENTS
1. What kinds of listening activities do my students like?	▪ How do students' feelings about particular activities affect their listening comprehension? ▪ What kinds of listening activities do students feel improve their listening comprehension?	These questions examine **second-order** issues of how students perceive their progress in a particular skill. As phrased, they do not address the **first-order** issue of whether students actually progress in the skill with these activities.

2. What is the impact of praise on the group dynamics?	▪ How do students react when I (the teacher) praise (a) the entire class, or (b) an individual student? ▪ How do students react when I (the teacher) comment on the progress or achievement of (a) the entire class, (b) an individual student to (c) the entire class, (d) an individual student, or (e) other student(s) about an individual student?	These questions become elaborate as they try to spell out what the two **place holders,** *praise* and *group dynamics,* mean for the purposes of the research. It is important to have operating definitions of these two key terms in order to determine what kinds of data to collect.
3. How much oral correction helps students learn?	▪ Does oral correction affect students' learning? If so, how? ▪ What do students learn from oral correction and how do they learn it?	This question focuses on learning, although that masks a lot of complexity. Oral correction is a clear phenomenon; what happens as a result is the question.
4. Why do students take so long to break into small groups for group work?	▪ What happens when students are breaking into small groups? ▪ What is going on as students pass from one social structure— the whole class—into another—small groups?	This **rephrasing** focuses on the transition in social structure from large to small groups. It leaves open the actual dimensions of that transition (e.g., time, who does what, interaction with peers and teacher, etc.)

4.3 *RESHAPING QUESTIONS*

This Investigation continues the series on developing a research plan; it focuses on how teaching and research-able questions differ from one another.

Using your list of questions from Investigation 4.2, sort them into teaching and research-able questions using the criteria just discussed. Start with the questions that seem clearly to be one or the other type; then work those questions you are less sure of. Remember that finding the distinction between teaching and research-able questions is not absolute; it is a matter of practice and judgment.

Recast each question so that you have both a teaching and a research-able version. Pay close attention to making the research-able version neutral, dropping the assumptions and judgments.

If you are working with others, you may want to pool all of your questions for the sorting process. Then select a subset of all the questions to recast into the two versions.

Any question, whether it is teaching or research-able, has a point of view. In research-able questions, that point of view should direct you toward inquiry, being off-balance with the status-quo, and reexamining the givens in the classroom situation. Within research-able questions themselves, however, there are also important differences in perspective that shape the inquiry. Two of these distinctions—**first-order** versus **second-order** and **emic** versus **etic** perspectives—help to orient you toward where the data or information that can respond to a particular question can be found.

For an example of working with teaching versus research questions, see Wagner Veillard's account, Chapter 3, pp. 47–48.

LOOKING AT QUESTIONS:
FIRST-ORDER VERSUS SECOND-ORDER PERSPECTIVES

My family spent a year in Brazil when my two children were in elementary school. My children entered Brazilian schools speaking little Portuguese and quickly found the classrooms quite different from what they were used to in the United States. My older daughter, who was eleven at the time, befriended a classmate who spoke some English. Early on, her friend told her not to worry, that "the teachers sound like they're angry all the time, but that's just the way they teach." My younger daughter, who was eight, confirmed this observation saying that her teachers had three ways of talking, "loud, louder, and loudest." After some months in school, however, these distinctions disappeared, although the kids would occasionally comment that their friends in the United States would find the Brazilian classrooms really loud, with "lots of yelling going on."

Ference Marton is an educational researcher who is interested in how people understand things around them, and particularly the teaching and learning that they engage in in classrooms. In his work, Marton makes the distinction between researching *what people do,* which he calls **first-order research,** and researching *how they perceive what they do,* which he calls **second-order research.** Distinguishing between accounts of activity and behavior and accounts of thinking and perception requires a shift in research perspective, as Marton (1981) explains:

> In the first, and by far most commonly adopted perspective, we orient ourselves towards the world and make statements about it. In the second perspective, we orient ourselves towards people's ideas about the world (or their experience of it). Let us call the former first-order and the latter second-order perspectives. (p. 178)

First- versus second-order research

When my daughters said that Brazilian classrooms were really "loud" and had "lots of yelling going on," they were making second-order observations. While this may have been the case from their North American point of view, to their Brazilian classmates these same classrooms sounded "normal." The Brazilian friend who told my daughter that "the teachers sound like they're angry all the time, but that's just the way they teach" was actually bringing together two second-order perspectives, the North American—"the teachers sound like they're angry all the time"—and the Brazilian—"that's just the way they teach." Both second-order perspectives are accurate depending on who you are. To introduce a first-order perspective into this discussion, one would need to describe the sound level in the classroom in more standardized terms, using decibels, for instance.

I use the term "standardized" here on purpose. It is important to realize that we cannot equate first-order with being "objective" and second-order with being "subjective." Both perspectives are based on assigning meanings to what is observed or experienced. The difference is that first-order perspectives use categories and forms of description that others outside the situation can verify if they employ the same ones, while second-order perspectives use the categories and forms of description the people in the situation use themselves. I can describe the same situation in two ways: "Yi Feng sat next to Katrin." (first-order: "sitting" and "next to" are terms most observers can understand and match to what they see) or "Yi Feng sat next to her friend, Katrin." (second-order: whether Katrin is a friend depends on what Yi Feng tells you, and on what Katrin herself thinks). If they are second-graders, "friend" can mean one thing; if they are high school students it can mean another. Thus second-order perspectives capture, as Marton says, "people's ideas about the world (or their experience of it)," while first-order perspectives label that world.

On Whorf, see Fishman (1982)

The world does not operate on first-order information alone; in fact, second-order information is often critical, as the following story illustrates. Benjamin Lee Whorf was a well-known linguist in the early twentieth century who developed the concepts of "linguistic relativity," that although there are elements that all languages have, which Whorf called "universals," different languages portray the world differently. Whorf's ideas have had a substantial impact in the fields of anthropology, linguistics, and education. When Whorf was starting his career, he supported himself as an insurance claims investigator. He wrote of a case in which a tannery insured by his company had had several fires of unexplained origin. Whorf was sent to look into the circumstances of the fires before settling the claims. He found the tannery well-organized, with careful attention paid to safety issues. There was, for instance, no smoking permitted inside the building because of the highly flammable solvents used in the tanning process. Workers were permitted to smoke, but they had to do so on a loading dock outside the building.

Like the other claims investigators who had examined the plant before him, Whorf was perplexed, since there were no obvious causes for the fires and indeed everyone seemed to be quite safety conscious. As he was leaving the building one day, he noticed workers smoking outside. They were standing beside some barrels, above which a sign read "Empty barrels." As he finished his cigarette, a man tossed the butt on the ground beside the barrels. This practice, it turned out, had been the unintended cause of the fires. The problem was that the barrels were not empty; rather, they *were* empty of tanning solvent, but they still contained highly flammable fumes. Thus a stray cigarette butt that landed in an "empty" fume-filled barrel could cause a fire. Whorf's point in recounting the story was that the word "empty," although accurate in general English usage, was misleading in this situation. The workers, with the best of intentions, took the word at face value. It stood for the real situation and people acted accordingly; however, in this case the "real situation" was different. The barrels were empty of liquid solvent but still full of combustible vapors. Thus, in Marton's terms, tannery workers were taking first-order actions on the basis of second-order perceptions.

I find Marton's distinction useful because it makes clear that any inquiry can exist on two planes: the level of action and the level of perception. As with the tannery workers, there are the actions that people take and there are the reasons, the thinking, the explanations that surround those actions. Teacher-research clearly investigates both realms. It examines the impacts of actions, like Betty in her study of the comprehensibility of directions, and it also probes perceptions and reasons as Vera does in trying to understand how her students define "good" conversations. More often than not, however, teacher-research spans both the first-order realm of actions and the second-order realm of perception and reasoning within one inquiry. Joan's study of emerging literacy is a good example. As described, her study looks at what students are doing as they figure out reading and writing in English. If she were to ask the children about their reading and writing, what is easy or hard for them and why, and so on, she would be generating second-order information for the study. If she were to also interview other teachers or the students' parents and caregivers to get their perceptions of the children's work, she would add further second-order information. All these data are second-order because they capture people's perceptions and thinking about emerging literacy in these students. When the data come from the students themselves, they are firsthand; when they come from other people, such as teachers or parents, they are secondhand. Taken together, first-order and second-order data can paint a rich and complex picture of a phenomenon, which is why Marton and his research colleagues refer to their work as *phenomenography*, blending the words *phenomenon* and *ethnography*

Refer to Vignettes; Chapter 2, page 25

The four questions, discussed as teaching and research-able (pp. 62–63), offer good examples of first-order versus second-order questions. In the following discussion, I analyze the orientation of each question. As you can see, these are parallel distinctions: teaching versus research-able is one, first- versus second-order is another. Both can apply to the same question, which is to say, a teaching question can have a first- or a second-order orientation, as can a research-able question.

1. *What kinds of listening activities do my students like?*

This is a second-order question because it focuses on students' opinions, what they like. If the question were recast as "What kinds of listening activities enable my students to make the most progress in listening comprehension?" it would then be a first-order question evaluating the impact of certain activities on students' listening comprehension.

2. *What is the impact of praise on the group dynamics?*

This question has a second-order perspective because it leads to examining students' perceptions and experiences. In order to answer it, the teacher-researcher will have to examine the phenomenon from the students' point of view: What do they see as "praise"? How does it affect their learning? It would not be possible to investigate this question except by getting into each student's frame of mind and understanding the various points of view.

3. *How much oral correction helps students learn?*

This question sits in the middle; it can include both first-order and second-order perspectives. Students' learning can be assessed using such external measures as test scores, grades, amount of participation in class, time on/off task, and so on. Likewise, oral correction strategies can be defined as teaching behaviors: peer correction, modeling the correct answer, coaching to correct, and so on. These are first-order aspects of the question. But the core of the question is the verb, *helps*, and this is a second-order issue. What the students perceive as "helping" them learn may differ from what teacher sees as useful and/or what the external measures show. Similarly, what the students see as "correction" may differ from what the teacher thinks she is doing to correct. This difference in perspective lies at the heart of second-order research. To study, borrowing Marton's words, "people's ideas about the world [of the classroom] (or their experience of it)" is what makes teacher-research so fascinating. Without this perspective, teacher-research can become mechanical documentation of what is going in teaching and learning and can miss the inner worlds of the participants that animate and make meaningful those processes.

4. *Why do students take so long to break into small groups for group work?*

If you contrast this question with question #2, you can see the difference between first- and second-order orientations that Marton talks about. This question is posed in a first-order perspective. It involves time—"students take so long"—and behavior—"breaking into small groups for group work." The data may show that they don't have their books, or that they talk a lot to peers as they shift activities, or that they walk very slowly from one group to the other. All of this first-order information will point to the physical world for responses to the question "why?" Not having books, talking a lot, and walking slowly are all data of actions and the material world. As findings, these can suggest actions to address the situation: Students should have all the necessary books with them, not talk, move more quickly, and so on.

The second-order perspective introduces parallel and fascinating dimensions to the same question. For instance, you might ask students what they see happening during the passing times, or whether they see these transitions as taking a long time. You might examine their perceptions of the differences between large and small groups as two social settings, and so on.

Second-order information is based in perceptions; it contributes to what anthropologist Clifford Geertz (1977) called a "thick description" of the situation. The thickness comes from getting at the complicated texture and interplay of actions and perceptions, of what people do and how they understand what they do and why they do it. Second-order information will point to the social world of beliefs, values, meanings, and interpretations for responses to the question "why?" Together, first- and second-order orientations to a question create a mosaic of information that can get at the messy complexity of life in classrooms.

4.4 *First- and Second-Order Questions*

Continuing the series on developing a research plan, this Investigation focuses on distinguishing between first- and second-order perspectives as a tool in developing research questions.

Using your recast list of questions from Investigation 4.3, sort them into first-order and second-order questions. Start with those you are most certain of and then work with those that seem to go less clearly in one group or the other. Remember that finding the distinction is a matter of practice; there are no absolute answers.

If you are working with others, you may want to pool your questions for the sorting process, and then select a sub-set to work with.

LOOKING FOR DATA: EMIC VERSUS ETIC PERSPECTIVES

Emic versus etic perspective distinction

First-order versus second-order perspectives refer to the orientation of the inquiry, and thus to the questions that evolve within it. **Emic/etic** is a related distinction that frames this issue from the data side of the process. The basic question is: Whose experiences and views of the world are we capturing? It reminds me of doing homework with my children; I would say, with some desperation, "But look, this problem isn't hard. You did one just like it yesterday." To which the retort would be, "It's not hard for you because you already *know* math!" This distinction between insiders' and outsiders' perceptions has been adapted to qualitative research from the field of linguistics by anthropologists and educational researchers. In looking at the sounds used in a language, linguists talk about distinctions between the chunks of sound that are meaningful to speakers of that language, which they call *phonemic* distinctions, and those distinctions that can be made among sounds but do not necessarily carry meaning in that language; these they call *phonetic* distinctions. In English, for example, the difference in the initial sounds in *she* and *he* is a phonemic distinction; it gives us two different words that label different genders. Whether we say *she* with a level tone or a falling-rising tone makes no difference in meaning in English, but it does in Mandarin Chinese, where *she* with a falling-rising tone means "to like," whereas with a level tone it means "west." So tone is a phonetic distinction; it can be produced by speakers of any language. In Mandarin tone produces a phonemic distinction, while in English it doesn't. Any language is a system of distinctions in sound. *Phonetic* distinctions are those that can be made among sounds, while *phonemic* distinctions are those that carry meaning for the insiders who are users of that language.

Anthropologist Kenneth Pike (1963) adapted these definitions to the study of how cultural groups assign and interpret meanings to their environments and experiences. His analogy was that language is a system of distinctions in sound that its users take for granted as normal, while culture is a system of distinctions in meaning that members of that group take for granted. Pike used the term *emic,* from phon*emic,* to refer to meanings that the insiders of a particular sociocultural group assign to a situation. He contrasted it with *etic,* from phon*etic,* to refer to externally observable or documented aspects of a situation or phenomenon. Thus, *etic* is what outsiders *see; emic* is what insiders *know.*

I had a clear experience of this distinction when one of my children started nursery school. She used to come home talking about something she called "the blue lion." All I knew about "the blue lion" was that when you sat on it, "you had to be quiet." From her emic perspective as an insider to the nursery school classroom, that was all there was to say about it. When I asked her etic questions about "the blue lion" as an outsider, I would draw blank looks or one-word responses. "How big is the blue lion?" I would ask, envisioning a stuffed animal. "Big," she answered. "Everybody sits on it at the same time." I tried to imagine thirty nursery-schoolers sitting on a stuffed blue lion. "When do you get to sit on it?" "Everyday. We sit there everyday." I was getting nowhere in trying to grasp what it was. As an insider with her emic understanding of nursery school culture, the blue lion was a fact of life. From an etic point of view, to me as an outsider, it made no sense. I could not attach the idea to anything I understood. Then, some weeks later, when I happened to be in her classroom, my daughter pointed to some worn blue tape that marked a large circle on the carpeted floor. "That's the blue lion," she said. And it all made sense. This blue circle or line ("lion") of tape was where the children sat at the start of each day for "circle" or sharing time (Cazden, 1988). So her emic and my etic perspectives converged, but they did not replace one another.

First- and second-order orientations serve to organize the kinds of questions we ask and how we approach gathering information to respond to them. Emic and etic perspectives describe the point of view intrinsic to the information we gather. Together these two sets of distinctions sensitize us to that fact that what we see and hear will depend on where we sit, what we can ask, and what we can say. The following research memo was written by Ann Hoganson, who conducted a teacher-research study with high school students studying Spanish. The first paragraphs detail how Hoganson used her assumptions to define the researchable questions within her line of inquiry. You can see her moving between first- and second-order orientations and proposing emic and etic ways to capture data.

Ann Hoganson

Account #4.2: Ann Hoganson, "What does 'knowing Spanish' mean?"

When I began my research project, *I assumed* the students would be unable to communicate using memorized chunks of material and that once they had studied a unit they would forget the material and be unable to use it in a communicative situation later. *I assumed* that by memorizing language, students would be unable to retain it and thus would not truly progress. *I also assumed* that teaching grammatical paradigms would be more useful than asking the students to memorize the structures without explaining them. *I supposed* students learned best by inventing and practicing dialogues or short skits and that students would define "knowing" Spanish as being able to read, write, speak and understand the language in an authentic context. In other words, "knowing" Spanish meant being able to communicate with Spanish speakers using the four skills and in a culturally appropriate manner.

My original **line of inquiry** was:

What happens when novice-level (ACTFL, 1986) foreign language students memorize chunks of language?

Next, I broke my inquiry into **five research-able questions:**

1. What does "knowing Spanish" mean?

2. How does memorizing material affect creativity with the language?

3. What activities help students memorize material?

4. How can students apply memorized material?

5. How do students communicate when they only know memorized material?

I began my research by focusing primarily on what knowing Spanish meant to the students and which activities they believed helped them learn the language. These two questions (#1 and #3) became my actual line of inquiry because I realized my concept of "knowing" a language differed from the concept held by my students (Hoganson, 1996; original emphasis).

4.5 *MAPPING EMIC AND ETIC PERSPECTIVES*

This Investigation combines examination of first- and second-order orientations toward the inquiry with emic and etic perspectives. on gathering data.

Read through Ann Hoganson's memo (Account 4.2).

1. Decide which of her questions carry first-order and which carry second-order orientations. It can be useful to sketch a diagram or flow chart showing how the questions interrelate and which orientation (first-order or second-order) they come from.

2. Think about how Hoganson will need to blend emic and etic perspectives to gather her data. Which question(s) will require her to take on the insider's point of view (emic) and which to take on the outside (etic) perspective? It is useful to sketch a chart with the questions down the left side, and to include notes on emic or etic data gathering.

Hoganson establishes a first-order orientation with her original line of inquiry. She focuses on how her students manipulate chunks of memorized language, which would lead to gathering etic data on how they perform in Spanish using this language. As she unpacks the inquiry into research-able questions however, she begins to probe the second-order realm of their perceptions by asking her students "What does 'knowing Spanish' mean?" (#1). The other questions carry forward the first-order orientation toward activities (#3), applying material (#4), and using memorized material (#2 and #5). Accordingly, questions #2 to #5 would probably lead to gathering data from an etic perspective on material taught, how it was taught, and student performance using it. Question #1, however, recasts the inquiry; it would require data from an emic perspective on how students define "knowing Spanish." In her last paragraph, above, Hoganson moves that second-order orientation forward when she writes, "I realized my concept of 'knowing' a language differed from the concept held by my students." Hoganson illustrates nicely how the focus can redefine itself, always within the same line of inquiry. She also shows how probing a phenomenon as a teacher-researcher can uncover issues that might be missed or overlooked as a teacher. How students view the subject-matter they are learning is clearly important in teaching it. In fact, successful instruction depends in part on understanding their point of view so that, as a teacher, you can address it.

Emic/etic relationships

A final observation about emic and etic. Although they often are characterized as a dichotomy, and I have presented them here as such, that stark view can be misleading. In the world, whether you stand inside or outside a setting, activity, or phenomenon is more a relative than it is an absolute. It is a matter of perception, both your own and that of others. Do you see yourself as an insider to this setting? Do others see you as one? That perception is based on an opposition; in other words, you may be more of an insider than someone else, or less one than another person. Going back to the homework example: When I help my daughter with her math homework, I find the long-division problem causing difficulty to be pretty straightforward. My daughter tells me that I think it's easy because I already "*know* math." Between the two of us, I am in an emic position as an insider to the world of long division. Hers is etic: it doesn't make sense to her. Then, after I explain how I would solve the division problem, she may say, "But that's not the way Mr. G. taught us. That's not the way we do it in our class." Suddenly my knowledge and understanding become etic, while my daughter's math classroom becomes the emic frame of reference. To solve the math problem in the proper way, I need to understand how the insiders do it. "Look, both ways will work," I say a bit petulantly. "Yeah, but only one is the right way," she retorts.

Emic and etic are always comparative. They contrast membership in a particular world of meaning, like my daughter and me in relationship to her math class. That membership, no matter how transitory, creates a point of view on the setting, activity, phenomenon, or even information. It thus establishes the distinction between those for whom a world of meaning makes sense as insiders (they know Mr. G's way of doing long division) and those who see, label, and interpret it from the outside (like my way of doing the math problem). One view, the emic, is the way those who are in the context make sense of it. The other expresses how those same events, issues, or phenomena make sense to people who are outside them. What is interesting is that both ways may well arrive at the same "answer," as when we both solved the long-division problem. But the ways of getting there differ. One way makes sense to one group—the math class and the textbook authors—the other way works for me with my dated long-division skills. These different interpretations of the phenomenon can lead to the same result. The knowledge of long division being taught and learned here is not the result, but how we get there. So, as my daughter says, the differences between our ways of solving the problem are significant. There is a right way for her community, in her world of meaning, and that is the one she needs to learn.

The profound importance of teacher-research is that it can offer public access to emic understandings of life in classrooms. It can thus make local sense of these things to a wider world. When teachers research their own teaching and the learning of their students, they reposition themselves. Their emic insiders' views make others' views etic. Most educational research speaks on behalf of teachers and students. The way it is done, the classroom is a tourist stop and what happens there becomes local life and customs to be viewed and interpreted. Its norms, practices, and activities are explained by people who are not natives of the culture. Even though many educational researchers have been practicing teachers, or may collaborate closely with teachers, theirs is always an etic view of classrooms. They do not work there. With teacher-research, the emic is explained by those who live in the classroom (Elbaz, 1992; Freeman, 1996). This means that other views become etic. When teachers speak for themselves through the research process, others cannot claim to speak for them. Like the math example, the end results in many instances will not be different. But *how* these results are arrived at will differ, and that is crucially important. Because, like the math example, that is where the knowledge actually lies. In that process of insiders making sense of what happens in classrooms, different knowledge is created and valued. We turn next to how that actually happens.

DEVELOPING RESEARCH PLANS: GUIDING INQUIRY INTO ACTION

In a grand sense, the research plan is how you go about creating knowledge through your inquiry. Although we have devoted a good deal of attention to them, developing research-able questions within a line of inquiry is only half of what is involved in getting started in the teacher-research process. The other half involves determining the kinds of data that can respond to those questions. In a sense, laying out a research plan is like a conversation, in which the questions are one voice and the data are the other. If the questions ask for something that the data cannot respond to, or if what the data say does not connect to the questions, then there is a mismatch between how the inquiry is conceived and how it is carried out, between the research-able questions and the research plan. Such cases become dangling conversations that are inconclusive.

See Investigations 3.1 and 3.2 in this chapter.

Developing the research plan is like scripting the conversation. It is like outlining the talking points in advance so that the individual parts connect and support each other to create the larger argument. First and foremost, the research plan involves making a series of decisions—some more tentative, others more definite—that will guide the process of the inquiry into action. The fewer of these decisions that are made on an ad hoc basis, the more disciplined the inquiry will be because its structure will be clear and will carry forward the logic of the inquiry.

The framework of a research plan is simple and straightforward. Like the structural beams of a house, this framework supports the specifics of the inquiry. The framework follows the basic question words, as shown in Figure 4.3.

Frameworks

Developing a research plan

Figure 4.3: **Questions to guide research planning**

WHAT	What kinds of data will respond to the question?
HOW	How can/will I collect the data?
WHERE/FROM WHOM	Where and from whom will I gather the data?
WHEN/HOW OFTEN	When and how often will I gather the data?
WHY	What am I trying to find out? What will I do with the data? What is my "first-cut" analysis?

Decision #1: What kinds of data will respond to the question?

See Hawkins (1967).

Data are information that comes from various sources. The value of a specific piece of data lies in these two facets: what it says and where it comes from. When people talk or write about "sources of data," this distinction is often blurred, although it is a crucial one. Data are a blend of information and where that information comes from. A very simple example: If a student says "That homework was really hard," as the teacher you will hear the comment in light of who the student is, his or her background with the content, how hard a worker he or she is, and so on. Who provides the data is an important element in what the data are. Here a basic map of **student(s), teacher, content, activity, and setting** can be useful. Figure 4.4 suggests that information can be found in five basic areas: the student or students, the teacher, the class content, the activity, and the classroom or school setting.

Three of these areas, content, activity, and setting, are in the public world; they produce first-order data. The other two, student(s) and teacher, have inner worlds. While they take part in the public world, they have opinions, feelings, beliefs, and so on about what they do. These data about their experiences provide second-order information about how they perceive the public world. Balancing and blending this public and private information is part of deciding what types of data can respond to your research question.

The issue of how questions and data line up is central to structuring the research design. Given a particular question, certain data will respond to it. For instance, the question "What is the impact of praise on the group dynamics?" requires data on three items: on "praise," on its "impact," and on "group dynamics." From the question, however, it is not self-evident exactly what the data should be or who specifically they should come from. What are data on "praise," for example? Or "group dynamics?" And what does "impact" mean? Impact on whom? . . . on strong students, on weaker students, on the class as a whole? None of these issues are self-evident, which reveals the first challenge of developing a research plan.

Figure 4.4: Sources of information: A basic map

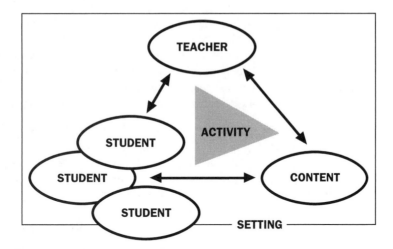

Often the research questions speak a different language from the lived reality of the classroom, so that it can be difficult to know where exactly to find information that responds to them. In the case of this question, the place holders (see p. 62)—"praise," "impact," and "group dynamics"—make it evident that these concepts will need definition in order to locate data on them. What you determine the data to be will, in turn, shapes what the place holder concept means in the research. If, for example, you take data on "praise" to be the *teacher's positive verbal comments* to students, such as "Good job!" or "Your work is excellent!" you have defined *praise* in a particular way so the research question becomes "What is the impact of the teacher's positive verbal comments (praise) on the group dynamics?" Just as questions and answers build on each other in a conversation, decisions about what constitute the data are shaped by—and likewise shape—the research question. This refines more precisely what you mean.

4.6 *Developing a Research Plan . . . Data*

Note on Investigations 4.6–4.10

The following five Investigations (4.6–4.10) form another series. The aim is to help you to think through developing a research plan. This series of Investigations can be done in three ways, represented in this chapter by the diamond symbols below:

A. individually ;

B. individually in consultation with peers ;

C. as a group project .

In the case of B (two diamonds), peers use one another to help clarify their own work and thinking. In the case of C (three diamonds), the group selects one question to pursue collectively by gathering data in their respective classrooms and pooling those data to address the common question. In this sense, C becomes a small-scale multisite research project.

As you read this series of Investigations, you will see that version A tells what the Investigation is and versions B and C provide suggestions for how to do it in groups. All five Investigations refer to the matrix in Appendix B (p. 200); use it to accumulate your work on the plan as you go through the series.

The first Investigation in the series examines what are the data in your plan.

Choose a research question from your list of questions in Investigation 4.3. Use this question as the foundation for a draft research plan. It matters less whether the question is one you will actually research than whether it occupies enough of your interest to practice designing a research plan around it.

A. With the question in mind, think about what kinds of information will respond to it. Use the template for a data collection matrix (Appendix B, p. 200) to write down your responses in the first column, labeled "data." Figure 4.4, p. 75, can be useful in orienting your thinking and discussion about the kinds of data you will need.

B. If you are working with others, you will want to work through this Investigation one person at a time. After the individual chooses a research question, together you can brainstorm the kinds of information that might address it.

C. If you are doing a group project, select one question for the group to plan around. It must be a question that everyone can address in his or her teaching context. Determine the kinds of information you will gather, bearing in mind that you would each be doing so in your individual classroom settings.

Decision #2: How can/will I collect the data?

When asked what the data of the study are, sometimes the response will be "interviews with students," "a journal," or "a questionnaire." The problem is that these are not data; they are means of collecting data. There is a crucial difference. Data are information from a source; but that same information can be *collected* in several different ways. For instance, if you want second-order data on students' opinions on what makes group work useful for them, you can collect these data through interviews, by having them write reflectively or keep a journal, or with a questionnaire. Figure 4.5 uses the basic data map (Figure 4.4) to outline the types of data (in **bold**) and possible means of collecting them (in *italics*).

Figure 4.5: Sources, types of data, and methods of data collection

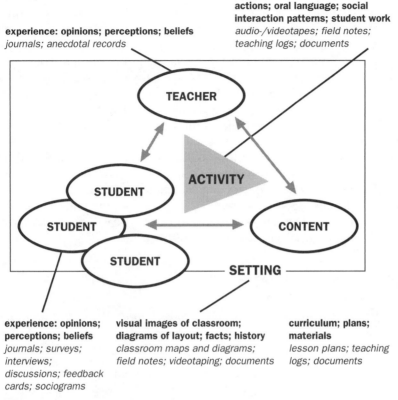

experience: opinions; perceptions; beliefs
journals; anecdotal records

actions; oral language; social
interaction patterns; student work
*audio-/videotapes; field notes;
teaching logs; documents*

experience: opinions;
perceptions; beliefs
*journals; surveys;
interviews;
discussions; feedback
cards; sociograms*

visual images of classroom;
diagrams of layout; facts; history
*classroom maps and diagrams;
field notes; videotaping; documents*

curriculum; plans;
materials
*lesson plans; teaching
logs; documents*

Note:
The data are in **bold** type; the data collection techniques are in *italics*. Most of the data
collection techniques are described in detail in Appendix C, pp. 201-218.

If you study Figure 4.5, you will see that one means of data collection, journaling, for example, can be used to collect data from several sources. Student journals, oriented to the inquiry, can produce data about their experiences and perceptions, while a journal kept by the teacher can generate data about his or her experiences. The type of data, second-order data on experience, is similar; the means of collecting it, through journals, is the same. But the sources, whether students or teacher, are quite different, and thus they will produce different information. Since each means of collection will reveal a slightly different facet of the data, it is important to bear in mind that the means of collection is not the data. This point becomes central when we examine the question of triangulation.

On triangulation, see Chapter 5, p. 96ff.

Another challenge in data collection is to be realistic when you ask yourself how you can or will collect the data. Often in teacher-research, the "can" and the "will" of data collection collide with one another. It is difficult, for example, to interview individual second graders while you are responsible for the whole class; it can be hard to take substantial class time to use a questionnaire with a class that you see very infrequently, and so on. The realities of teaching often proscribe the ways in which data can be collected, so it is important to hold your teaching context firmly in mind as you determine both the data and how you want to collect them. In Chapter 5, we will look at ways of collecting data more closely. For purposes of developing the research plan, however, you can proceed in one of two ways, using a both-ends-toward-the-middle approach. You can review the data you think you will need to respond to your question, and identify a means to collect each data type. Or you can settle on two to three ways you might collect data, and then examine each way in turn to determine the various types of data it could generate. Returning to the example above, depending on their focus, student journals can provide second-order data on participants' perceptions of the class and activities. Journals can also provide first-order data on students' writing skills, spelling, syntax, vocabulary usage, and so on. Because time is always a factor in getting the work of teacher-research done, efficient use of data sources and collection is critical. Having one activity serve multiple purposes is important; but it is equally important to be clear what those purposes are. Distinguishing between what the data are and how you will collect them is a crucial step towards that efficiency.

On data collection techniques, see Chapter 5, pp. 93–98, also Appendix C.

Data Collection Strategies

4.7 DEVELOPING A RESEARCH PLAN . . .
DATA COLLECTION STRATEGIES

The following Investigation examines **data collection.** *You will want to refer to the matrix in Appendix B (p. 200) to complete this Investigation. Refer to Investigation 4.6 for an explanation of the options (A), (B), and (C).*

A. For each of the kinds of data you have listed in the first column of your data collection matrix, write down a way to collect them. Use your imagination; think of the realities of teaching, the activities you might use in class, and how they might provide access to the data you want. If you can't think of a way to collect a particular type of data you have listed, leave the space blank on the matrix. If you can think of several ways to collect the same data, list them all for now.

B. *If you are working with others,* work through the data on one person's draft matrix at a time.

C. *If you are doing a group project,* consider each type of data you have listed in turn. Discuss the type and decide how each person might collect it in his or her classroom. Keep in mind the realities of each person's situation.

Display visually this information about who will be collecting which data in which ways in two forms:

Grid #1: *To get organized,* create a grid with the types of data across the top and the means of collection down the left side. Fill in the each cell with the names of group members and their research sites/classrooms. Set this grid aside.

Grid #2: *To keep track of the group research plan*, create a grid with the names of group members and their research sites/classrooms across the top and the types of data down the left side. Make the cells fairly large because you will be adding more information to each one in Investigations 4.8–4.10. Enter the means of collection in each cell where it applies. Leave blank those cells on the grid that do not apply.

You will use this grid in the remaining Investigations in this chapter.

Decision #3: *Where and from whom will I gather the data?*

By now it should be clear that data are inextricably linked to their sources. In the phrase "who says/does what," "who" is as important as "what." Decisions about where and from whom to collect data are a central part of focusing the research process; it is here that the research plan is useful. Working through these decisions in advance can help to keep you realistic and anchored in your setting. There are a couple of guidelines to keep in mind:

- *Think about how many people you actually need data from.*

It helps to begin by thinking about the "universe," or total group, from whom this particular type of data might be collected. In the example of students' experiences of group work, the universe would probably be all the students in the class. However, it may not be necessary to collect data from the whole universe on this question. In fact, you may be better served in terms of time and energy to start with a subset. So the first question is: Given this universe, what can be a useful and representative subset? Do you need data from everyone in the class, or could you focus on four or six students? If so, how would you choose them?

In the case of large-scale quantitative studies that use statistical measures, this question of how to reduce the universe of a study to a reasonable size is known as "sampling." The basic principle of sampling is representativeness, which is generally achieved though randomization. In other words, selecting the sample on a random basis from a given universe of the study theoretically gives everyone in that universe the same chance to be picked as a source of data. However, as a procedure to guarantee representativeness in teacher-research, randomness usually doesn't make sense, given the limited size of the universe and the numbers of students. Therefore, representativeness will depend on other factors, the most basic of which is the question "Why am I selecting this source of the data?"

On sampling, see Kerlinger (1986), Chapter 8.

- *Think about where you can reasonably collect the data.*

Where and when, the next decisions, are often directly linked. Can you collect the data you have in mind during the lesson? If the data are samples of student work or a short reflective writing, then you probably can. But if they involve interviews, it may not be possible in the classroom setting. So determining where you can collect the data can help you to be realistic about the process.

- *Less data well collected are more valuable than more data gathered haphazardly.*

It is a natural reaction to feel as if you have to get everything—student work from *every* student, interviews with *all* the boys in the class, your own journal entries after *every* lesson, and so on. Quantity can easily overtake quality, with the mistaken impression that more data, no matter what the quality, is better than less data, from a thoughtfully selected sample, collected rigorously and carefully. While it is crucial to have *enough* data, it is equally important to have the *right* data from the *right* people. Therefore, the useful axiom is: less data well collected can be more valuable than more data gathered haphazardly. The axiom comes with a caveat, however, that sometimes, due to the realities of working at the hyphen of teaching and research, one can undercollect data. Strategic and realistic choices about sources of data will guide the research process by focusing on what is essential. Like anything, that skill grows with time and experience.

Investigations

Data Sources

4.8 DEVELOPING A RESEARCH PLAN . . . DATA SOURCES

This Investigation examines data sources. Refer to Investigation 4.6 for an explanation of the options (A), (B), and (C).

A. For the data you have listed in the first column of your data collection matrix (Appendix B, p. 200), think about from whom and where you will collect those data. Enter your decisions in the third column on the data collection matrix. Think about *why* you would choose this or that source. If you were to explain why you had chosen that source, what would you say?

When you have finished, review what you have listed. Think closely about your teaching situation: Is this realistic? Can you do it? Remember the axiom about quantity and quality: Less data well collected are more valuable than more data gathered haphazardly. This is not meant as a reason to undercollect data, but simply to be realistic about what you set out to do so that you can protect the quality and thoroughness of your efforts.

B. *If you are working with others,* work through these questions for the data on one person's matrix at a time. Then discuss each source using these questions as a guide: Why have I chosen this source? Is this realistic, given my teaching situation? Can I have reasonable access to these sources, given my other responsibilities?

C. *If you are doing a group project,* identify sources for each type of data you have listed. Keep in mind that the sources should be comparable across all teaching situations. In other words, you don't want to interview the boys in one class and the girls in another. The aim should be to establish comparable sources for each means of data collection in each teaching situation.

Enter this information on Grid #2 that you started in Investigation #4.7.

Decision #4: When and how often will I gather the data?

As we have noted, time is a—perhaps even *the*—central issue in teacher-research. There is no way around the fact that teachers' lives are filled with many, often conflicting, demands. Adding research to the mix can intensify the sense of being pulled in too many directions at once. While it does not erase these demands, the fact of scheduling your data collection carefully and thoughtfully can help to reduce that feeling of things spinning out of control. Decisions about *when* and *how often* to collect data are crucial ones. They need to be shaped by two forces: the reality of the demands of teaching and the necessary discipline of the research inquiry. It isn't good enough, from a research standpoint, to collect the data when you have the time or when the opportunity arises. Like a savings plan or a diet, you need to forecast what you will do when. But from a teaching standpoint, it may not be realistic to forecast collecting data constantly. It is a balancing act. You need to account for what seems workable for you in your teaching context, given the demand of your work life. And you need to balance these decisions against the discipline and structure of your inquiry.

Here the axiom is "well begun is half done" or "well-scheduled is half the battle." Think through the process. Place the data collection within the context of your teaching duties and the demands of your life. Be reasonable with yourself. At the same time, be disciplined about what you will do. Plan to collect data at regular intervals, with a rhythm that has a logic to it. Pace yourself: Look at the long-haul of your total research plan and the time available. Then make solid decisions and stick to them. Time is also a factor in triangulating data collection, which we will consider in Chapter 5, (pp. 96-98), but for now it is enough to forecast a reasonable collection schedule.

4.9 *Developing a Research Plan . . .*
Scheduling Data Collection

Scheduling
Data Collection

Refer to Investigation 4.6 for an explanation of the options (A), (B), and (C).

◆ A. For each of the ways of collecting data you have listed in the second column of your data collection matrix (Appendix B, p 200), decide *when you will collect those data*. Think realistically of the data you need and how often you can—and need to—collect them. Here again, keep your teaching context firmly in mind. Temper your enthusiasm with realism to create a schedule that is feasible for you and meets the discipline of your research.

◆ B. *If you are working with others,* work through these decisions on one person's draft plan at a time. You can be helpful to one another by gently asking your colleague whether the proposed schedule is doable, and also by monitoring the discipline and regularity of the data collection plan.

◆ C. *If you are doing a group project,* determine the schedule for each means of data collection you have listed. Bear in mind what will be realistic as well as what will be comparable across your teaching situations. As in determining sources of data, the aim should be to establish a comparable schedule for each means of data collection in each teaching situation.

Enter this information on Grid #2 that you started in Investigation 4.7.

First-cut analyses

Decision #5: What will I do with the data? What is my "first-cut" analysis?

Although it may seem premature to think about what you will do with the data once you have collected them, it isn't. There is nothing less productive than leaving the data you have collected to sit around and get stale. For one thing, you lose out on the excitement of seeing what you have. Like berry picking, it can be highly motivating to look in the bucket from time to time to see what you have collected. For another, you lose the opportunity to let the data you have collected shape what you need to do next. Often the data will reshape the questions, so it is crucial to plan ahead and consider what you will do with data as you are collecting. This is what is called "first-cut analysis."

Doing the first-cut analysis is a way of seeing what is in the data. It is not necessarily, or even often, the ultimate way in which you will analyze the data; rather, the first-cut analysis is how you will get started. It creates forward momentum in the research process that will carry you from collecting data into analyzing them. You can think of first-cut analysis as similar to the process by which you review your mail. When you pick it up, you find that you need to open some of the mail to read the contents, while with other mail, like catalogues or supermarket circulars, which come already open and accessible, you can flip through them. Still other mail, such as bills or bank statements, which you can identify just from the envelopes, you may set aside. This type of review, which is almost second nature with your mail, is essentially a first-cut analysis. It allows you to see what is there, according to the categories of action that each piece of data demands. Occasionally a letter will trick you—like the advertisement which is made to look like a bill—and this can cause you to reflect on the categories you take for granted. This, too, is part of first-cut analysis. As you review the data you have, you want to be alert to information in them that challenges your expectations, categories, or assumptions.

First-cut analysis usually involves commonsense strategies such as **reading through the data**, **counting instances** (how many people answered . . .), **listing** and/or **grouping common themes** or ideas together, **sorting responses by some characteristics** (all the girls said . . .), **underlining similar words or themes**, **comparing X with Y**. To figure out an appropriate first-cut analysis, you need to hold the data up against the background of the research question and the inquiry. If you look at the data, you can see what is in them: Can you count them? Can you make lists from them? Can you read them for themes? Are there things that you can compare within one data set or among data sets? These are all ways of unpacking the information that is in the data you are collecting. As you ask these questions, think about your inquiry and what you want to know. Whatever you do with your data needs to be guided by the inquiry that triggered your work in the first place.

The metaphor of unpacking data helps to conceptualize the process of determining first-cut analyses. If each type of data is like a suitcase, unpacking the data is like taking things out of the suitcase. Before you unpack, however, you usually scan the room to see where you can hang the clothes that need to be hung up, whether there is a chest of drawers, where you can put the socks and T-shirts, and so on. Underlying this process is the fact that you know what you have in the suitcase, so you know what you need in order to unpack its contents. Determining the kinds of first-cut analyses you will pursue to unpack your data is like figuring out the hangers and drawers you need to unpack the contents of the suitcase. As you take things out of the suitcase to hang them or put them in drawers, you may notice that you didn't include something you need. Perhaps the hotel has a swimming pool and you didn't pack a bathing suit. This, then, is the second critical function of first-cut analyses. As you unpack the data you have, you can see what other data you may need to collect. Doing first-cut analyses on your data as you are collecting them serves two functions: It helps you to see what you have and it helps you to notice what you don't have and may want to collect.

4.10 *DEVELOPING A RESEARCH PLAN . . . FIRST-CUT ANALYSIS*

This is the final Investigation in the series on designing a research plan. Refer to Investigation 4.6 for an explanation of the options (A), (B), and (C).

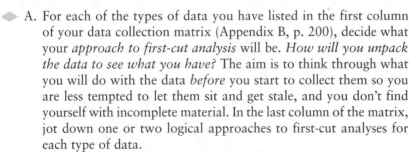

A. For each of the types of data you have listed in the first column of your data collection matrix (Appendix B, p. 200), decide what your *approach to first-cut analysis* will be. *How will you unpack the data to see what you have?* The aim is to think through what you will do with the data *before* you start to collect them so you are less tempted to let them sit and get stale, and you don't find yourself with incomplete material. In the last column of the matrix, jot down one or two logical approaches to first-cut analyses for each type of data.

B. *If you are working with others,* work through these decisions on one person's draft plan at a time. Use colleagues to brainstorm several first-cut analyses for each type of data.

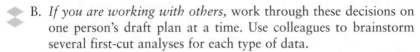

C. *If you are doing a group project,* determine one or two approaches to first-cut analysis for each type of data you plan to collect. Then, enter this information on Grid #2 that you started in Investigation 4.7.

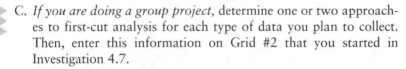

Note: In a group research project, first-cut analyses work in two stages. First, each person should do his or her own analysis on the data he or she is collecting. This is like (A), above. Second, group members can pool similar data to do first-cut analyses on them. Keep in mind that the data come from different settings—classrooms, and teach-ers—so they must be treated individually before they are treated col-lectively, otherwise their individual origins will be muddied or lost.

The first-cut analysis is your preliminary visit to the data to see what they say. Where you go from here is the subject of the next chapter.

Suggested Readings

On second-order research, Ference Marton's work on phenomenography is not as widely known in the United States as it is in Europe. A 1981 article, "Phe-nomenography: Describing conceptions of the world around us," (*Instructional Science* 10. pp. 177–200) gives an excellent overview of this approach of ethnog-raphy which focuses on participants' experiences and perceptions. Marton's book with S. Booth, *Learning and Awareness* (Mahwah, NJ: Lawrence Erlbaum, 1996) provides a more in-depth examination of his approach to researching people's con-ceptions of their work and their worlds. There is also a Web page that provides an up-to-date list of phenomenographical research conducted by Marton and his col-leagues (phenomenographica: http://www.ped.gu.se/biorn/phegraph.html).

The classic work which launched the emic/etic distinction is Kenneth Pike's *Language in Relation to a Unified Theory of the Structure of Human Behavior* (The Hague: Morton, 1963). In his book, *Tranforming Qualitative Data* (Thou-sand Oaks, CA: Sage Publications, 1994), Harry Wolcott weaves together exam-ples from his long career as an educational sociologist with a discussion of ana-lyzing and presenting data (see also Chapter 7, pp. 146ff. in this book). Finally, Vivian Paley's article, "On Listening to What Children Say" (*Harvard Educational Review* 56 (2) pp. 122–131) is an excellent discussion of collecting data from young children by a leading teacher-researcher.

There are many ways of thinking about the interrelationship among the stu-dent, the subject matter, and the teacher. Science educator David Hawkins, wrote what is now a classic article on this constellation of relationships which he called the 'I-Thou-It' relationship, (Hawkins, 1967). Also Pam Grossman's *The Making of a Teacher: Teacher Knowledge and Teacher Education* (New York: Teachers College Press, 1990), mentioned in Chapter 1, talks about how teachers construct their understandings of what they are teaching. In 1990, Mary Kennedy prepared a very readable survey of research in this area, *A Survey of Recent Literature on Teachers' Subject-Matter Knowledge* (East Lansing, MI: National Center for Research on Teacher Learning).

Many of the books on qualitative research in educational settings contain sec-tions, some more elaborate than others, on developing research questions. Two that I have found particularly useful and clearly written are Chapter 4 (pp. 49–61) of Joseph Maxwell's *Qualitative Research Design: An Interactive Approach* (Thousand Oaks, CA: Sage, 1996) which overviews the process of developing a research question, and the section (pp. 295–335) of Michael Quinn Patton's *Qualitative Evaluation and Research Methods* (Thousand Oaks, CA:

Sage Publications; 1990, 2nd ed.) on how to word research questions and on research interviewing (see Appendix C: Interviews, pp. 216-218). Both books are also excellent resources on research design and developing research plans. Maxwell's book is straightforward and accessible. Patton's book is now a classic in the field; he writes in a way that is clearly grounded in his enormous experience of evaluation and research design.

5

COLLECTING AND ANALYZING DATA

If we begin with certainties, we shall end up in doubt.
But if we begin with doubts and we are patient with them,
we shall end in certainties.

Sir Francis Bacon

Doing teacher-research can feel like juggling. In previous chapters we have talked about how teaching and research can impose seemingly contrapuntal demands: Teaching draws you into taking action and doing things in the classroom, based on what you know and need to accomplish; research pulls you in the opposite direction, toward questioning the bases of those actions and what you assume to be true. Their essence is captured in Francis Bacon's statement. Doing teacher-research means maneuvering between doubting what you are finding and what you are becoming certain of. Orchestrating this opposition is a skill and initially, like most new skills, it can feel contradictory, like patting your head while rubbing your stomach. With time and practice, however, the oppositions begin to support one another and can become second nature. But the tension is usually sharpest when you are collecting data and starting to analyze them.

Orchestrating
oppositions:
Data collection
and analysis

Once you are launched into the research process itself, the work entails two complementary activities: data collection and data analysis. Normally these are thought of as sequential activities, which they are to some degree. It makes sense that you have to collect information first in order to analyze it, like shopping for food before you can prepare the meal. However, given the demands of teaching and integrating research into it, and given the need to balance doubting and becoming certain, it is important to see data collection and analysis as integrated and mutually reinforcing activities. It is thus more like mentally reviewing what you have in the refrigerator, what you feel like cooking, what you cooked yesterday, and how much money you have in your wallet, in order to make decisions about what and how much to buy as you shop for the meal.

This chapter is about how to carry out the work of teacher-research. Given your research question and your research plan, how will you go forward with collecting the data and with analyzing them?

The chapter is organized around the basic movement from data collection to data analysis seen in Figure 5.1. It will constantly remind you how that movement is more recursive than linear. As you collect data in response to your research question, you will be pushed to think about collecting more or other related data to fill out the picture.

From data collection to analysis

Figure 5.1: The teacher-research cycle: Collecting and analyzing data

5.1 *Getting Oriented to the Relationship Between Data Collection and Data Analysis: Applying an Analogy*

In this Investigation I use the analogy of shopping for dinner to look at the relationship between data collection and data analysis.

Think about the above analogy. You can approach the analogy in two ways. In the first, the parallels are not drawn; in the second, they are. You may approach it (1) by making the connections as you see them and then referring to what I have done, or (2) by reading the parallels I have drawn and applying them to your own situation and thinking.

If you choose Option 1: Cover the right column of scenarios A and B below and read through the left column. Think about, or talk through with a colleague, the following question:

What parallels can I draw between this step in the scenario and the steps in collecting and analyzing data?

If you choose Option 2: Read through both columns of the scenarios. Then think about, or talk through with a colleague, the parallels I have drawn between the steps in the scenarios and the steps in collecting and analyzing data.

Scenario A: From shopping to preparing the meal

*In this scenario the analogy is **linear**. It follows the "classic" sequential relationship between collecting data and analyzing them.*

You go to the store with a shopping list . . .	You are in your classroom with your research plan . . .
A. You select several ingredients on your list . . .	A. You collect the data called for in your plan.
B. and put them in your shopping cart.	B. You keep the data together (tapes, journals, field notes, etc.).
C. After paying for them at the check-out, you bag them and take them home.	C. You take the data out of the classroom to work with them.
D. Once at home, you take out what you have bought . . .	D. Away from the classroom, you sort the data according to what you have, and do the first-cut analysis.
E. and use what you have bought, combining appropriate ingredients, to make a meal.	E. You draw connections between different types of data to see how they illuminate one another. For instance, perhaps the interviews shed light on the journals, or the field notes suggest something about students' work.

Scenario B: What's in the fridge?
What do we feel like cooking or eating?

*In this scenario, the analogy is **recursive**. It illustrates the multiple ways in which data collection and analysis are embedded in teaching context and in work as a teacher. It is worth paying special attention to the ways in which previous knowledge and experience, as well as the teaching context, shape the relationship between teaching and researching when both functions are done by the same person.*

You go to the store with a rough shopping list. As you enter the store, you start thinking about . . .	You are in your classroom with your research plan, but you are also thinking about . . .
A. what you had for dinner last night and the fact that you will be going out tomorrow.	A. the classroom setting and students, what happened recently in class, what will happen tomorrow or next week.
B. You select several ingredients on your list, but decide not to buy something that will spoil if you don't use it today,	B. You collect some of the data called for in your plan. You hold off on some data—e.g., the interviews. Given the energy of the students, interviewing will be more productive tomorrow.
C. and put the items in your shopping cart.	C. You keep the data together (tapes, journals, field notes, etc.).
D. You decide not to buy something you had on your list because you already have a closely related item at home— e.g. You forgo the sour cream and plan to use the yogurt you have in the fridge instead.	D. You revise your collection strategies to take advantage of an existing data source—e.g., students will be polling their peers for a math exercise and you embed some questions relevant to your inquiry.
E. As you head to the check-out line, you review what you have in the shopping cart against the menu that is forming in your head. You have decided not to have green beans but broccoli instead, and to use up the yogurt, but also to have the chicken as the main dish as you had planned.	E. In the classroom, you review your data as you are gathering them, doing first-cut analyses to quickly preview what you are getting. You make adjustments as necessary. However, these are always according to your research question and in keeping with the structure and discipline of your data collection.
F. You bag what you have bought and take it home.	F. You take the data out of the classroom to work with them.

DATA COLLECTION

Collecting data is collecting information that relates to your inquiry, information that you believe will respond to your research question. The data are not the answer to the research question; they are the raw material out of which responses to your question will probably emerge. The process of drawing responses out of the data, or finding them in the data, is called *data analysis*. Thus, separating the gathering of the information from working with it to find a response is a key part of the structure and discipline of the research process. If you are haphazard or incomplete in collecting data, you may not have adequate information to address your research question. On the other hand, if you do not look carefully, or you jump to conclusions, you may shortcut the analytical process. Collecting data will probably push you to attend to aspects of your teaching and your students' learning that you might otherwise overlook in the usual day-to-day work of teaching. Because it asks you to step back, make connections, and develop interpretations, analyzing data often leads to new perspectives on familiar things. So both steps are critically important in this process of making familiar things seem new and strange. Together these processes can make you question what you are certain about, and lead you to greater certainty about some aspects of teaching and learning that you might have doubted.

By its nature, collecting data needs to be a disciplined undertaking. You need to be aware both of what you are doing as you collect any particular information and why you are—or are not—doing it. This is the heart of the "discipline" of the research inquiry because it will allow others to see how you arrived at your interpretations and findings. The challenge in data collection is twofold. First, you need to stick *to* your plan; second, you need to stick *with* your inquiry. You may find that the second process redirects the first. Often you will find you need to adjust what you had planned for data collection for any of myriad reasons: There isn't enough time that day; a key student is absent; the tape recorder doesn't work; you need to do something else and so can't take field notes at that time, and so on.

Sticking *to* the plan/Sticking *with* the question

Changes are part of the research process; managing them in a conscientious way is one of the major challenges of doing research well. The key is to make changes reasonably and systematically, which I am calling sticking *to* your research plan. Whether—as in the scenarios—you go grocery shopping with a list or with a rough idea in mind of what is in the refrigerator and what you need, the aim is the same: to have adequate food on hand to prepare a meal. In doing teacher-research, the aim in making changes is similar. Whether the adjustments are anticipated or spontaneous, they must advance the inquiry and they must fit within the structure and discipline of the research plan. If there isn't time that day, then perhaps you reschedule the data collection for the next day or plan it into a teaching activity. But you don't just abandon that instance or form of data collection, or do it halfheartedly. If a key student is absent, consider why he or she is central to the inquiry. Depending on what you decide, you may reschedule the data collection or you may focus on another student. But don't just substitute one student for another without some thought and reason. If you mean to survey a whole class and only half the students return the questionnaires, you need to figure a way to get the other half to respond, and so on. This is what sticking *to* your research plan entails. Data collection cannot be a casual undertaking; it needs to be organized, sustained, and well-managed. The discipline of doing teacher-research means that you think through changes as they happen or are forced upon you, and that you keep track of departures from your research plan by making note of them. What you don't or aren't able to do is part of the picture of the research, and you will need to take it into account in the data analysis.

On developing a research plan, see Chapter 4, pp. 75–84.

Changes in data collection happen against the backdrop of your inquiry. They are adjustments in the overall scheme, substitutions within the given menu of the research plan. Sticking *with* your inquiry provides direction and coherence to these adjustments as you make them. The research plan provides the structure for data collection; the inquiry provides the reasoning behind it. The plan manages the ongoing nature of the work by responding to the following questions: How (when) (where) (from whom) am I going to collect these data? What am I going to collect next? The inquiry keeps you anchored in your questions: Why am I doing this research? Why am I collecting these data? What am I going to do with the data? What do I assume/expect? How might I be wrong?

It is important to reiterate that the inquiry and the research question are not one and the same. The research question or puzzle is a point of entry into the inquiry. It expresses the inquiry in a form that allows you to investigate it, take action to understand it, and collect information that may shed light on it. In the course of doing this work, you may well find another way to phrase the question, another puzzle, that provides a more fruitful entry point into the inquiry. Thus the question or puzzle may well redefine itself; however, the inquiry remains constant. For this reason, sticking *with* the inquiry does not mean sticking *to* the specifics of the research question. The inquiry houses the question, and the question furnishes the inquiry with specific direction. Indeed, more often than not, the specifics of the research question will change through the work of data collection and analysis. However these shifts can—and should—be traced back to the inquiry itself. In the following account, beginning teacher-researcher David Mathes describes this process of reframing research questions within an inquiry.

On inquiry and questions, see Chapter 2, pp. 34–35.

Account 5.1: David Mathes, "Doing pair work in a sixth-grade class"

My inquiry on the subject of pair work in my sixth-grade French classes (students ages 11–12) at Guilford Central School emerged from a loop writing exercise (for procedure see Appendix A, p. 198). The following **line of inquiry** developed:

> **What are the factors that contribute to effective group work in the foreign language classroom?**

In this teaching experience, I wanted to experiment with using group work to work effectively with mixed-level classes. However, as my teaching progressed, I found, for different reasons, that I was doing

David Mathes

far more pair work than group work. The French levels in the classes were not as diverse as I had predicted, and I found that pair work gave the best results for the amount of time I spent with each class. Therefore, I substituted the words "pair work" for "group work" in my inquiry.

I began with the following **research questions:**

1. What motivates students in mixed-level foreign language groups?

2. How does student-centered group work influence students' performance in traditional teacher-centered foreign language lessons?

3. How do social relations out of class influence group work interactions in class?

As I got into the data-collecting process, I found that not all of my questions were clear. Or they did not reflect the reality of my classes, or the data I was collecting. I found it hard, for example, to define the word "motivates" in (1) "What *motivate*s students in mixed-level foreign language groups?" And there was the problem of defining the universe of students I wanted to study. In my classes at Guilford school, students ranged in age from 9 to 15 years old, and I found it difficult to break down data from such varied ages. The scheduling helped to focus matters. Since I had much more contact with my two sixth-grade classes (ages 11–12), I decided to concentrate my research in the sixth grade.

The **data** I had collected at that point suggested that the students' attitudes toward school in general, and their prejudices for or against classmates, influenced their attitudes about working in pairs. For that reason, I decided to concentrate on question #3:

(3) How do social relations out of class influence group work interactions in class?

From the data I had collected in one sixth-grade class, I found that I could compare the boys' attitudes to those of the girls. I thus came up with the following subquestion based on question (3):

(3A) How do boys differ from girls in their approach to pair work?

These data came from only one of my sixth-grade classes (of about 15 students), so I decided to focus on just that one class. Because I often alternated pair work with more traditional teacher-centered lessons, I could contrast the students' attitudes and performances to these two types of instruction. So I also focused on the question derived from #2 above:

(3B) How does student-centered pair work influence students' performance in traditional teacher-centered foreign language lessons?

This Investigation traces the evolving connections between a research question and data collection.

> *Working alone or in discussion with peers,* read through David Mathes's account (Account 5.1) in which he explains how and why he redefined his research questions in the face of his teaching and the data he was collecting. Identify the turning points in this redefinition and, for each of them, describe what led to the adjustment. It may help to make a bubble diagram or flow chart that shows the movement from one question to the next and the influences that caused the shifts.
>
> Trace the final research question (#3) back to the original inquiry. How are the question and the inquiry related? How has the inquiry been redefined through these adjustments in the research question? How have teaching context and data collection shaped these adjustments?

Your research question, and the inquiry that undergirds it, animate how you collect data. Your research plan frames the decisions you have made about how you will collect data in response to your question. In collecting data, you can draw from a range of possible techniques. Like teaching a lesson, when the techniques need to respond to the aim or objective, in gathering data you want the techniques to match the purposes for which the data are collected. Those purposes, in turn, respond to the question you are investigating and the inquiry driving the work.

Data Collection Techniques

Figure 5.2 gives an overview of data collection techniques available to you as a teacher-researcher. It is drawn from an Australian publication, *Teachers' Voices: Exploring Course Design in a Changing Curriculum*, edited by Ann Burns and Susan Hood (1995).

Figure 5.2: Methods and techniques used in action research

METHOD	DESCRIPTION
journals/diaries	regular dated accounts of teaching/learning plans, activities and classroom occurrences, including personal philosophies, feelings, reactions, reflections, observations, explanations
teaching logs	more objective notes on teaching events, their objectives, participants, resources used, procedures, outcomes (anticipated or unanticipated)
document collection	sets of documents relevant to the research context, e.g., course overviews, lesson plans, students' writing, classroom materials/texts, assessment tasks/texts, student profiles, student records

observation	closely watching and noting classroom events, happenings or interactions, either as a participant in the classroom (*participant observation*) or as an observer of another teacher's classroom (*nonparticipant observation*). Observation can be combined with field notes recordings and logs or journals.
field notes	descriptions and accounts of observed events, including non-verbal information, physical settings, group structures, interactions between participants. Notes can be time-based (e.g., every 5 minutes) or unstructured according to the researcher's purpose.
recording	audio or video recordings, providing objective records of what occurred, which can be re-examined. Photographs or slides can also be included.
transcription	written representation of verbal recordings, using conventions for identifying speakers and indicating pauses, hesitation, overlaps or any necessary non-verbal information
surveys/questionnaires	sets of written questions focusing on a particular topic or area, seeking responses to closed or ranked questions/options and/or open-ended personal opinions, judgements or beliefs. Used in non face-to-face situations
interviews/discussions	face-to-face verbal sessions conducted by the researcher as unplanned, planned or structured interactions. The researcher can use previously planned questions, structured interview schedules or allow the interview to unfold spontaneously
stimulated recall	use of previously recorded or transcribed data to prompt responses from participants on actions, feelings, thoughts, attitudes, beliefs, following events or activities being researched

On the pros and cons of various techniques, see Marshall and Rossman, 1989, pp. 102–106.

Like teaching techniques, you can examine each of these data collection techniques for its purpose (*why* use it?), its procedure (*how* to use it?), and the advanced preparation and/or setup it may require. Appendix C (p. 201ff.) describes these data collection techniques in detail. Since many people have used these techniques, given their experience, there is also advice on the pros and cons of each technique.

Figure 5.3 outlines basic techniques for data collection in and out of the classroom and provides a good starting point for cataloguing the various ways in which you can collect data in your teaching. Each technique addresses five areas: (1) What you do in the classroom, (2) what you think about what you do,

Figure 5.3: How, where, and when of data collection techniques

WHERE IS THE DATA?	TEACHER'S ACTIONS (First order) 1) What you do/say	TEACHER'S THOUGHTS (Second order) 2) What you think about what you do/say	STUDENTS' ACTIONS (First order) 3) What student(s) do/say	STUDENTS' THOUGHTS (Second order) 4) What student(s) think about what they do/say	STUDENTS' LEARNING (First or second order) 5) What student(s) are learning/have learned?
		HOW TO COLLECT IT?			
WHEN? IN THE CLASSROOM/ WHILE TEACHING	▪ keeping teaching logs; lesson plans ▪ making audio/video recordings ▪ writing field notes (by observer, or teacher depending on involvement in activity)	(These depend on the activity and the teacher's involvement in it.) ▪ keeping journal/diary ▪ making anecdotal records	▪ keeping teaching log; annotating lesson plans ▪ writing field notes ▪ making audio/video recordings ▪ conducting interviews/discussions ▪ making classroom diagrams and maps	▪ having students keep journals or do feedback cards ▪ doing surveys or questionnaires ▪ conducting interviews/discussions ▪ gathering data for sociograms	▪ having students keep journals/ diaries or do feedback cards ▪ collecting documents; student work; test results ▪ doing surveys or questionnaires ▪ conducting interviews/discussions
OUTSIDE THE CLASS- ROOM/ AFTER TEACHING	▪ listening to/ transcribing audio recording; reviewing video recording	▪ keeping journal/diary ▪ doing stimulated recall with audio/ video recordings	▪ conducting interviews	▪ having students keep journals ▪ doing stimulated recall with audio/ video recording ▪ conducting inter- views ▪ making sociograms	▪ having students keep journals ▪ conducting interviews

(3) what your students are doing in the classroom, (4) what they think about what they are doing, and (5) evidence of what they are learning. The table shows how the techniques cluster in each of these five areas.

TRIANGULATION

5.3 *EXPLORING TRIANGULATION*

The following Investigation prepares you for the concept of triangulation in data collection and analysis.

Working alone or with peers, think about and then discuss what makes the following physical objects sturdy and able to stand independently:

Group A: a bird bath; a telephone pole; a hat stand; a tree

Group B: a fence; a dry stone wall; a sign board; a bicycle

Group C: a three-legged stool; a traditional native American tepee; a tripod; a tricycle

Group D: a table; a car; a chair; a cat or dog

Triangulation

At its most basic level, triangulation is about what makes something sturdy, able to support its own weight, and therefore dependable. In the physical world, things that are "triangulated" are better balanced and physically more dependable than things that are not, because they are able to stand by themselves. In the conceptual world of research, triangulation simply builds on this principle. The term was imported from land surveying, where, as evaluation specialist Michael Patton (1990, p. 187) explains, quoting from Fielding and Fielding (1986, p. 23), "a single landmark only locates you somewhere along a line in the direction from the landmark, whereas with two landmarks you can take bearings in two directions and locate yourself at their intersection." In research, triangulation means including multiple sources of information or points of view on the phenomenon or question you are investigating. There are, in fact, three layers on which you can triangulate your research: the level of the data sources; the level of data collection, or research methods; and the level of data analysis, or theoretical triangulation. Of the three, triangulating data sources and collection is the most common. Qualitative researchers Catherine Marshall and Gretchen Rossman (1989)define "data triangulation" clearly and simply as "the act of bringing more than one source of data to bear on a single point." (p. 146)

Triangulating data sources is a matter of where you get your information; triangulating collection methods is a matter of varying the ways in which you gather that information. Researchers Matthew Miles and Michael Huberman (1984) make a great comparison to detective work. They explain that the notion of triangulation is linked to eliminating—or at least minimizing—bias in findings and thus to increasing your confidence in what you are finding as you analyze your data:

Bias is not inevitable. Detectives, car mechanics, and general practitioners all engage successfully in establishing and corroborating findings with little elaborate instrumentation. They often use a modus operandi approach which consists of triangulating independent indices. When the detective amasses fingerprints, hair samples, alibis, eyewitness accounts and the like, a case is being made that presumably fits one suspect far better than others. Diagnosing engine failure or chest pain follows a similar pattern. All signs presumably point to the same conclusion. Note the importance of having different *kinds* of measurements, which provide repeated verification. (p. 234)

The classic framework, outlined by sociologist Martin Denzin (1978) details four basic types of triangulation (quoted in Patton 1990, p. 187).

(1) **Data triangulation** makes use of *several sources of data.* In a first-order study of student writing, you might use the writing itself, your corrections (and notes on how it was written), and the assessments of another teacher. In a second-order study, you might use the writing samples, students' perceptions, and your views.

(2) **Investigator triangulation** uses *more than one investigator* to gather the data. In addition to yourself you might have a fellow teacher make field notes on the writing class, or you might have a student conduct some interviews, for example.

(3) **Methodological triangulation** uses *multiple ways to collect data,* and thus to study the problem. You might conduct observations and interviews, and collect student work to study the question you have. Like the detective example, this type of triangulation is the one we most commonly think of when designing studies; however it is not the only—or even, in many instances, the best—one to use.

To these first three types of triangulation, I would add :

(4) **Triangulation in time and/or location** means collecting the same form(s) of data and/or using the same method(s) *over a given time period* or with the same sources *in several different locations.* For example, the former might mean tracking a student or group of students for a term; the latter might mean shadowing the student(s) in several different class settings with different teachers.

Denzin's final form of triangulation occurs in data analysis:

(5) **Theoretical triangulation** uses *more than one perspective* to analyze the data. You could analyze a videotape for the sequence of activity; for gender and participation; and for topic, language used, and errors made, for example.

As you consider these five types of triangulation, it is important to keep two things in mind: First, the aim of triangulation is to strengthen your study; second, the types of triangulation you use will depend on your inquiry and the focus and design of your study. Figure 5.4 (p. 98) shows how the different types of triangulation can strengthen research planning.

Figure 5.4: Research planning and types of triangulation

	RESEARCH PLANNING	TRIANGULATION
What	What kinds of data will respond to the question?	*Data* triangulation
How	How can/will I collect the data?	*Methodological* triangulation; *Investigator* triangulation
Where and from whom	Where and from whom will I gather the data?	Triangulation in *location*; *Investigator* triangulation
When and how often	When and how often will I gather the data?	Triangulation in *time*; *Methodological* triangulation
Why	What explains these data? How can I best unpack them?	*Theoretical* triangulation

5.4 *Applying the Ideas of Triangulation*

This Investigation builds on the research plan developed in Chapter 4, Investigations 4.2–4.6, to apply triangulation to your plan.

Working alone or with peers, review the research plan you developed in Investigation 4.4. Think about the types of triangulation above:

- How does each form of triangulation apply to the study you are designing?

- How could you improve triangulation in your study using one or more of these forms?

Using the framework in Figure 5.4, mark the places on your own research plan where you could strengthen the triangulation. Be specific about what you would do and how.

The important points to keep in mind about triangulation are these: It can build stability and confidence in how you interpret your data and thus in what you find. It illuminates problems and anomalies, and thus raises new questions to pursue. Triangulation is recursive and not linear; in other words, you don't just decide on a triangulation strategy at the beginning; rather, you keep returning to the question of how you can know more, have more confidence in what you are finding, and thus how you can collect more or different data, or how you can look differently at the data you already have. Therefore, you should think about triangulation as you plan your research, as you are carrying it out, and as you analyze your data. At its heart triangulation is a question of the discipline with which you design and pursue your inquiry, which is why it most often comes to the fore in planning the investigation and in collecting the data.

DATA ANALYSIS

To triangulate data in analysis, you have to do two things, which orchestrates another seeming opposition. You have to consider the information that you have collected so you can see what there is. And you also have to put it back together in new or different ways in order to more fully understand it. Data analysis can seem counterintuitive and even, sometimes, counterproductive. The impulse in teaching often is to say "I know what this means . . ."; "I know why that student said or did that . . ."; "I know why that activity turned out as it did . . . and I know what to do about it." In conducting teacher-research you are pushed to examine this sense of certainty, to expose it to scrutiny and questioning—not necessarily because you might be mistaken but to find out what is true and why. Disassembling and reassembling are essential steps in this process of uncovering reasons and explanations.

The nineteenth-century Russian literary Formalist poet Mikhail Lermontov argued that the purpose of literature was to make the "familiar" appear "strange." By taking familiar aspects of life and setting them down as a printed text, using particular rhetorical forms, Lermontov hoped that the author could encourage readers to see these daily commonplaces in new ways. Anthropologists also have worked with this dynamic relationship between the familiar and the strange. In the first part of this century, early ethnographers like Boas (1943) and Malinowski (1960) studied so-called "primitive" cultures to counter the views of them imported through the colonial exploration and exploitation of the nineteenth century. Their work sought to understand the fundamental similarities between these cultures and Euro-American sensibilities, to underscore that, in fact, they shared comparable structures and social goals and thus that what seemed "strange" could in fact be quite "familiar." Although that idea has continued to be a major focus of ethnographic anthropology since that time, turning their skills to our own society, ethnographers have sought to reverse the process, to make what is "familiar" and commonplace seem "strange" or different, and thus worthy of remarking on and better understanding (Wolcott, 1994).

The same process can apply to the teacher who examines and analyzes the data from his or her own students, classroom, and teaching. The aim is to make the regular appear new, to put a different frame around what is usual and taken for granted in everyday teaching and learning, and thus to perceive and understand it in new ways. For these reasons data analysis can often be the most engaging, and simultaneously the most challenging, part of the teacher-research process. It can literally feel manic: as if things are falling apart, then coming back together, only to fall apart again. Veteran qualitative researchers talk about this phase of the research process as cycles of disintegrating and reintegrating understandings. It can be simultaneously exhilarating and frustrating, confusing and insightful, energizing and exhausting; but it is guaranteed not to be boring or routine. It can thus be helpful to have an overview of the basic process. Four elemental activities make up data analysis: These are **naming, grouping, finding relationships,** and **displaying.**

Four key concepts in data analysis

Naming involves labeling the data in some way. These names are called "**codes**"; in qualitative research they can come from three basic sources: from categories outside the data such as the setting, the research question, previous research, and so on; from the data themselves; or they may be created by the researcher. If, for instance, you are coding an audio transcript of a class discussion, you might do so according to who is talking. Thus you might code the turns by student names or by gender; the names or the terms "boy" and "girl" are categories from outside the data, from the class setting. Within the second option, if you code the transcript according to topics discussed you might use words that occur in the transcript; these codes come from the data itself. The third option involves codes generated from the data by the researcher. In this case, you might find in the transcript that some students are interrupting others, or "cutting each other off," or others are reacting sarcastically, or "putting other's comments down," while others are trying to manage the discussion, or "trying to make it work." These codes, in quotation marks, are your terms; you are giving names to patterns you see in the data. The second and third options are similar in that the codes come from data; for this reason they are called **grounded codes.** In the first option, on the other hand, the codes come from outside the data themselves, from the setting, for example; they are called **a priori codes.**

For discussion of emic/etic, see Chapter 4, p. 69–73.

Naming involves taking the data apart. **Grouping** involves reassembling the names you are giving to parts of the data by collecting them into categories. As with codes, the **categories** can be **grounded,** emerging from the data, or they can be **a priori,** from outside. Grouping the names you are giving to or finding in the data begins to create a structure around the data, like the scaffolding on a building as it is being constructed. In this instance, the structure is building toward an interpretation of the data that accounts for what is going on in them. To strengthen that structure, you need to find relationships in the data, to identify patterns among these categories. Finding relationships among groups or categories is like putting cross-braces on the scaffolding, which strengthen it so it will be less likely to twist or shake.

Outliers

As you name, group, and find relationships in the data, however, it is critically important to look at what does not fit into the emerging structure of the analysis. These pieces that don't fit are called **outliers** because they lie outside the analysis. Often outliers will provide important insights about your analysis; they can show you where the interpretation you are building is weak or incomplete, and how it needs to be redirected. However, the temptation is to reject these outliers as the things that do not fit, in order to maintain the momentum of discovery and to confirm the architecture of analysis and interpretation you are building. It is here that you need to recall Francis Bacon's injunction: "If we begin with certainties, we shall end up in doubt. But if we begin with doubts and we are patient with them, we shall end in certainties."

As the data analysis progresses, you will need to lay out what you are finding in order to see the emerging whole of the interpretation. This step is called **data display;** the aim is to set out the patterns and relationships you see among the categories. These displays make the interpretation concrete and visible; they allow you to see how the parts connect into a whole. Data displays are both processes and products, which means that making them is as important as having them completed. As processes, displays are like rough sketches that can point you toward the finished drawing. The act of drawing can show you what you want to draw and how to put it on the paper. Often, in subsequent sketches, you will pick up, reincorporate, and perhaps rework and improve something you had drawn earlier. The act of drawing creates the evolving sureness of the image. Similarly, in making and remaking displays of the data, you are refining the interpretations that fit the data in response to your question and inquiry.

Displays are also products. They are maps of the emerging landscape of the data and, like maps, they can be created to different scales depending on the purpose. Maps can show the streets and buildings of the town, or they can show the major highways and geographical features. Both are valid; their usefulness depends on the intended purpose. You would not use a street map to drive from Chicago to Atlanta; nor would you use a highway map to find your way around Denver. In view of this dual quality of process and product, with any data display you need to be aware of how you are creating it, even as you consider the purpose in putting it together. You need to remember that no display is singular or exhaustive; displays are dynamic and always open to rethinking and remaking. As you display data you can ask yourself, to what question am I trying to find a response? How are these patterns, categories, and codes fitting (or not fitting) together? Is this interpretation pointing me in the direction I mean to go?

5.5 DATA ANALYSIS: USING A GROUNDED APPROACH

The following five Investigations (5.5–5.9) focus on three different approaches to data analysis. Each makes use of data found in Appendix D (pp. 219-223).

This Investigation introduces the basic steps of **grounded data analysis**. It refers to the four elements in data analysis discussed above (pp. 99–101).

In Appendix D (p. 219) you will find a series of nine letters that appeared in the *New York Times* as part of an article on how people cope with becoming unemployed. The letters are divided into two groups. Treat the four letters in the first group, Set A, as a data set on which to practice the basic process of grounded data analysis. For this Investigation, assume that the inquiry focuses on what it is like to become unemployed after holding a regular job. The research question is:

- How are the writers of these letters experiencing unemployment? What are the central issues and concerns for them?

Set A: Grounded data analysis

1. Read through the four letters in Set A (p. 219–221).

2. Reread the first letter in set A, underlining phrases and ideas that strike you. For each thing you underline, **name** the theme or concept with a key word. Write this **key word** in the margin.

   As you continue with the process, you may reuse key words and add new ones. However, do not go backward to change key words you have already assigned. Let the reading and finding the themes and

Grounded
data analysis
procedure

concepts move you forward. If you notice that you have read a passage and you have *not* identified any themes or concepts in it, push yourself to do so. You should not leave any passage unlabeled.

This process is called **grounded analysis** because you are surfacing themes and concepts from the data as you read them. The aim is to unpack the data according to themes and concepts you see.

3. Repeat the process with the rest of the letters in Set A. As you read several letters, you will probably notice similar themes or patterns. Write these on a separate piece of paper. Often you can trigger **patterns** by asking yourself as you read: *How do these data relate to others I have seen? What similarities or differences am I finding in the data?*

4. When you have finished reading all four letters, make a list on a separate piece of paper of the **keywords** you have generated. As you list them, you will discover clusters and affinities among the words, so put similar or related keywords together. Name these groups so that they become **categories** of your analysis. At the same time, you should keep track of the key words that don't seem to fit in any of the categories; these are the **outliers.** They can be as important to your analysis as the categories themselves.

5. Finally, make a map of the categories (#4) and patterns (#3) to show how you see them connecting to one another. Again keep track of any categories or patterns that don't fit into the emerging scheme. *Remember:* Don't force things to fit; try to let the connections surface.

The map can take several forms: a flow chart; a bubble diagram with arrows; an outline of headings; a matrix which shows how the categories intersect; or simply arrows among the various categories to show the emerging relationships. This map is called a **data display.**

These four activities, **naming, grouping, finding relationships,** and **displaying,** are the basic elements of any data analysis. Although you will enter the process at different points depending on the purpose of the analysis, the four activities remain the same and stand in the same relationship to one another. The difference will be in the order in which you move through them. That order is animated by the type of study you are doing, which, in turn depends on the inquiry you are pursuing.

For an example of grounded analysis, see Investigation 1.1 in Chapter 1, pp. 4–5.

Figure 5.5 illustrates the two basic approaches to data analysis. In one you work to ground the analysis in what is in the data. In the other you apply preexisting or a priori categories to the data. Regardless of approach, however, it is critical to recognize that when you name what you see in a particular piece of your data, you are taking the first step in establishing what the interpretation will eventually be. If you take a grounded approach to build up an interpretation out of what you are seeing in the data (as in Investigation 5.5), the names for the themes and concepts you are finding will evolve as you work through the data. On the other hand, if you take an a priori approach, you will apply a set of names and/or categories you already determined to the data. Broadly put, in a grounded analysis you are uncovering what may be in the data; in an a priori analysis you are looking for things you have determined in advance. This echoes the distinction between emic and etic views of data discussed earlier. These two approaches mark an important fork in the road of data analysis. The choice of which to use should be determined by your purpose, or what it is you want to find out from the data, which, in turn, is linked to your research question and your inquiry. The choice is not exclusive; you may start in one approach and shift over to the other. However, that redirection should be guided by your inquiry.

Figure 5.5: **Basic paths of data analysis**

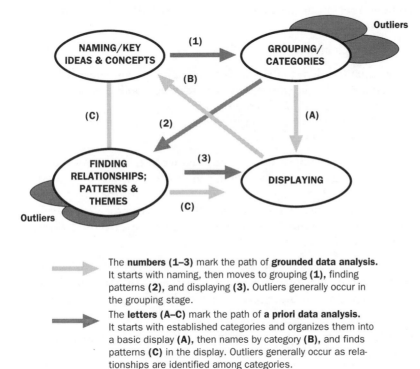

Grounded and
a priori approaches
to data analysis

The **numbers (1–3)** mark the path of **grounded data analysis.** It starts with naming, then moves to grouping **(1),** finding patterns **(2),** and displaying **(3).** Outliers generally occur in the grouping stage.

The **letters (A–C)** mark the path of **a priori data analysis.** It starts with established categories and organizes them into a basic display **(A),** then names by category **(B),** and finds patterns **(C)** in the display. Outliers generally occur as relationships are identified among categories.

5.6 *DATA ANALYSIS: USING AN A PRIORI APPROACH*

This Investigation focuses on approaches to data analysis. It uses the material in Appendix D, p. 219, as data for an a priori data analysis. You may want to refer to Figure 5.5 for a map of the process you are engaging in.

Treat the five letters in the second group of letters, Set B (pp. 221–223), as a data set on which to practice the basic process of a priori data analysis. For this Investigation, as in Investigation 5.5, assume that the inquiry focuses on what it is like to become unemployed after holding a regular job. But the research question is:

■ How are self-esteem and interactions with other people (family members, peers, etc.) affected by becoming unemployed?

A priori
Data Analysis
Procedure

Set B: A priori data analysis

1. Set up a sheet of paper with two columns. Title the first column "self-esteem," and the second "interactions with other people." These are the **groups** or **categories** you intend to focus on in your a priori analysis.

2. Draw five horizontal rows—one row per letter down the paper—so that you create a **matrix display.** The intersections of the rows and columns create cells in the matrix; you now have one cell for each letter writer.

3. Read through all five letters in Set B.

4. Reread the first letter in set B. Underline phrases and ideas that fall into either of the categories. For each item you underline, name the idea with a key word and write the key word in the appropriate cell in the matrix. As you go through the process you may reuse key words and/or add new ones.

5. If a passage does not seem to relate to either of the categories, mark it. Name the theme or concept in it, and record these names on a separate list of **outliers.** The aim is to read the data for the two a priori categories identified in the research question. This process is called a priori analysis because you have determined the categories *before* you analyze the data.

6. Continue the process with the rest of the letters in Set B, naming what you find and entering the names in a new cell of the matrix for each letter. On a separate piece of paper, keep track of the patterns that emerge. Ask yourself:

   ■ What patterns am I seeing within and between the two main categories, "self-esteem" and "interactions with other people"?

   ■ What can I say about the data that don't seem to fit into these categories?

   ■ How do these data relate to the main categories or to other outlying data?

7. When you have finished the letters in the data set, read through each column on the matrix and make a note of the patterns that emerge on a separate piece of paper: *What do the themes and concepts in this column say about the column heading?* As you read, you may discover clusters and affinities among the themes and concepts. If so, count those that are alike or related. Give these groups names to label these categories as they develop.

8. Summarize what you have found in each column. You may want to make a map or simply write a couple of statements. Then look at how findings in the two columns may interconnect. Make any statements you can about their interrelations.

9. Finally, return to your list of **outliers,** the key words that didn't fit in either category. Read through them to see how, if possible, they may connect to your findings in #8. Be sensitive to these outliers; they can hold the seeds of important answers and may refocus your analysis.

A common form of analysis within an a priori approach involves measuring quantities or counting instances in the data. Determining the quantity of items in particular categories entails using numbers as a way to **name** what is in the data. When numbers are counted and compared to the total possible in the category, they become **frequencies.** Surveys and questionnaires provide perhaps the clearest examples of data collection methods that can be analyzed quantitatively; however, virtually all data have quantitative dimensions and can be analyzed accordingly.

For an excellent discussion of using numerical analysis in teacher-research, see McDonough and McDonough (1997).

5.7 DATA ANALYSIS: USING QUANTIFICATION WITHIN AN A PRIORI APPROACH

Investigations

This Investigation uses the material in Appendix D, pp. 219–223, as data for **quantification** *as a form of a priori analysis.*

Use all nine letters in Appendix D as your data set, Set C, on which to practice the basic process of **quantifying data.** For this Investigation, as in Investigations 5.5 and 5.6, assume that the inquiry focuses on what it is like to become unemployed after holding a regular job. In this case, however, the research questions are:

■ How often do writers refer to financial issues or to family issues?

Set C: Quantitative data analysis

Frameworks

Quantitative Data Analysis Procedure

1. Set up a sheet of paper with two columns. Title the first column "financial issues" and the second "family issues." This sheet displays the **groups** or **categories** you intend to quantify in your analysis. To do the analysis you will count the number of times these two issues are mentioned in the letters.

2. Draw horizontal rows across the paper—one row per letter—so that you create a matrix display. The intersecting rows and columns create a cell for each respondent in a 2 x 9 (two categories by nine respondents) matrix.

3. Read the names of the letter writers and indicate the gender by writing M or F at the left of the first column.

4. Read through all the letters.

5. Reread the first letter, underlining any mention of financial or family issues. For each mention, put a check mark in the appropriate cell in the matrix.

6. If a passage does not seem to relate to either of the categories, pass over it. Focus only on mentions of the two themes: financial or family issues.

7. Repeat the process with the rest of the letters, marking checks in the new cell for each respondent.

8. When you have finished, total the checks in each column. These totals are called **frequencies;** they indicate *how many times* the theme was mentioned.

9. To display your findings, make a chart of the following frequencies:

   ▪ Frequency (number of mentions) of financial or family issues.

   ▪ Frequency (number of mentions) per issue, per gender of the letter writer.

To convert your frequencies into percentages, add the frequencies of the columns to get the total number of all mentions of either issue. This is called the **N,** for the total number of responses. It is critical in displaying a numerical analysis because it tells how much weight to give the particular frequency. If, for example, the N is 5, then 1 out of 5 equals 20%. If the N is 60, 12 out of 60 equals 20%.

Using the N as 100%, convert each frequency to its percent. To display percents, write them as follows: e.g., 80% (N = ##).

Maggie Cassidy
(see Freeman, 1992)

Navigating shifting approaches to data analysis can be unsettling, in large measure because it often throws you back on your research question and how you have articulated your line of inquiry. Some years ago I did a research project with a colleague at the local high school. It was not strictly a teacher-research project in our definition because I, as the outside researcher, brought an issue to Maggie Brown Cassidy, a French teacher at the high school, and asked if we might collaborate in the inquiry to examine classroom management and student discipline in her foreign language classroom. My line of inquiry stemmed from my interest in how the social and the cognitive intersect in the language class. Since language is so firmly embedded in social relationships because learning a language is highly interactive, and since adolescence can be a stage of such interpersonal affect and drama, I was intrigued by how an experienced teacher might manage the social setting of the classroom to support language learning.

Cassidy agreed to the collaboration, and we began to collect data on what was going on in the classes and on factors that might cause students to be asked to leave classes for disciplinary reasons, thus removing them from the learning environment. We were working from an assumption we both shared as high school teachers, namely that to some degree students "manage" presence or absence in class through accepting or violating classroom norms; this management is based on social rather than academic reasons.

I sat in Cassidy's French classes, taking field notes, and I interviewed groups of students from those classes. Cassidy kept records on her teaching and on discipline issues, which we discussed together. We approached the data we were gathering a priori, looking for evidence of discipline issues in what the kids said or did, and how Cassidy had responded. After a month or so we realized that there was a problem. Our a priori analyses showed quite clearly that there were no major discipline problems. In fact, students were not being asked to leave Cassidy's classes, for disciplinary or other reasons. Attendance was very high and seemed to remain so. I questioned whether Cassidy might be acting differently because I was in class as an observer, but both she and the students said she wasn't. I also wondered whether these students were simply well behaved; however, discipline records and their own self-reports revealed that they were a normal group who did get in trouble in other classes and were asked to leave those classes from time to time. Cassidy and I were at a loss; it looked as if the research question was not leading anywhere, and that there might be nothing to understand about student discipline and language learning in this context. Our data analysis was leading to a dead end.

The breakthrough occurred one day during a group interview when, at the end of the discussion, I asked the students what it would take for Cassidy to ask one of them to leave class. The students promptly detailed a number of classroom norms, most of which were tacit, and they all agreed that challenging those norms would be serious enough to warrant temporary expulsion from the class by Cassidy. The list included things one might expect such as use of physical force against other students, throwing things, breaking things on purpose, expressions of disrespect to the teacher, and so on. But it also included questioning another student's abilities as a language learner (e.g., calling someone "dumb"), not being helpful to others ("not playing along"), and not engaging in the lesson ("not trying."). I showed the list to Cassidy who concurred with the group on all of the norms they had listed. In fact, the list was relatively stable. Neither she nor other groups of students could think of other issues to add to or subtract from it. So the class had a clear contract: The students knew what it would take to be asked to leave the class and their teacher agreed. The contract seemed to include normal high school disciplinary issues, but it also included norms of social interaction and participation.

These data stood our research question on its head: If everyone agreed on these disciplinary norms, and if these students were being disciplined for such issues in other classes, why not in Cassidy's French classes? What was keeping them involved? Why didn't they transgress these limits? Thus our inquiry into student discipline in the language classroom refocused on what engaged these students in language learning so that there were minimal classroom management issues. We needed, then, to reorient our data analysis from our a priori look for factors that would cause students to be removed from the class to those that seemed to keep the students involved. But we didn't exactly know what those might look like or where we might find them. So we adopted a grounded approach to look at what was going on in these classes. We used the names that the students had supplied, using "dumb," "not playing along," and "not trying," as codes to reanalyze the data we had. These codes provided starting points to gain an emic view of the students as insiders to the social interactions in the classroom. I won't relate the outcome of the study—a full account is available in Freeman (1992)—however, the story illustrates the interconnected web of inquiry, research questions, and data analyses: How an inquiry drives the research process, although the specific research question may change. How data analysis can interact with and reshape research questions and, likewise, how it is possible—and indeed necessary—to combine a priori and grounded approaches to data analysis within a single study.

The main differences between grounded and a priori approaches to data analysis lie in how you approach the data and how you lay out what you find. In grounded analysis, you approach the data to look for meanings that surface through the process of naming, grouping the names into categories, and finding relationships among them. When you approach data in an a priori fashion, you take the categories as the basis for the analysis and look for instances, or names, of those categories in the data, and then for relationships among the categories (see Figure 5.5). In a grounded analysis the display or mapping involves assembling the connections you are finding among the categories from the data. Displaying these patterns and relationships serves to crystallize the analysis, to create a gestalt out of the different pieces, and to assemble an integrated interpretation. In an a priori analysis, the display serves a different function. It lays out the amount and kind of data that fall in each category. This provides weight, emphasis, or textured detail to some categories over others, which in turn serves to build the connections among them. So the two forms of analysis start at different points and generally yield different results.

Teachers' Voices

Clare Landers

Clare Landers is a beginning teacher-researcher who wanted to look at a particular student in her high school Spanish class. Although the boy, whom she calls "Tim," was not learning disabled, Landers found from observing him that he demanded special attention from both her and her mentor teacher. Landers's research question centered on the learning environment; she asked "How does the learning environment affect this student and his learning?" She collected field notes along with samples of the student's work, her own teaching journal entries, and an interview with her mentor teacher, who knew the student well. When it came time to make sense of her data, Landers found that she was overwhelmed. There was a lot of information, and it was difficult to know where to start or how to proceed. She decided to create a series of maps to display her data in order to start to find the relationships among the parts.

Account 5.2: Clare Landers

In the three maps, you see the evolution in Landers's grasp of the data she had collected. You can see how the various themes and patterns came together to create a comprehensive view of the student's role in her classroom. Landers observes, "The mapping was the most interesting and difficult aspect of the research process. As I was doing it, I didn't know what I was going to find, or even if I was going to find anything. It reminded me of free-writing and not knowing what information and answers you have inside of you that will emerge in the process."

Figure 5.6: Clare Landers, On mapping data

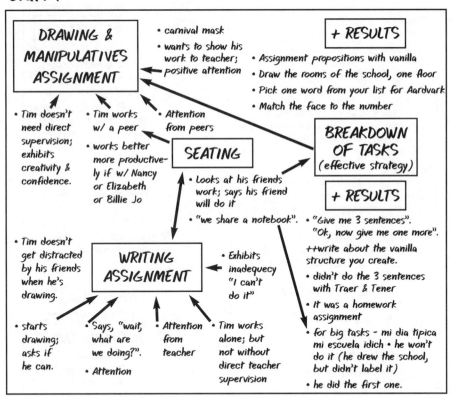

Draft 2

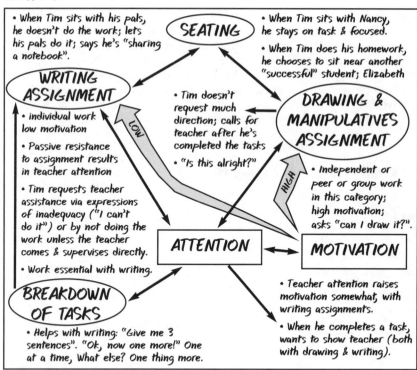

- When Tim sits with his pals, he doesn't do the work; lets his pals do it; says he's "sharing a notebook".

SEATING

- When Tim sits with Nancy, he stays on task & focused.
- When Tim does his homework, he chooses to sit near another "successful" student; Elizabeth

WRITING ASSIGNMENT

- individual work low motivation
- Passive resistance to assignment results in teacher attention
- Tim requests teacher assistance via expressions of inadequacy ("I can't do it") or by not doing the work unless the teacher comes & supervises directly.
- Work essential with writing.

- Tim doesn't request much direction; calls for teacher after he's completed the tasks
- "Is this alright?"

DRAWING & MANIPULATIVES ASSIGNMENT

LOW

HIGH

ATTENTION ↔ **MOTIVATION**

- Independent or peer or group work in this category; high motivation; asks "can I draw it?".

- Teacher attention raises motivation somewhat, with writing assignments.
- When he completes a task, wants to show teacher (both with drawing & writing).

BREAKDOWN OF TASKS

- Helps with writing: "Give me 3 sentences". "Ok, now one more!" One at a time, What else? One thing more.

Draft 3

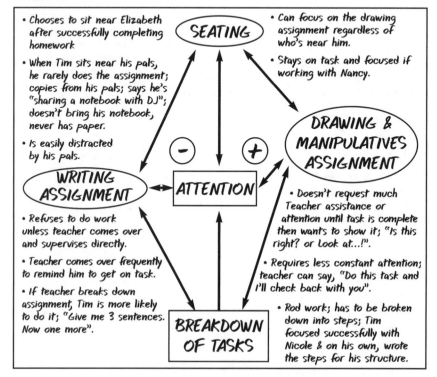

- Chooses to sit near Elizabeth after successfully completing homework
- When Tim sits near his pals, he rarely does the assignment; copies from his pals; says he's "sharing a notebook with DJ"; doesn't bring his notebook, never has paper.
- Is easily distracted by his pals.

SEATING

- Can focus on the drawing assignment regardless of who's near him.
- Stays on task and focused if working with Nancy.

DRAWING & MANIPULATIVES ASSIGNMENT

(−)   (+)

WRITING ASSIGNMENT ↔ **ATTENTION**

- Refuses to do work unless teacher comes over and supervises directly.
- Teacher comes over frequently to remind him to get on task.
- If teacher breaks down assignment, Tim is more likely to do it; "Give me 3 sentences. Now one more".

- Doesn't request much Teacher assistance or attention until task is complete then wants to show it; "Is this right? or Look at...!".
- Requires less constant attention; teacher can say, "Do this task and I'll check back with you".
- Rod work; has to be broken down into steps; Tim focused successfully with Nicole & on his own, wrote the steps for his structure.

BREAKDOWN OF TASKS

This Investigation continues the focus on approaches to data analysis by comparing the two data analysis displays generated in Investigations 5.5 and 5.6 through the grounded and a priori data analyses.

Take the data analysis displays you created in Investigations 5.5 and 5.6 and lay them side-by-side in front of you.

If you are working with peers, put the grounded displays together and the a priori displays together. It is best to focus on one group of displays at a time, and then to compare the two groups.

A comparative look:

Working alone or with peers, list the ways in which the two displays are *similar to* and *different from* one another. Consider the following questions:

- What does each display tell you? What does it *not* tell you?

- What information is available in both displays? What information is available in one but not the other? Why?

- What further questions are triggered by each display?

Talking through a display:

As part of the data analysis process, it can be invaluable to talk through what you are finding. This activity pushes you to articulate your emerging understandings of the data.

Two important caveats: Talking through a data display is not the same as having a conversation. It is important to stay close to the data, to voice what you are finding in it and to not elaborate. It is equally important to keep track of the insights and ideas that surface in the process, to note questions and half-formed notions and ideas. The discipline of talking through a data display lies in balancing two needs: staying close to the data and actively pursuing all interpretations.

- Find someone who has not worked with the data and who might be interested in your findings on the topic. Select *one* of the two displays to explain to him or her.

- Begin by stating the inquiry and the research question that drives the analysis. (These are stated at the start of the respective Investigations.)

- Then talk this person through the display. Let the person ask questions.

You should respond only on the basis of what you know from the data and your analysis. Do not introduce any external information. If you don't know the response to a question (which will be quite likely), note the question as one for further study.

You may want to repeat the process with a different person, using the other data display. The point here is to have the experience of working from both displays to see how they are similar and how they differ, and what questions they trigger in your respondent.

After you have finished, make notes for yourself about the process of explaining a display. Think about the strengths and issues involved in each type of display. Also consider where each display leads you in analysis: What are the next questions that arise out of each one?

Finding patterns in data

Putting together emerging understandings of data, whether through mapping, as Landers did, or comparing data displays (as in Investigation 5.8) is crucial to arriving at comprehensive and viable interpretations. Researchers talk about the viability of interpretation in terms of its "robustness." A robust interpretation or finding is one that is founded on strong and recurrent patterns of evidence. Finding patterns and relationships in data is the essence of data analysis. Patterns and relationships will take different forms depending on the content of the study, the research question, and the inquiry. However, they share a deep structure of three basic characteristics. Patterns in data can be **superior/-subordinate, co-occurring,** or **sequential** or **recursive.**

In a **superior/subordinate** relationship, something seems to cause, direct, or include something else. In the data from the unemployment letters, for instance, there may be patterns, such as a number of writers who say they are angry about losing their jobs, while others write that losing their jobs has opened new directions in their lives. These patterns can be characterized as superior/subordinate relationships in which losing one's job can make a person angry and/or create a sense of redirection in one's life. A **co-occurring relationship** is a less strong or hierarchical version of the superior/subordinate relationship. Co-occurrence refers to when one topic occurs often in the data in proximity to or in a relationship with a second topic. In the example, if many of the letter writers talk about having financial difficulties in the context of being angry about losing their jobs, this may be a co-occurring relationship. Lack of money is not the only reason the writer is angry, but it may be a related reason.

Often, in the complexity of learning and teaching in classrooms, and in schools as social environments, it is hard to firmly establish clear superior/subordinate relationships in data analysis. It is often more accurate and useful to talk about co-occurring relationships in order to show how patterns and aspects in the data relate to one another without having a definitively causal relationship. Establishing causal connections in data through a superior/subordinate relationship usually requires reference to a norm or standard that is accepted by the disciplinary community. In the case of statistical analyses for example, the concept of probability provides such a norm. **Probability** is used to define how likely things are to co-occur in relation to one another, compared to by chance. Statisticians, and the research community at large, generally use the standard of $p < 0.05$ to talk about probable relationships that are "statistically significant." This means that the probability of this particular relationship between the categories in the analysis occurring by chance is less than 5 percent; in other words, it occurs by chance in less than 1 of 20 cases. So phenomena that co-occur by chance in less

Probability as a co-occurring relationship

than 5 percent of the cases are described in statistical terms as having a "probable" co-occurring relationship. The less the probability, as it drops below $p < 0.05$, the stronger the possibility of superior/subordinate relationship.

The third type of relationship among data in analysis, a **sequential** or **recursive** one, is based on patterns of order and time. In this relationship one thing precedes or follows another, which precedes or follows a third, and so on. When the pattern continues linearly, the relationship is **sequential;** when it connects back to itself, it is **recursive.** In analysis, these types of patterns connect data or categories often through the order of things and not through a hierarchy. Thus the sequential or recursive types of relationships can be quite common. For teachers, sequential and recursive relationships are familiar parts of classroom life. The daily or weekly class schedule is a recursive cycle; the curriculum, when it is presented in a book, for instance, is usually organized sequentially. Often, however, language curricula will be spiraled so that topics and skills are returned to in increasingly depth and complexity, thus combining sequence with cycle.

5.9 *PATTERNS OF RELATIONSHIP IN DATA ANALYSIS*

This fourth Investigation in the series on data analysis examines the types of relationships found in data analysis displays.

> *Working alone or with a peer,* use the two data analysis displays you created in Investigations 5.5 and 5.6 to examine the kinds of patterns and relationships you find in them. Start with the display of your grounded analysis and identify an example of each of three types of relationships: **superior/subordinate, co-occurring,** and **sequential** or **recursive.** Depending on how you made your map (see Investigation 5.5, step 5), you will probably be able to identify some or all of these three types of relationships.
>
> *If you are working with others,* focus on everyone's grounded analyses.
>
> Turn to the display of your a priori analysis and do the same thing. Given the matrix of this display, you may find it difficult to find a sequential or recursive relationship; however, the superior/subordinate and co-occurring relationships should be easier to identify.
>
> *If you are working with others,* focus on everyone's a priori analyses.

These three types of relationships can help you to understand the various patterns you may find in the data. In this sense, they can serve as archetypes, against which you can examine the specifics of your data and the interpretations you are building. At some point, however, the analyses of different types and sources of data must be put together. Coalescing these separate interpretations into a version of the whole is where we turn next.

PUTTING TOGETHER ANALYSES: BUILDING A VERSION OF THE WHOLE

Eric Bass is a highly skilled performer who works with puppets of various sizes which he designs and makes. Bass generally begins by fashioning the head and then develops the body to accompany it, although he will also work from a scrap of cloth or other material to make the puppet's torso and then develop a head to go with it. Bass then builds stories to engage the puppets. He is quite emphatic on this point: "You don't decide on the story and then do it. You recognize it in the puppets . . . or in a sound, like the notes of a flute, or an image, or a song." Bass's work is like that of a teacher-researcher or indeed anyone who is **building interpretations** out of particular information or evidence. There is, as we have seen, a stage of assembling the parts, of arriving at viable interpretations of each data set by type and by source. And there is a stage that entails building a whole interpretation to encompass these, sometimes, disparate parts. Getting to this second stage can be challenging because it requires taking the skills of analysis to another level, beyond the specifics of one set of data or one group of insights, to examine how all the information can fit together.

Building interpretations

J.D. Klemme

J.D. Klemme was studying teacher-research while interning as a French teacher at Wilmington High School. He was interested in what and how his students were learning about French through the dialogue journals he was using with them. He explains how the inquiry arose out of his own experience with dialogue journals as a language learner in a graduate French class.

Account 5.3A: J. D. Klemme, "Journaling and Prior Knowledge"

This study was inspired by a journaling technique that I experienced first-hand in my Advanced French class. The professor would ask for a journal entry each week, and then respond to my writing with a flattering perspicacity that inspired me to write more thoughtful, longer entries. Since he was responding to my ideas and questions, I read his comments with special care, often picking up useful vocabulary and stylistic formulae which I would then recycle in my own subsequent entries.

I was so impressed by what I learned from this process that I decided to use journaling during my teaching internship. I was quite curious about how well the high school students I was teaching would respond to the same technique, and this curiosity became a natural area for inquiry. I began the study with the research question: *"What happens to students' errors when journaling?"* I have to concede, however, that I really hoped to find evidence of *How students were using their journals to correct their own mistakes* as I had done in my graduate French class.

Klemme's research plan and data collection were straightforward, as he describes.

Account #5.3B: J. D. Klemme, "Journaling and Prior Knowledge"

Data collection

I collected between three and five journal entries from each of my five sophomore high school students. I did not not grade the entries, but they were required assignments. The students could choose to write about an assigned topic, or they could choose to keep an "open journal." The journal was assigned once every two weeks and the students always had at least 48 hours to complete the assignment. I photocopied each entry for data collection, and then wrote a lengthy response to each student's journal entry. The first part of my response was in English, while the second part was in French. In total, each of my five students was assigned five entries. I received 18 entries. These entries, plus a series of final short interviews, made up my data.

Data analysis

I began coding my data after receiving the students' second entries and immediately I began to doubt my initial assumptions. I was not seeing any evidence of improvement. Indeed, some of the second entries seemed to be more poorly written than the first. I did not easily abandon my assumptions, however, and I held firm, believing that great progress would come in the next round of data collection. There were spurious advances, but nothing like the clear, incremental progress for which I had hoped. It was only after finishing teaching the class, when I began final coding, that I realized that my data would shed little light on *how students correct errors through journaling*. Indeed, given the data at hand, I was more inclined to discover *why students do not correct errors*. I decided to pull back and open up my research question by asking, *"What is going on when students are asked to write a journal entry?"*

In analyzing his data, Klemme was very explicit about how he assembled the various strands of his findings. At each juncture he built a cumulative analysis that pointed toward his research question, almost as if he were building a bridge from the information he had toward what he wanted to understand. His diagram, in Figure 5.7, outlines the flow of his findings.

Figure 5.7: J. D. Klemme, "Journaling and prior knowledge": Data flow chart

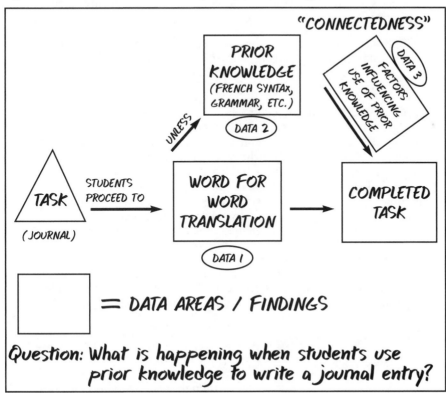

Klemme explains the development of his analysis as he built up the comprehensive picture from the three strands of this analysis, which he calls "Findings."

Account 5.3C: J. D. Klemme, "Journaling and Prior Knowledge"

Findings

Finding #1: The first thing that I discovered in my coding was that sentences in the journal entries had strong English syntax, as in the following example:

> "Dans le film *French Kiss* une personne du Français est representé si un aggressive, alcoolique avec un grand accent."

We could translate the sentence almost word-for-word following English word order:

> "In the film *French Kiss* a French person is represented as an aggressive alcoholic with a big accent."

In other entries, the student really is translating directly and actually plugs English words into the sentences when the French equivalent is not immediately retrievable. There were some exceptions to my students' word-for-word translations. An example of this, in the sentence above, shows that the student has some knowledge of French syntax. Although "une personne du Français" is not accurate French, it does show that the student knows something about how French adjectives are used.

These observations allowed me to conclude that *my students seem to be translating their thoughts word-for-word into French except in places in which they have prior knowledge of how French varies syntactically from English.* (**Finding #1**)

Finding #2: I began my coding hoping to find evidence of student progress in learning French. I thought that the common mistakes made in the students' first and second entries would disappear in later writings. This was not the case. Mistakes that never appeared in the first and second entries suddenly appeared in the fourth entry. I concluded that students were not making full use of their linguistic knowledge. I decided to test this hypothesis with a series of short interviews in which I asked individual students to correct mistakes similar to the ones they had made in their written entries. Most students were able to correct these mistakes quite easily. For example, one student chose to use the English words *monster, witch* and *dream* in a journal entry, yet during the interview she was able to come up with each of these words in French. I therefore concluded that *my students do not always make use of their prior knowledge.* *(Finding #2)*

Finding #3: I now knew that my students were using word-for-word translation except when they had prior knowledge of French. I also knew that they were applying this prior knowledge inconsistently. I decided to choose the entries that I thought made good use of prior knowledge to see if there were any commonalties among them in how the students used the French they knew. In this way I thought I might find what caused students to make better use of their prior knowledge. I selected one entry each from the three students who handed in their journals consistently. From these journals, I selected the entries that I found to be the most "French," by which I mean the entries appeared to strive to use French vocabulary and syntax accurately.

I noticed first that the three entries were quite different from the other fifteen. Entries D1 and D2 were quite personal, and entry D3 had a very original, even whimsical format. Also, in each case the entry I had chosen was the longest entry written by that individual. Because each of these long entries was either personal or creative, I hypothesized that the student was able to "connect" the topic with the writing in some personal way. I arrived at this conclusion, however, after I had finished my data collection and so I was unable to verify it with these student writers. Still, it certainly appears that *students were better able to access prior knowledge when they "connected" with what they were writing. (Finding #3)* The reason for this remains unclear and needs further study. Perhaps, for instance, the students took more time and tried harder when communicating ideas that were important to them.

Creating an integrated analysis of your data involves putting the pieces of your various insights and findings together into a possible whole. If you now return to Klemme's diagram (Figure 5.7, p.115) you can see clearly how he brought the three findings together through an integrated display. As he explains, this iterative process pushed him to rework his research question once again, although the overall direction of the inquiry remained constant:

Account 5.3D: J. D. Klemme, "Journaling and Prior Knowledge"

Integrated data analysis

I needed to narrow my research question again, to see how my findings might help me to answer it. When I diagrammed my findings and how they interacted [see Figure 5.7, p. 116], I found that the data seemed to fall into a pattern which responded to the question, *"What is happening when students use prior knowledge to write a journal entry?"* I found that students will proceed to translate their thoughts directly from English (**Finding #1**), unless they have prior knowledge of the French structure (**Finding #2**). In turn, the degree to which they use this prior knowledge was partially determined by how "connected" they felt to their entry (**Finding #3**).

Even though it can seem complicated and somewhat overwhelming, this step of putting together the various data analyses to build an overall interpretation is a critical one. For at this point, you gain—and create—an overall perspective on your work and begin to see what you have, what is missing, and how can you interpret it all together.

Examining the
what-how-why
of your analysis

The integrated display of your data provides the basis from which you can make them public, whether through writing them up, presenting them verbally or visually, or simply using what you know to argue for what is important in your teaching and your students' learning. For this reason, it is important to go beyond the data themselves to the level of findings, to examine *what* you know, *how* you have come to know it, and *why* you believe it is so. Working in this way accomplishes two important things. First, it compels you to think through the discipline on which your research is based. By being explicit to yourself about not only *what* you have found, but *how* you found it—in other words your research methods—and *why* you believe it is true, you move your work from assertion to argument. It will now be possible for you to discuss both the findings and the methods of your work. Second, this explicitness should raise questions. By determining what you know, you see more clearly what you don't know: the areas that remain open or unclear in your work. This is a crucial step in examining the **validity** of your work, as we will discuss in the next chapter. It also propels the teacher-research cycle forward into the next phase, for good inquiry leads to further inquiry, just as questions lead to certainties, which in turn lead to more questions.

Investigations

5.10 *Assembling Data Analyses: Creating an Integrated Display*

Review the three displays of data analysis you have completed on the unemployment letters (Investigations 5.5, 5.6, and 5.7). Bear in mind that the inquiry has focused on what it is like to become unemployed after holding a regular job. Within the inquiry, there have been three slightly different research questions:

- How are these writers experiencing unemployment? What are the central issues and concerns for them? (**Investigation 5.5**)

- How are self-esteem and interactions with other people (family members, peers, etc.) affected by becoming unemployed? (**Investigation 5.6**)

- How often do writers refer to financial issues and to family issues? (**Investigation 5.7**)

1. Read through each display separately. After you have read all three, on a separate sheet of paper list common or repeating themes, patterns, or issues that emerge. Also list any specifics that do not appear to be repeated in these analyses. It is most useful to do this step on your own, even if you are working with peers.

2. Referring to the types of relationships in data analysis (**Investigation 5.9**), organize the information from (#1) above and create an integrated display for it.

   If you are working with peers, it is most useful if each person creates his or her own display (or at most with one other person). Creating a display with more than two people generally becomes unwieldy.

3. Find a colleague who is not familiar with the data and talk through the integrated display (see Investigation 5.8, *Talking Through a*

Display, p. 111). Keep in mind that the aim is to articulate the links that you see. Often talking through these connections will make them more apparent to you. For this reason, you may want to pause periodically to take notes on what you have just said. (You can also use a tape recorder to record your narration.)

If you are working with peers, have one person serve as notetaker while a second person talks through his or her display and the others respond with questions and comments. Then rotate roles.

4. Reread your notes, referring to the integrated display, to see what makes sense and what questions you have. Draft a second version of the display, which now includes: (a) the relationships of themes or patterns in the data; (b) the *what-how-why: What* you know about these relationships, *how* you know it, and *why* you think this is the case, and (c) the new or remaining questions that you have. Finally, list ways you might investigate each of these questions. This can now serve as a basis for writing up your work.

TOWARD MAKING ANALYSES PUBLIC

Displaying data through analysis moves inquiry towards understanding, and a research question towards a response. These procedures serve to build a picture of what you are finding. They allow you to see what you have and, perhaps, what additional data you will need. In this sense, data analysis marks an important turning point in the teacher-research cycle. It takes you out of the specifics of data, toward the bigger picture of what you are finding out through the process. As such, qualitative researchers will talk about the relentless ways in which data start to come together, when you start to see many connections, patterns, or themes simultaneously, only to have these interpretations fall apart as more data are added that cannot be accommodated or accounted for. This is the tension that Francis Bacon talks about, in which certainties spawn questions (Bacon's "doubts") which spawn certainties. These are the turnings of the research process, and of teacher-research in particular. They are the rhythms by which knowledge is built. In creating knowledge from local understandings, analyzing data also accomplishes something else in the research process, however. It prepares you to make public what you are finding and the understandings you are generating.

Suggested Readings

There is a tremendous amount of work available on research design and research methods, and on qualitative and interpretive research in educational settings. On the issues of research design, I'd recommend two titles. Ruth Hubbard and Brenda Power's book *The Art of Classroom Inquiry* (Portsmouth N. H.: Heinemann, 1993) does an excellent job of laying out design issues in teacher-research, particularly chapters one through three. Joe Maxwell's book, *Qualitative Research Design: An Interactive Approach* (Thousand Oaks CA: Sage Publications, 1996) is a good general guide; however it is more oriented to educational research. Marshall and Rossman's *Designing Qualitative Research* (New York: Cambridge University Press, 1989) is also a very readable account of designing and carrying out qualitative research projects.

On data collection, I'd recommend two books: Jo McDonough and Steven McDonough's book *Research Methods for English Language Teachers* (London: Arnold, 1997) is an excellent compilation of data collection strategies. The other is Michael Quinn Patton's classic book, *Qualitative Evaluation and Research Methods* (2nd edition) (Newbury Park, CA: Sage Publications, 1990) which provides detailed advice, gleaned from extensive experience, on data collection and analysis. Patton writes in a very readable style; however I would recommend this as a source book to consult. Also, please see Appendix C (pp. 201–218) for a fuller discussion of data collection techniques and related references.

On data analysis, the classic sourcebook is Matthew Miles and Michael Huberman's *Qualitative Data Analysis* (1st edition) (Newbury Park, CA: Sage Publications, 1984). This is a thoroughly comprehensive and thus somewhat daunting book; however it is well-worth consulting as a source. Harry Wolcott's book, *Transforming Qualitative Data: Description, Analysis, and Interpretation* (Thousand Oaks, CA: Sage Publications, 1994) is a wonderful account from an experienced practitioner of how to approach the analysis and writing up of qualitative data. Wolcott intersperses his technical discussions with examples from his extensive work.

6

RESEARCHING TEACHING CONTINUED: TEACHER FEEDBACK ON STUDENT WRITING

Wagner Veillard

Wagner Veillard

PREAMBLE:

Dear reader,

If you have been reading the chapters in this book in order, you will have gone through a process very similar to the one I went through when I took part in the teacher development program in São Paulo, Brazil, which I mentioned at the beginning of Chapter 3. As I explained, the program lasted ten months and was divided into four modules. The first and third modules involved intensive course work, during school vacation. We spent the second and fourth modules in our schools, doing teacher-research. In Chapter 3, I described the carnival rides I took as I moved my thinking from a teacher's to a teacher-researcher's point of view. Now, in this chapter, I am again doing the "work at the hyphen," doing a teacher-research project in my school as part of the last module of the teacher development program. This time the focus of my inquiry is the influence of teacher feedback on students' writing.

Yours,

Wagner Veillard

6.1 *REVIEWING RESEARCH DESIGN*

This Investigation, which is the same as Investigation 3.2 (pp. 50-51), asks you to analyze this chapter from the point of view of research design. You may want to familiarize yourself with the Investigation before you read the chapter, or you may want to read the chapter first and then return to the Investigation in order to complete it.

The following questions can be responded to in any order. They provide a framework to move an inquiry toward a planned research project. (I use the terms "you/the researcher," because the questions can apply equally to reading other people's research.)

- **WHAT?**   What is the inquiry?
  What are the research-able question(s)/puzzle here?
  What are the supporting questions/puzzles?

- **WHY?**   What is the background or rationale of the research?
  Why are you/the researcher interested in it?
  What motivates the work?

- **WHERE?**   Where will the research be done?
  In which particular classroom(s) or site(s)?

- **WHO?**   Who will be the participants in your study?
  What role—if any—will colleagues play in the study?

- **HOW?**   What data are relevant to the research questions?
  How do you/the researcher plan to collect them?
  How will you/the researcher analyze them?

- **WHEN?**   What is the provisional time line or schedule?
  When and how often will you/the researcher gather data?

- **SO WHAT?**   Why will the research matter?
  To whom might it make a difference?
  What might you/others understand differently as a result?

Answer these questions, as far as possible, from the information in the chapter. As you do so, make note of things that you find missing. Which—if any—of these questions does Veillard *not* address in this account? It can help to do this task in a 7 (rows) x 3 (columns) matrix, in which you list the guide question words down the left side, the information you find in this chapter in a second column, and things that are missing in a third column.

---

1. What is the purpose of this report?

I am writing this paper to help the reader understand what happened to me as both a teacher and a novice teacher-researcher during the last module of the teacher development program. It is also my intention to share who my research partners were, the environment in which we were working, the reasons for my original inquiry, and the literature on which I based my ideas. After that, I intend to describe my research plan, what we actually did, how my students felt about the class, and how I managed to keep the project going in the midst of other teaching and curricular demands. In displaying some of the data I gathered and explaining the reasoning behind my analytical process, I want to show how my students and I perceived the changes that occurred in their writings.

After drawing a few conclusions, I will suggest improvements I feel would be necessary were I to investigate the same topic again. In the last part of the chapter, I will outline how I plan to continue my efforts as a teacher-researcher once the teacher-development program is over.

This chapter is divided into seven sections of which this is the first; each one consists of a question and an answer. I chose to write about my experience in this manner for two reasons. First, I had a hard time figuring out how I could present everything I wanted in a coherent form. In drafting my report, I found that I kept jumping from one topic to another, going back to previous items which I had not fully explained, and generally making a mess out of what I wanted to say about my students, their writing, and myself as a teacher-researcher. Second, I thought it would be good to use a format that permitted readers to determine the order in which they would read the chapter. The arrangement of questions that follows seemed logical to me as a writer, but I encourage the reader to find his or her own way through these questions. By choosing what to read next, readers can decide what information they need or want.

On formats for reporting research, see the discussion of Wolcott in Chapter 7, pp. 160–164.

2. What was my research question and why did I choose it?

In my first attempt at researching my teaching, described in Chapter 3, my question was "How can my students assess their own writing?" There were major flaws in this inquiry. Because of the poor quality, in my judgment, of the work they handed in, I had assumed that students did not already evaluate what they wrote. I also found juggling teaching and researching a real challenge. Trying to cope with my research project and, at the same time, the school demands for assessing and grading students was tough. Furthermore, my inquiry, which combined working with self, peer, and teacher feedback, was more than I could handle. As a teacher I do use all of these forms of feedback on student writing, but for research purposes, this time I focused only on the last type: teacher feedback. Compounding my problems in my first project, I was inconsistent about data collection. As a result, at the end of the process, it was almost impossible to make meaning of the evidence I had collected. So as I began this project, I felt I needed to prove to myself that I was capable of designing a research plan, even if not a very creative one in my opinion, and of being disciplined enough to follow it to completion.

See Investigation 3.2, pp. 50–51.

I realized that a focused research question would be crucial if I were to avoid the problems I had encountered the first time. So I decided to frame my research question as

> What happens to my students and their writings when they receive different types of feedback from the teacher?

However, once again I found I was trying to cover too much ground if I wanted to consider all the possible ways a teacher can provide feedback on what students write. For example, teachers talk to students, cross out incorrect spelling, underline improper grammar, write comments about content, list questions on the margins, put letter or number grades on compositions and so on. They often use more than one of these forms of feedback in a mixed format, or they provide no feedback at all, and sometimes do not even return students' assignments.

In discussions with my advisors on this project, Donald Freeman and Silvia Corrêa, I realized that I was setting myself up for a potential failure if I did not narrow the focus of my research. I adapted my question to:

What happens to my students and their writings when they receive teacher feedback either on form only or on content only?

I thus separated the focus of the feedback I would give into feedback on the form of the students' writing, including spelling, grammar, organization, coherence, and so on, and feedback on the content of what they wrote. I established that students would produce five writing pieces, and in order to reduce the number of variables, these writings would consist of descriptions and narratives only. Before rewriting each one, they would receive a response from me, the teacher. For the first writing piece, students would get feedback on the content only; for the second, feedback on form only. Then they would tell me which type of feedback—form only or content only—they preferred to receive on the next three assignments. They would also explain why they had chosen that type of feedback. I would give the other writing assignments and would correct them, focusing on either form or content according to what the student had requested. After they had revised their fifth piece, I would ask students if they saw progress in their writing, what kind of progress they saw, and if they would like to continue receiving the same type of feedback and why.

On first- and second-order questions and research, see Chapter 4, pp. 65–69.

My idea was to investigate what type of teacher feedback my students felt helped them the most. I was interested in finding out whether what they perceived as helpful actually made a difference in the quality of the writing they produced. In other words, I wanted to examine whether my students saw improvement in the same way that I did. This point alone demonstrates that, although struggling to be less teacher-centered, I still viewed my role as a very important one in the classroom. I took for granted that they needed my feedback on their writing in order to make progress. My questions were just which type of feedback students would prefer receiving, which kind I would feel more comfortable giving, and what our impressions would be when the writing was analyzed according to an established set of criteria for what constitutes good writing.

As in my first project, the core of my inquiry again rested on writing because I enjoy it immensely. I write a lot myself and am always anxious to discover why certain procedures work for me so that I can help other people find out what works for them and why. To top things off, I was asked to teach a writing class at the school, and I felt it was perfect timing to have those students be my research partners.

3. *When and where did I conduct my research?*

According to my initial plan, the objective was to spend one week on needs assessment and then five weeks to collect students' writings at the rate of one assignment per week, for a total of six weeks. Due to a series of interruptions—holidays and classes being canceled because of school events—it took me nine weeks to gather all the data I had planned. I started collecting information on August 2 and finished two months later, on October 6.

I carried out my research at an international school located in the southern part of São Paulo, the same site as the work reported in Chapter 3. The school has an enrollment of 700 students, distributed from kindergarten to twelfth grade. The school offers a Brazilian curriculum, an American one, and an International Baccalaureate. The latter is geared toward pupils who plan to go to Europe for college. The school facilities include two libraries, an auditorium, a cafeteria, two computer labs, an indoor gym, a soccer field, a chapel, and about 40 classrooms. There is always a nurse available for minor emergencies and since it is a Catholic school, there are two priests living on campus.

Somewhere in the middle of this institution is Room 29; it is on the second floor, down the hall at the corner, by the stairs. It is fancier than most classrooms at school, and, although nowadays various subjects are taught there, the space was originally set up for French classes only. It has a TV, a VCR, and a stereo system. There are ten posters on the walls and they show maps and photos of places in Europe. Inside the room there is a bookshelf, a fan, and the U.S. and Brazilian flags. Looking out the window, one can see a grove of trees. My students and I meet in this world every morning, Monday through Friday, from 8:00 to 9:05 A.M. The high school principal reads the announcements of the day from her office at 8:05 A.M. and we listen to her through the speaker. She has the habit of ending the announcements with a prayer, and then class starts.

On displaying data, see Chapter 7, pp. 154–164.

4. Who were my research partners?

Figure 6.1: Background on students in the writing workshop

Total number of students: 13

Gender		Year in High School	
Male:	4	Juniors:	7
Female:	9	Seniors:	6

Age	Number of students	Nationality	Number of students
19	1	Brazilian	7
18	5	Chinese	4
17	4	Mexican	1
16	2	Bulgarian	1
15	1		

How long have you been a student at this school?	Number of students
Less than one year	3
Between one and five years	5
Between five and ten years	3
More than ten years	2

As Figure 6.1 shows, my students were all upperclassmen. They were in school from 8 A.M. to 3:10 P.M. and had eight periods of 45 minutes each, seven for classes and one for lunch. Some of them would stay at school as late as 5 P.M. to take part in activities such as art or sports. Eight of them took the school bus, one drove her own car, and the others were brought to school by parents or drivers. Most of the students could be described as upper-middle class or wealthy. They had all been abroad, either as tourists or as residents. Only two students, like me, did not have a computer at home. In order to respect their privacy, all students' names have been changed. The class, Writing Workshop, was offered for the first time. Although it was supposed to be an elective, I soon found out that students had registered for the course because "We didn't have a choice," as Juliana said. Sônia added, "The superintendent did not want us to have a free period."

5. What happened?

The skeleton of my research plan is divided into six parts, one for each week of the project. Likewise, I will divide this answer into six parts, but each "week" will cover more than five lessons because it actually took me nine weeks to collect all the information I wanted. So I have divided the actual data collection into the six "week" segments of the project design. As you may recall, in week #1 my feedback would be on content only; in "week #2," on form only; and then for weeks #3 to #6, the students would choose the type of feedback they preferred—on form or content—and I would respond accordingly. The goals, objectives, and activities of the course, along with my classroom observations and journal entries, have become the flesh around the few bones I had put together before classes started.

Week #1: The course activities included the following:

- Learn basic information about my students and assess their needs. Ask them to write a letter to a friend telling the person their expectations for this class. After that, I hand out my syllabus and we look for similarities and differences in our expectations.

- Encourage writing by asking them to keep a journal and allowing them time to do so daily in class. Journaling prompts must be diverse and interesting.

- Provide opportunities for interaction; encourage sharing; show respect for the individual; accommodate differences; create a team spirit; build a safe environment. Each person prepares a question and has a chance to survey everyone in the class. We record the answers and share our findings. My question is "What languages do you speak at home?" and I use it to gather some background data on my students and as an informal needs assessment, since it helps me to find out who considers English as his or her mother tongue, as Figure 6.2 indicates. Since some students speak more than one language at home, the totals add up to more than 13, the number of students.

Figure 6.2: Home languages of students in writing workshop

Languages	Number of students
Portuguese	10
Chinese	5
Korean	3
English	3
Bulgarian	1
Spanish	1

- Distribute course book, *Viewpoints: Readings Worth Thinking and Writing About,* by W. Royce Adams (Addison Wesley: 1993). Ask them to find something they like about the book and share that with the class.

- Homework assignment for the weekend: Learning Memo #1. Think about what we did in the first week of classes and answer the following question: "What did you learn about yourself, other classmates, the teacher, and the subject (English writing)?"

The following excerpts were taken from three students'—Sônia, Shimoko, and Nadine—Learning Memos:

The most important thing I learned in this class is that you cannot judge a person by first impressions. There were a couple of people in the class that I did not know before and now I have a better opinion about them. Also, working in groups is not so bad like I thought. It's always good to know other points of view.

During one week of class at first I thought that I would do really bad because, I do not write well. But, gradually I realized that I feel comfortable in the class with other students and that I am not the only one with writing problems.

I also learned that Pedro likes to play soccer and all this year I didn't know that Pedro was Bulgarian until I had learned about him in this class.

Week #2: This week we do the following activities:

- Students write a description of a special object. I ask them to draw their objects. They exchange papers and each partner makes a drawing based on what he or she has read. The drawings are compared and we have a group discussion on how they feel about the activity and what improvements they plan to make on their descriptions. They change whatever they want; I collect their work and write extensive comments in the margins about the content only. I put a lot of effort into showing that I am interested in *what* they write, not on *how* they write it. Martha writes about how special her telephone is to her, and how her parents do not let her use it as often as she wants. An excerpt from her description, with my comments in italics, is below:

. . . you must be thinking so what? The problem is that I have strict parents and they are <u>totally oriental types</u>. So they have a lot of rules (*I'm Brazilian, so I don't understand what "totally oriental" means. Could you explain it a little more, please?*) and one of them is they prohib me to use the telephone, well sometimes they let me use it, but they . . . (*What is "a lot of rules"? How many? of what kind?*)

I return the papers and they rewrite them. Most of the additional sentences appearing in their second drafts stand out from the rest of the paragraph because they are clear-cut answers to my questions and comments. In spite of that, I am happy for the dialogue we have established. The following is part of Martha's second draft.

. . . problem is that I have strict parents and they are typical Chinese. When I say typical Chinese I am referring to those who follow the oriental culture and their way of thinking are more strict. So they have a lot of rules, for instance I have to obey them, I can't go out at night, I have a limited time to get home whenever I am with my friends and they prohib me to use the telephone. Sometimes they let me use it, but they make a lot of questions such as "Who are you talking to?", "Who is she?", "What does she want?" and "Why do you guys take so long to hang up?". But since I have this special telephone, I simply can call whoever I want without letting them know. And because of it, I can also call my boyfriend everyday.

We start reading unit one in the course book, "Viewpoints on Reading Essays," and try to discuss it in class. Students seem reluctant to participate. My journal entry for that day starts like this:

Maybe I should be asking myself what I mean by "reluctant." What are my expectations? How much "talking" do I want to see? I feel discouraged. They don't seem to care about anything I do. I have tried changing the pace of the lesson, my tone of voice, and even the way they are seated in the classroom. I have chosen personal topics, and I have given them the chance to work individually, in pairs, and in groups of four. I see no difference in attitude towards the class. I know I may regret writing this, but I feel as if they know what I want, but are simply refusing to do it. The reasons are unknown to me.

In talking to colleagues about it afterward, I realize that I might be using "participation" and "speaking" as synonyms.

Week #3: The students write a narrative on the topic "What is your morning routine?" They get in groups of four and read one another's papers. I tell them to look for similarities and differences in the things they do in the morning from the moment they wake up to the time they arrive at school. There is some discussion in the whole group. I collect their work and read the papers, focusing on form only. I pay careful attention to spelling, capitalization, punctuation, subject-verb agreement, and sentence fragments. I return the papers and they rewrite them. The following show Andrezza's entire first and second drafts. The underlinings and punctuation in bold show my feedback on the form of her writing:

First Draft:

I wake up at 6:00 a.m._ Then, I get up, take a shower, brush my teeth, and get dressed. At about 6:20 a.m._ I eat something_ and at 6:30 a.m. I take the bus_ to school.

I stay in the bus for about an hour and a half listening to my Walkman_ and sometimes I fall asleep. I arrive at school at 7:50 a.m._

Second Draft:

I wake up at 6:00 a.m. Then, I get up, take a shower, brush my teeth and get dressed. At about 6:20 a.m., I eat something, and at 6:30 a.m. I take the bus to school.

I stay in the bus for about an hour and a half listening to my Walkman, and sometimes I fall asleep. I arrive at school at 7:50 a.m.

Like Andrezza, the other students simply change the items I mark and recopy the rest of the composition as it was. At first, I feel upset because 10 of the 13 students write less on this second assignment. In five cases, there is a 50 percent decrease in the number of words. Later, as a teacher, I feel a bit pleased with what has happened because I find it quite boring to correct form only. Nevertheless, I want to make sure they write more next time.

We are able to finish Unit One in our course book, and I ask them to vote on the type of teacher feedback they wish to receive on their next three assignments. Trying to make their job easier, I make the mistake of using a black pen to write comments on content and a red one for the comments on form. You can probably guess what happens. By hoping to make a clear distinction between the two types of feedback, I have directed the focus of their analysis toward the color of my pen. After patiently explaining the choice of form or content, the students remain unconvinced. Antônio, Shimoko, and Nadine write:

> "... Feedback?! ... I would rather have the "black" feedback [on content]. It seems less shocking. The red color [on form] has a "STOP" kind of meaning, evil, it seems that something is terribly wrong, as for the "black" it's a more "comprehensive" color. The black is "less" teacherlike, it looks like you wanted to really understand us."

> "I prefer that the teacher marks in red [on form] grammar and spelling. It shows all my mistakes. I like the comments, but not the detailed questions about a certain essay."

> "For the next three assignments, I prefer in black feedback [on content] because it's easy for me to see my mistakes and in black feedback the teacher wrote questions."

Out of the 13 students, only Camille and Shimoko opt for feedback on form, and I feel like giving up the whole research process for the first time. How can I compare a group of two to a group of eleven? I feel even more discouraged when I come across an article in the school library. The text describes in detail the experience of middle-school teachers teaching writing in California, and lists the numerous advantages of using self, peer, and teacher feedback throughout the writing process. The teachers in the article declare that, according to extensive research, students produce more and better writing when the teacher provides feedback on content only. Although I was struck by what I read at the time, I neglected to note the actual reference. I have since realized the importance of making note of information when you see it so that you can refer to it later. It seems to be part of joining the conversation of research on a certain topic. I talk to my advisor and colleagues once again, and we decide that it is better to stick to the original plan. I end one of my journal entries with the following sentences.

> "I am not that happy about working on this research project, but I don't think there is enough time to change directions now. I will be reflecting about my teaching anyway. In order to finish the program, I will stick to the original plan, and have this be a rehearsal for something I can call my own. Despite the fact my results may seem irrelevant, I am certain that I will at least learn something about my students. This alone should force me to remain interested in this project."

Week #4: I have students go through a series of activities before they turn in their next assignment, an essay based on the question "Who are you?" I ask them to answer the topic question, using a maximum of five words. Then, I ask them to answer it again; this time their minimum is 300 words. I play some background music from the movie *Out of Africa* as they write. The next day, they have to answer the same question using any language other than English; they have a 10-minute time limit. I hand out small green cards and ask students to write something nobody in the class knows about them. I take the cards home and prepare a matching exercise. One column has all the students' names, and the other has the secret facts about them. I use this exercise as a quiz at the beginning of the following class. The information is listed below:

(1) Antônio   ( ) I don't like to read books.

(2) Rob   ( ) I had a dog called Shope.

(3) Pedro   ( ) I lived in Mozambique for about four years.

(4) James   ( ) I had three dogs, but they died.

(5) Myrthes   ( ) I would love to go to Las Vegas when I'm 21 years old.

(6) Nadine   ( ) I studied at Paca for eleven years, and it was terrifying.

(7) Martha   ( ) I had my head shaved in 10th grade.

(8) Andrezza   ( ) I like to write in my diary.

(9) Camille   ( ) I learned to ride a bicycle in New Jersey.

(10) Helen   ( ) Nobody knows why I was absent yesterday.

(11) Juliana   ( ) I love stuffed animals.

(12) Shimoko ( ) My room is almost done, which means I can move in very soon.

(13) Sônia ( ) I have a scar on my head because I bumped into a picture frame.

(14) Veillard ( ) I almost died this summer because of a "faulty" landing.

I ask the students to prepare questions using the formula "If you were Z, what kind of Z would you be?" My question is: "If you were a color, what color would you be?" Once each person has a question, we walk around recording everyone's answers. When this phase is over, we put all the answers of each participant on individual slips. For instance, Antônio's answers to his classmates' questions might include: Antônio—blue, zebra, BMW, Monday, hamburger, etc.

I distribute the slips randomly and, based on the answers, each person has to write about somebody else. In a short paragraph, they respond to the question "Who is (Antônio)?", and they guess and justify personality traits of the person whose slip they have. When they are finished, we exchange paragraphs to see what their classmates have guessed about them. We end the process by having a discussion on which activity they enjoyed the most and why. They hand in their essays on the following day. I provide feedback comments in the manner they selected, form or content. I hand the essays back to them, and they rewrite them using the feedback.

We start work on Unit Two of the course book, "Viewpoints on Writing Essays," and I still do not understand why students are reluctant to speak when I open the floor for comments. After some thinking, I decide to step back and get a view of the whole picture. My students have seven classes per day. How different is my class from the other six? In an attempt to find out how other teachers provide feedback to what these students write, I develop a questionnaire for my fellow teachers with the following questions:

An example of questionnaire (re)design

Questionnaire: First version (to faculty)

Surveying fellow teachers

1. Which subjects do you teach?
2. How long have you been a teacher?
3. How long have you been teaching at this school?
4. Do students have to write in your class?
5. How often?
6. In which form?
7. Do you read what your students write?
8. How often?
9. How much of what they write do you read?
10. Do you respond to what they write?
11. How often?
12. In which form?

This part is optional.

Name: _____

Age: _____

Nationality: _____

I show the questionnaire to the school superintendent and hand it out to 26 teachers (from kindergarten to twelfth grade). I am surprised that 10 teachers return it to me on the same day. Two of them come to me to offer suggestions. Great! After looking at what teachers say, I change the questionnaire slightly to get the students' views on the issue. They complete it in class.

Questionnaire: Second version (to students)
Instructions

Think about the following questions before answering them.

1. Write your name, age, and nationality.

2. How long have you been a student?

3. How long have you been a student at this school?

4. List the classes you are taking this semester and the teacher for each period.

5. Do you write [in these classes]?
   Answer "yes" or "no." Consider any and all writing you do related to school.

6. How often?
   Every day, once a week, once a month, etc.

7. In which form?
   Taking notes in class, answering textbook questions, writing essays, taking tests, etc.

8. Do teachers read what you write?
   Answer "yes" or "no."

9. How often?
   Every week, once per quarter, etc.

10. How much of everything you write do they read?
    All of it, tests only, homework, notes, 50 percent, etc.

11. Do teachers respond to what you write when they read it?
    Answer "yes" or "no."

12. How often do they provide any kind of feedback on your writing?
    Always, sometimes, etc.

13. In which form do they provide feedback?
    Orally; written comments about spelling, grammar, and/or content; a letter grade only; a number grade only; questions; they cross out what is wrong; they underline what is right; a mixture of any of the above; no feedback at all; etc.

Week #5: In order to assign another description, I ask students to bring a picture from a calendar to class. This time students have more options in brainstorming because we have reviewed listing, clustering, and freewriting in the textbook. In the middle of the class, Juliana asks me how they are going to be evaluated in this class. I understand her question as a desire to know what she needs to do to get a high grade by the end of the quarter. I tell her that it is a good question and ask if she minds waiting until the next day for an answer. In the following class I hand out copies of the "special object" description and the "waking-up" narrative. Each person gets his or her own writing back. I ask them to grade both drafts of each assignment using a 0 to 10 scale. In triads, they share the system they use, and Camille tells the class that "It is funny that nobody gave less than a 6." It is no coincidence because 6.3 out of 10 is a failing grade in this school, so it seems that everyone is intent on giving at least passing grades. We laugh about her comment and I ask why that happened. In the next activity, they are to grade their papers again using a form, the General Analytic Scale, I found in *Houghton Mifflin English 8* by Shirley Haley-James and John W. Stewig (1990). The grades are lower.

It is interesting to look back at what I have done and realize that, without noticing, I am once again veering toward my first line of inquiry, "How can my students assess their own writing?" from Chapter 3. To word it better, I realize I was searching for answers to the question "What happens when my students judge their own writing?" At the end of the grading activities, Juliana seems pleased. Because I am anxious to know the reactions of the entire class, I assign Learning Memo #2 for homework. My instructions are: "Look back over what we have done so far. Write a few sentences for each category and include examples of things that . . ."

On shifting research questions, see Chapter 4, pp. 63–69.

A) You liked (Why?)	Helped you (How?)
B) You liked . . .	Didn't help you . . .
C) You didn't like . . .	Helped you . . .
D) You didn't like . . .	Didn't help you . . .
E) Any additional comments?	

For example, "A" would be something that the student *liked* doing and that he or she believes *helped* in learning to write in English. "B" represents something the student *liked* doing, but believes *did not help* in learning. Students have to justify their opinions. The following excerpts were taken from their Learning Memos in response to this assignment.

> "This class makes me feel comfortable because I have my own diary which is the journal and in this journal I am free to write what ever I want."—Nadine

> "I liked when we made up a question to ask everyone in the class because it helped me to get to know them a little better."—Andrezza

"I enjoy the most when you let us write with music. It's so inspiring! I think it was a great idea."—Antônio

"Sometimes I enjoy the class, sometimes I just don't get the main point of the activity. Like, writing what do you feel or think. I see it as useless."—Shimoko

"I also liked to judge my own work and give it a grade. But I think it didn't help very much because it's not I who decide what grade I'll receive. It is interesting that the teacher is aware that to grade and judge a composition is not an easy task."—Juliana

"I liked writing an essay about 'Who Are You?' This helped me to learn things that I've never knew about myself. For instance, I didn't know before that I love writing."—Martha

We return to writing. I ask my students to brainstorm for 10 minutes about how they might describe the calendar picture they have brought to class. In pairs, they exchange pictures and journals. Without reading what is already there, each person is asked to brainstorm for another 10 minutes a description for the partner's picture. The journal, in which these additional ideas are written, and the picture are returned to the writer. We move on to discuss Unit Two in the course book, which we have finished reading. Then, I ask students to go back to their journals and look for similarities and differences from the two brainstormings. Students brainstorm on their own pictures for another 10 minutes and the class is over. They write their descriptions at home, and they hand them in on the following day. I return the papers with the type of teacher feedback each student has selected, and they rewrite their pieces.

I divide the class in half and each group prepares a test for one of the units we have covered in the course book. Once finished, the groups exchange tests and answer each other's questions. We discuss the difficulty of the questions, and then I hand out Bloom's taxonomy of thinking processes. Working in the whole group, the students classify the questions they have prepared to see whether they test knowledge, comprehension, application, analysis, synthesis, or evaluation.

Week #6: I am supposed to tell students the topic for their fifth and last writing piece, a narrative. However, I cannot think of anything I consider interesting enough for them to write about. So, I decide to have them suggest topics and then select one from the ideas they come up with. The plan is simple, yet it has taken me many unsuccessful trials to resort to it. Since oral participation is not overwhelming, we end up with three topics on the blackboard: friendship, the future, and summer vacations. I am baffled when students vote for summer vacations. First, they talk about the topic in pairs. Then, the entire class works together to brainstorm ideas, which I write on the blackboard. When it is over, they copy down whatever ideas they wish. The students write their narratives in class on the following day. I collect, add the feedback in the manner they have chosen, and return the papers. The students rewrite them for homework.

I assign some grammar exercises and after that, I spend a few classes on self-assessment. I hand out copies of everything students have written during the six weeks, and I ask them to look over their work in the order they wrote it. I give them specific tasks such as "Count the number of adjectives in your descriptions." This activity has two purposes. It will prepare students to write about their own progress in Learning Memo #3 and it will help me when I sit down to analyze the data I have gathered because a lot of information will already be coded. The third Learning Memo consists of five questions and is completed in class on green slips of paper. I present the guiding questions and allow time for them to write their answers before moving on to the next question. These are the questions:

A. Do you see any progress in your writing? If so, of which kind? If not, why?

B. Would you like to continue receiving the same type of teacher feedback? Why?

C. Look over your 10 writing pieces (two drafts for each of the five assignments). Which is your best piece? Why?

D. Select the best writers in your group and rank them.

E. What would you like to write about next?

Two students are absent for the entire week and therefore do not take part in the memo activity. The answers to question D from the other 11 students appear in Figure 6.5 and 6.6 (page 139), where I discuss data analysis. Before answering, students have to read one another's best pieces, as chosen by the author. I split the class in two groups in order to reduce the time spent on reading classmates' works. It is no accident that Camille and Shimoko are in different groups. They were the only two students receiving feedback on form and I wish to find out how readers see their writings as compared to the rest. I can hardly believe that the research project is almost over. I feel relieved for I just have to wrap up my analysis.

On discipline in research design, see Chapter 1, pp. 8–10 and Chapter 4, pp. 55–57.

6. What do my data tell me?

Although I will stick to the facts and try to be as objective as I can, I think a better wording for this question would be "What meanings can I construct based on the information I collected?"

Nine of the 13 students wrote more in the fifth assignment, the "summer vacation" narrative, than in any of their previous work. The other four students wrote more in the "Who are you?" essay. Since the number of words did not increase regularly according to the sequence in which the assignments were given, I cannot use cumulative practice or time in the course as a way to explain the difference in the quantity of writing between the first and last pieces. Therefore, I am led to believe that students wrote more in the last narrative simply because it was the only topic which they felt was their own. The "Who are you?" essay was probably the topic they saw as the most personal, in spite of the fact that I was the one to assign it. Ten students wrote less in the "morning routine" narrative and I think this might have been the result of poor pre-writing activities. In contrast, there was extensive work done before they wrote the "Who are you?" essay.

Figure 6.3: Quantity of students' writing in number of words

Student	Special Object	Morning Routine	Who Are You?	Calendar Picture	Summer Vacation
Martha	290	158	335	363	431
Helen	312	168	346	337	392
Camille	133	129	270	247	661
Myrthes	138	226	593	356	497
Juliana	257	315	603	416	624
James	n/a	218	380	300	517
Nadine	225	126	356	480	600
Andrezza	78	63	291	278	325
Antônio	193	113	452	346	293
Pedro	109	41	271	236	345
Sônia	179	103	452	n/a	419
Shimoko	227	159	492	303	370
Rob	n/a (joined class late)	455	700	418	880

The following table ranks students according to how much they wrote, as judged by the total number of words, over the nine-week period.

Top Five:	1. Rob 2. Juliana 3. Nadine 4. Myrthes 5. Helen
Bottom Two:	12. Andrezza 13. Pedro

The top five writers all chose to receive feedback on content. So did the bottom two. Therefore, I cannot confirm that if the teacher provides feedback on form, the students will necessarily write less, or vice versa. I should point out that Rob, who is ranked first, registered late for the class and only joined the group at the beginning of the third week. Maybe he just enjoys writing and as a result was able to produce more words in four assignments than many of his classmates generated over five pieces.

In the last week of my project, I asked students to judge their own writings because I wanted to look for similarities and differences between the way they evaluated their work and the way I did it. Therefore, I distributed grading sheets, taken from *Houghton Mifflin English 8–Teacher's Edition,* which had seven categories. I introduced minor changes to the sheets so that they would suit the needs of these junior and senior students. The categories on the grading sheets were:

FOR DESCRIPTIONS	FOR NARRATIVES
Capitalization	Capitalization
Punctuation	Punctuation
Spelling	Spelling
Five senses used	Beginning is interesting
Details are organized	Ending is interesting
Clear picture of subject	Details are included
Use of exact words	Use of linking words

Students read their papers and assigned a grade for each one of the categories. The grades ranged from 1 to 5, depending on whether the paper was: poor = 1; weak = 2; good = 3; very good = 4; excellent = 5. Students used the description checklist when evaluating the "Special Object," the "Calendar Picture," and the "Who are you?" pieces. The narrative checklist was used for the "Morning Routine" and the "Summer Vacation" assignments. Since they looked at both drafts of each assignment, this activity generated a huge amount of data, which I managed to put in one single grid, seen in Figure 6.4. Table 1, on the left side, is a condensed version of the grid; it contains only the number of excellents (5) each student gave to his or her writing pieces. Table 2, on the right side, shows the grades I assigned to their papers using a 0–10 scale divided into two parts: 6 points for content and 4 points for form. The pieces are labeled as follows: *SO:* Special Object; *WY:* Who are You?; *CP:* Calendar Picture; *MR:* Morning Routine; *SV:* Summer Vacation: An *X* on the table means that the student did not hand in the assignment.

Figure 6.4: **Summary of student *versus* teacher-assigned grades**

Writing Assignment	Table #1: Students assess own work Number of excellents given to pieces					Table #2: Teacher assesses students' work on a 0–10 scale (6 = content; 4 = form)				
Students	SO	MR	WY	CP	SV	SO	MR	WY	CP	SV
Martha	0	0	0	6	2	9	6	6	5	8
Helen	1	1	0	0	2	6	6	3	4	7
Camille	0	0	0	0	0	3	6	5	6	6
Myrthes	1	0	0	0	2	9	9	8	8	8
Juliana	3	3	2	3	2	9	6	8	6	5
James	X	2	2	4	4	X	9	5	5	7
Nadine	0	0	0	0	0	9	6	6	5	6
Andrezza	1	3	2	6	1	3	3	4	7	6
Antônio	2	6	2	3	2	9	6	6	5	4
Pedro	1	0	0	0	3	3	3	3	2	4
Sônia	0	0	0	X	1	6	3	6	X	8
Shimoko	3	0	1	0	0	6	6	6	6	7
Rob	X	1	X	3	2	X	9	8	6	9

Top Three Writers	
Students' view of own work	1. Antônio 2. Juliana and Andrezza 3. James
Teacher's view of students' work	1. Myrthes 2. Rob 3. Juliana and Martha

The figure shows that the top three writers, according to the students' view of their own work, were Antônio, Juliana and Andrezza, and James. According to my view of their work, the top three writers were Myrthes, Rob, and Juliana and Martha. I still have doubts about why Antônio, the student who gave himself the highest grades in the group, did not appear on my list. Likewise, Myrthes, the student to get the highest grades in my evaluation, did not appear on the students' list. Maybe it is a reflection of the fact we were using different scales. Maybe it is a matter of individual standards about what excellence in writing means and what my expectations as a teacher are. I use the expression "writers with highest grades" deliberately, because I am not confident enough to call them the best writers in the group. What is intriguing, however, is that if I did not have access to these data, and someone asked me to name the top writers in the class, I would say Antônio, Juliana, and Rob.

Actually, I don't think I would change my answer even after consulting the tables. I wonder if students' views of themselves or their work might have a greater influence on me than what my careful, almost mathematical, analysis of form and content tells me. It might even be that I end up showing how I perceive my students' work and this in turn makes them have a better image of themselves. These are scary thoughts, as a teacher! But these speculations might lead me into some interesting research in the future. A more down-to-earth explanation for the difference in our perceptions is that my 0 to 10 grading scale does not provide, for whatever reason, for a close account of what the majority of students think. This becomes more evident if I add another element, students' views of their peers' work, to the picture. I was able to get this information when students completed the third Learning Memo. They worked in two groups to read their peers' best writing pieces, and they were not required to resort to any scale when voting for the best writers in the group.

These answers on who was the "best writer" in the group allowed me to build a sociogram for the group. These sociograms are reported in table form, in Figure 6.5, and in diagrammatic form, in Figure 6.6. To develop the sociogram, I need to arrive at a total number of points for each student that represents the number of times he or she was nominated "best" writer by peers in his or her group. I calculated these total scores as follows. I took the number of times the person was chosen as #1, as the best writer, and multiplied it by three; then the number of times that student was chosen as #2, as second best writer, and I multiplied this number by two; and then the number of times he or she was chosen as #3, as third-best writer, and I multiplied that number by one. Finally, I added all of these scores together to get a total score for that student. In the case of Antônio, for example, his total score, 9, was constructed as follows: $(2 \times 3) + (1 \times 2) + (1 \times 1) = 6 + 2 + 1 = 9$ or $(2 \times$ "best writer" [3 points]$) + (1 \times$ "second-best writer" [2 points]$) + (1 \times$ "third-best writer" [1 point]$) = 9$ points total score.

Veillard here offers an excellent example of first-order *versus* second-order perceptions.

On the construction of a sociogram, see Appendix C.

Figure 6.5: Sociogram results (table): Students' perceptions of who is the best writer in each group

Students	Number of times chosen as:			Total number of points:
	#1	#2	#3	
GROUP A				
Antônio	2	1	1	9
Pedro	0	1	0	2
Myrthes	0	1	1	3
Camille	2	0	2	8
Andrezza	1	2	1	8
GROUP B				
Shimoko	1	1	3	8
Nadine	0	0	0	0
James	1	1	0	5
Rob	2	1	0	8
Juliana	1	2	1	8
Martha	1	1	2	7

As you can see, Antônio is considered the best writer in group A and Rob, Juliana, and Shimoko are considered the best writers in group B. Since both Camille and Shimoko appear among the top three writers, each one in a different group, one possible interpretation is that correct spelling and proper grammar have a greater impact on peers than they have on me as a teacher. Somehow this statement seems risky, but it is based on the information I collected.

Figure 6.6: Sociogram results (diagram): Students' perceptions of who is the best writer

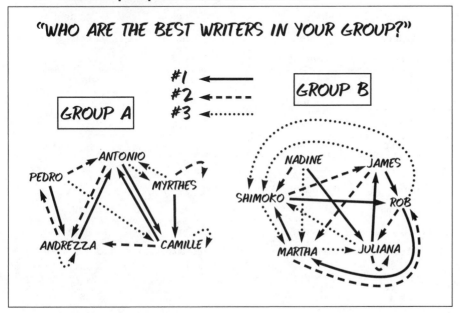

The sociogram data also call attention to Nadine. She is an isolate, whom no one chose as best writer in the sociogram for group B. Nadine is also one of only two students to give herself no excellents on any of the five writings, and I ranked her fifth according to my assessment on the 0 to 10 scale. Based on these facts, I would say that both she and her classmates have a poor image of her work.

When I asked students to select their best work over the nine-week period, their answers confirmed what other data, such as number of words per assignment (Figure 6.3) and number of excellents given to each piece (Figure 6.4), had already told me. Seven out of 11 students chose the second draft of their "Summer Vacation" narratives as their best writing pieces. Only three people, Juliana, Pedro, and Rob, did not see progress in their writing. Since I do not have enough information to explain this finding, I will refrain from ungrounded speculation. All the same, Rob offers an insight on awareness of progress in writing when he notes in his third Learning Memo, "In general, I don't really know what I am doing wrong." Camille adds, "Yes, there was some progress because my content got better." Please remember that Camille had feedback on form all along. My reply to these comments is "I need to do more research on students' awareness of their progress, if that's at all feasible."

Figure 6.7: **Summaries of students' preferences for style of teacher feedback (on form or on content) at the end of the term**

PREFERENCES BY STUDENT

Summary of findings by student

STUDENTS:	What type of feedback did you get for assignments 3, 4, and 5?	Would you like to continue getting it?	If not, which one now?
Martha	content	no	both
Helen	content	X	
Camille	form	no	content
Myrthes	content	no	both
Juliana	content	yes	
James	content	no	form
Nadine	content	X	
Andrezza	content	yes	
Antônio	content	yes	
Pedro	content	X	
Sônia	content	X	
Shimoko	form	no	both
Rob	content	no	form

(X means that the student was absent or did not answer. "Both" was not offered as an option)

**PREFERENCE BY TYPE OF TEACHER FEEDBACK
(ON FORM OR ON CONTENT)**

Choices	Number of students	Choices	Number of students
From content to both	2	Content only	4
From form to both	1	Form only	2
From content to form	2	Both form and content	3
From form to content	1		
Continue with content	3	Content (with & without form)	7
Continue with form	0	Form (with & without content)	5

Summary of findings by correction preference

Most interestingly, by the end of the project, students expressed a more even distribution about the type of teacher feedback they wanted to receive on their assignments.

> "Content I think is important, but grammar is what I really need to work on."—Rob

> "I want to have the "red" way [on form] which is the grammar mistake. I changed my mind because the "black" [on content] way didn't help me, so its hard for me [to see] my spelling errors."—Nadine

> "I would like to keep the comments as feedback. It helped me because it let me know how the reader feels about what he's reading."—Andrezza

> "I would prefer the type you put the little comments . . . based on those questions we try to improve the writing."—Antônio

> "I would like to change because to see which one is better the grammar or the content you need to try both."—Camille

> "I want to change to grammar and spell[ing] because my manner of putting in content is better than before."—James

If I had the energy, this would be the appropriate time for me to start a new research project with the same group so I could compare the results of this study with those at the end of another two-month period.

7. *What were some of my important mistakes?*

I say "important," because I made a lot of mistakes. Some of them turned out to be beneficial, showing me a new direction, for instance. Others I would definitely try to avoid, if I were to investigate the same topic again. I learned from all of them, which is why they were important. I have listed them below with subheadings.

- *Focus on students:* I would focus my research question even more on my students. I believe that my inquiry was still too teacher-centered. Moreover, I would work with my research partners for at least a week before finalizing my research plan. I can choose the topic in advance, and I still think it should be something I enjoy, like writing. However, if I want to call my students "research partners," they should have some influence on the shaping of my question. If, for example, I were to concentrate on needs assessment for the first week of the class, I would certainly have quite a few questions to choose from.

- *The intersection of teaching skills and doing research:* Also related to the research question, I should have a better understanding of "content" and "form" to clearly define the meanings attached to these words in light of my research question. As much as possible, I was consistent in the types of feedback I offered students. However, this meant I was not able to incorporate changes in the way I did things as I came to grasp certain ideas about correction. So I was perfecting my skills in correcting students' writing even as I was studying the impact of those skills on my students. This is a good instance of working at the hyphen of teaching and doing research.

- *Gathering data:* I could improve the questionnaire I handed out to teachers by having possible answers added after each question. This might help the people filling out the questionnaire without guiding them in a particular direction. I incorporated what I learned from this mistake in the questionnaire I handed out to students, which you can see in comparing the two versions on pages 131–132.

On the importance of doing first-cut analyses; see also Chapter 4, pp. 82–84.

- **Ongoing data analysis:** I could easily have responded to the question "What happened?" (#5) several times during the nine-week period, and not only at the very end of the project. While I did write journal entries and lesson plans throughout the research process, I did not analyze them on an ongoing basis. Thus it was a big job to go back and mesh them into one analysis at the end of the project.

- **Asking "why?"** I would ask myself "why?" on a regular basis because it throws me off balance, which I see as a major step leading to growth. I need to recognize that it can do the same for students, though I could ask them "why?" in a less aggressive manner than I did. I am sure I intimidated my students at the very beginning of the project, and in some cases it took a lot of time and effort to regain their trust.

- **Reading related literature:** Although I consulted books on writing and research, both in preparing for and in doing the project, in the future I would read even more literature related to writing than I did this time. From the standpoint of several years later, I can see, for instance, that work like the following would have made a difference to my thinking: Peter Elbow's discussion in *Writing with Power* (1981) of the doubting and the believing games in responding to writing; Tom Romano's *Clearing the Way: Working with*

Teenage Writers (1987), in which he talks about grading and evaluation; Donald Murray's ideas about conferencing in teaching writing, in *A Writer Teaches Writing* (1985); and Lucy Calkins's *The Art of Teaching Writing* (1986) on teaching writing to early adolescents.

At the same time, I would be more skeptical about what I read. For instance, I mentioned earlier the report I discovered in the school library by some middle school teachers in California who found that correcting student writing for content only was most effective. However, my findings here did not match theirs. In fact, I found that students gravitated toward input on form. But after reading the California report I was tempted to give up on my project; I felt, why am I looking for something other people have already found? But I ended up finding something different, which suggests that research knowledge is not absolute and demands a certain healthy skepticism.

On the orientation of valuing in teacher-research, see Chapter 8, pp. 188–191.

- **Working at the hyphen:** Perhaps the biggest mistake I made was assigning grammar exercises as a means of breaking the routine in our work with the course book. Only after I did so did I realize that I was providing explicit feedback on form. I wonder if I was unconsciously uncomfortable with the fact that my students would be living with incorrect spelling and improper grammar for three weeks if they had chosen to have my comments on content only. I think I felt a little like I was letting kids leave home without an umbrella when I knew it was going to rain. You, as reader, might rightly reply, "Well, let them get wet a couple of times and you won't have to remind them about taking an umbrella. In other words, you will not have to do what they are capable of doing for themselves." Nevertheless, I felt this pull between teaching the students through doing some explicit work on form, and studying how their writing developed when they received the type of correction they wanted. From their final comments, it is evident that their perceptions changed as well. Clearly the process is a dynamic one.

I know that there are many mistakes that I have not mentioned or even noticed. I hope that you, as the reader, will fill in the gaps in both the content of what I did and the form in which I chose to report it.

FROM HERE: FEELINGS AND THOUGHTS ABOUT DOING TEACHER-RESEARCH

As I did this research project, I mostly felt excited not only about the Writing Workshop, but also about all the other classes I was teaching because they became opportunities for discovery. I loved learning more about myself, my students, and the subjects we were studying together. Actually, I still feel excited about these discoveries and as a result, I continue writing on a daily basis in my journal. It is a record of the small miracles that might otherwise pass unnoticed. This journal is my daily homework assignment and in order to do it well, I must pay attention in class and listen to what pupils say. I feel like a student again, or better yet, like a learner. I enjoy teaching some classes more than others. However, I encounter new people in teaching all of them, and they are like books that no library could loan me. Even the textbooks I teach from seem new although I have used them for a while. Like any other learner, there are times when I feel discouraged because I can't understand or know what to do for my students. I feel worse when I make the mistake of slipping back into old ways of teaching.

In a sense, getting started doing teacher-research, which for me happened through the teacher development program, was like the traffic light I needed in my career. I have been driving along the highways of the teaching profession for some time and the roads, or should I say schools, are full of many things. There are holes: Things taught, and more importantly, things not taught. There are crazy drivers: Teachers who are looking for shortcuts and who use their power to break the rules they are paid to reinforce. There are also impatient people who honk their horns: Parents and administrators who expect institutions to produce miraculous results. And there are hitchhikers: People who are teaching but who have no idea where they are going or how they are going to get there.

I kept on driving, but I was no longer paying attention to the various signs along the way. That was when the light turned yellow. Somehow I awakened to the fact something was wrong, either with my car, my driving, or both. Maybe I had a flat tire or needed more fuel. The light turned red. It was time to stop, pinpoint the problem, and work on the engine to get the car moving again, maybe even get it running better than before. I found colleagues who were the mechanics who helped me to fix my own car. The experience was new for me because I was not used to getting my hands dirty in my own teaching; nevertheless, I enjoyed it enormously. I took a test drive while working on this project and now that it is over, the light has turned green again. My car has free mileage and I am on the road once more. This is what I see as I look ahead: more reading about writing, greater professional involvement, perhaps further education, and doing more teacher-research along the way.

A closing thought: While I have always found it boring to read a writer's or researcher's thanks to people I do not know, I now realize the importance of showing gratitude for the invaluable support one gets from others in doing this kind of work. Rosângela Valle pushed me to apply for the teacher development program; Terry Aranda, Silvia Corrêa, Donald Freeman, Kathleen Graves, and Donald Occhuizzo were terrific advisors; Celina Teixeira, a teacher of French, piloted my questionnaire; Cláudia Vitoriano e Silva, a colleague, supported me regularly; and to my sister, Katia Cristina Veillard, many thanks.

6.2 *LESSONS LEARNED IN DOING TEACHER-RESEARCH*

In this Investigation, you use Chapters 3 and 6 to examine what the author, teacher-researcher, Wagner Veillard, has learned about doing teacher-research.

In Chapters 3 and 6, Wagner Veillard offers two forthright and candid accounts of his own movement into teacher-research. He is open about both the strengths and the challenges as he develops the skills and orientations necessary to do work at the hyphen of teaching and research.

Working alone or with others, review both chapters. Create two lists of "lessons learned." The first list should detail what you believe Veillard has learned from one account to the next. The second list should detail what you have learned about doing teacher-research from reading these two chapters.

7

GOING PUBLIC

In a way, research is like fishing:
What you uncover depends
on where you cast your line.'

J. D. Klemme

Perhaps because I came to research through being a teacher, I have often felt susceptible to, and slightly intimidated by, public presentations of research findings. Sitting in an audience of parents and teachers from our local school district recently, listening to the state commissioner of education and the local superintendent of schools, I realized what troubled me. It was not so much the content of what they were saying, which had to do with school reform and strengthening teaching in schools, but the unbridled assertion of knowledge to reinforce a particular argument. As they spoke, I was jarred by the phrase, *"The research shows (or tells) us,"* as if there were one unified body of "research," or that "it" had the human ability to "show" or "tell" anything without someone to speak for it. In their comments the speakers did not acknowledge that research is a product of human experience, and that the knowledge it produces comes packaged in a point of view. Whether intended or not, the phrase "the research shows (or tells) us," stifled discussion and cast us, as listeners, in the subordinate role of having to accept what was being said as fact without alternative explanations or interpretations. Although I was uncomfortable, at the time I did not counter their statements. Perhaps I was silent because I basically agreed with their arguments; perhaps it was because I did not have any counterevidence with which to build an alternative view. Perhaps it was the form of interaction and the social use of knowledge as power that discouraged me from responding. I do not know why I was quiet in this instance, but I do know that such public expressions of knowledge are important business. They have everything to do with how teachers and others create access to knowledge that is publicly recognized and valued.

This chapter is about this dynamic, and the issues and processes involved in going public with what you have learned, or are learning, through doing teacher-research. While this step appears to be the final one in the teacher-research cycle, it is also a beginning. It marks the point at which you make what you know, have learned, or are learning through inquiry, accessible to others. So it launches the public face of the private undertaking. This part of the cycle has two interrelated impacts. First, making public your understandings can push you to be clear about what you know, how you found it out, and why it matters. Thus, second, this public voicing can compel you to be both articulate and accountable for your work. It is important to recognize that, while it is not imperative, going public with understandings is where the teacher-research process gains much of its power and social impact. You can certainly take what you have learned through inquiring into your teaching and channel it directly back into your own classroom without any public display or ownership of your findings. This is a valid approach to developing your own understanding of what you do as a teacher and how your students learn. However, as noted in Chapter 1, if part of the agenda of teacher-research is to make what teachers know and can understand about learning and teaching in classrooms more public and influential in education, then going public with the learnings that result from doing teacher-research is a crucial step.

Figure 7.1: Teacher-research cycle: Going public

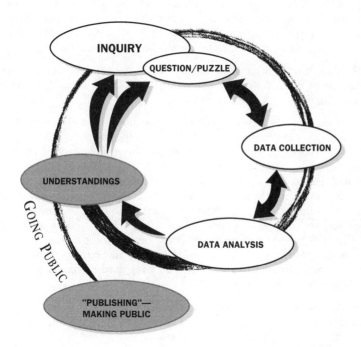

Going public can reorient attitudes—your own as a teacher who is researching teaching as well as those of others who encounter your work. On a basic level, being public about what you are doing can uncover different dimensions within teaching and learning situations that might appear problematic on the surface. The teacher in the following account consciously used the teacher-research process to illuminate a situation that, in the usual life of school, might have been difficult because it was out-of-the-ordinary. When Kristen Fryling began teaching Spanish to sixth graders, ages 11 and 12, in a rural elementary

Kristen Fryling

school whose students were almost entirely English-speaking, she found a Spanish-speaking boy had recently joined the class. As the teacher, Fryling wanted to figure out how she might draw the boy into the Spanish class, to recognize his language expertise and thus to give him a role with his classmates that he would not have as an ESL learner. As a teacher-researcher, Fryling was intrigued by how this role would evolve and be defined throughout the term. However, she had not counted on the attention her teacher-research would generate among other teachers and staff members.

Account 7.1A: Kristen Fryling, "Chico's story"

When I began teaching Spanish at an elementary school, I discovered that a twelve-year-old boy had just arrived from Venezuela. This boy, whom I will call Chico, would be in one of the sixth-grade beginning Spanish classes which I was scheduled to visit twice a week for 45 minutes. When I got to the school just after Christmas vacation, I heard the news of the new arrival from two of the sixth graders. Ned and Zev approached me that day and said, "Guess what? There's a new kid in our school and he speaks only Spanish; no English!"

"I asked him in Spanish what his name was, and he said, 'Chico,'" Zev continued. "So, using Spanish works?" I replied, somewhat facetiously.

After hearing the news, I was excited to think that we would have a native speaker who was the same age as the children in my Spanish classes. However, I also wondered how he might react to my teaching Spanish to his classmates. I had heard stories from other seasoned teachers who had been often corrected by native speakers while conducting Spanish classes. My questions began . . .Would my accent sound strange or terrible to him? Would he be bored by what seemed to him the slow pace of the class? Would he be intimidated by his English-speaking peers? Would he not want to stand out or be different from them? What would happen in Spanish class when he was there? How would his classmates respond to him if he took on the role of peer teacher?

So the **inquiry** was born: *How do I incorporate this native Spanish speaker into my teaching of the class?* At several points, I wondered if Chico was even going to be *in* my class because the ESL teachers were taking him out a lot in an attempt to ease his adjustment to the school. But I held the hope that he would want to assist me in teaching Spanish, and indeed, over time, he began to help out a little more each lesson. The **research question** soon emerged: *What is going on when Chico is taking the role of teacher with his peers in the novice Spanish class? And how does his role evolve?*

In her account, Fryling makes public the arrival of a new student in the school, thus opening up the possibilities in this commonplace event. Her musings and wonderings show how her inquiry took shape as she contemplated the role that Chico might play in her Spanish classes. By publicly discussing the issues she faced as Chico entered her class, Fryling establishes the event as one that can be investigated and understood, rather than simply assumed to be part of the status-quo of school life. The balance of her case study examines how Chico's role evolved in her class over a three-month period, as he moved from observer to interlocutor to teacher of his peers. Fryling views this movement as evidence of his successful integration into the social fabric of the sixth grade, and indeed the school, as Chico assumed the publicly recognized role of peer teacher. She concludes her account with an excerpt from an interview with Chico, just before the end of her teaching, in which she comments on "Chico's preoccupation with his present role as a Spanish teacher."

Account 7.1B: Kristen Fryling, "Chico's story"

As the other sixth-grade students review the lesson, I ask Chico if there is a better way we can use the posters of greetings we made. These posters show simple vocabulary for greeting and leave-taking in Spanish:

Chico: "Ah-ha . . . Eso fue también lo que quería decir. Yo quería que enseñaras el calendario, los días, los meses . . ."
[*Yes, that's what I wanted to say. I'd like you to teach the calendar, the days and the months.*]

Kristen: ". . . el tiempo"
[*Weather*]

Chico: ". . . el otoño, el verano, el invierno, la primavera . . ."
[*Fall, summer, winter, spring*]

Kristen: "¿Habrá tiempo para que puedas hacerlo en la primavera?"
[*But will there be enough time for you to do that in the spring (when you're teaching)?*]

Chico: "¿Para qué? ¿Qué? ¿Dar clases de español?"
[*For what? To teach Spanish?*]

Kristen: ". . . que puedas enseñar a tus compañeros?"
[*When you teach your classmates . . .*]

Chico: "Sí."
[*Yes*]

Fryling anticipates how Chico's role as Spanish teacher to his classmates will continue after she leaves the school. The brief exchange between them shows the school as an ongoing context in which research is not easily bounded; it does not begin or end in neat ways. Indeed, the players and situations that spark the inquiry generally continue well beyond the period of the teacher-research cycle itself. By making the work public, as she did in a report to the school faculty, Fryling showed the progress and accomplishment in this teaching situation, even as she subtly created conditions for these innovations to continue. Her work shows the skillful use of the public face of an inquiry, and suggests the possible usefulness that going public with the teacher-research process can have. It also suggests the challenges and complexities of how best to capture the fluid and ongoing quality of the work.

GENRE

If only going public were as simple as telling what you have found; but it isn't. Anything written, indeed anything made public, comes in a package. It comes in a given form that enables others to recognize what it is—or means to be—and thus to place it within the category of similar things. Because of the packaging and the responses it triggers, the form can accomplish certain intended results.

7.1 *THINKING ABOUT GENRE*

*This Investigation is a **thought experiment** (see Chapter 2, p. 28–33); it involves giving a gift to someone you know. To imagine the recipient, think of someone you know fairly well—a friend, colleague, or family member, for instance. Imagine that you are giving this person a birthday gift. For purposes of the experiment, it doesn't matter what the gift is. Now imagine each of the following four scenarios. In each scenario, the gift is the same but the circumstances surrounding the act of giving it differ. The thought experiment is to examine what might happen under each set of circumstances.*

Think each scenario through by itself and consider the following questions:

- What would happen?
- How might the recipient react?
- What might trigger the reaction?

After each scenario, you may wish to jot down some notes.

If you are working with others, you should complete each thought experiment by yourself before you discuss them together.

Scenario (A): The gift is elaborately wrapped in beautiful paper with ribbon and a large bow. You are carrying it when you happen to run into the recipient by chance. You give the gift to the recipient on the spot, saying "This is for you."

Scenario (B): The gift is unwrapped; you have it in a recycled, brown paper bag without tape or string. You are attending a large birthday party for the recipient. Gifts are being presented formally, one after the other. When your turn comes, you give the gift to the recipient, saying "This is for you."

Scenario (C): The gift is elaborately wrapped in beautiful paper with ribbon and a large bow. You are attending a large birthday party for the recipient. Gifts are being presented formally, one after the other. When your turn comes, you give the gift to the recipient, saying "This is for you."

Scenario (D): The gift is unwrapped; you have it in a recycled, brown paper bag without tape or string. You are carrying it when you happen to run into the recipient by chance. You give the gift to the recipient on the spot, saying "This is for you."

This process of creating something within a form, matching that form to its social expectations, and thereby triggering responses to it is called **genre.** Sunny Hyon (1996) examined genre from three perspectives: the view of English for Specific Purposes (ESP), the view of North American rhetorical studies, and the view of Australian systemic linguistics and its related genre research. From the ESP view, genres are seen as communicative events that use particular language-patterns or forms to accomplish certain purposes (Swales, 1990, p. 58). The view of North American new rhetoric studies expands the idea of a form used to accomplish a purpose to include the social actions a given genre accomplishes. Proponents of this view of genre are interested in how the actions provoked by a genre are shaped by and within a particular social context or setting (Miller, 1984). The Australian view of genre has its roots in the systemic study of language (Halliday and Hasan, 1989), which looks at how linguistic structures accomplish particular functions or purposes in social settings. This view of genre emphasizes the connections between the form of language and what it can achieve. Hyon summarizes the Australian view, as captured in the work of Jim Martin (Martin, Christie, and Rothery, 1987), who has led much of the Australian work on genre, as follows: Genres are "staged, goal-oriented, social processes, structural forms that cultures use in certain contexts to achieve various purposes" (Hyon, 1996, p. 697).

Taken together, these points of view suggest that genres include three interconnected elements. First, a genre has a given **form** usually—but not always—in language. Second, the form is used for a **purpose,** to accomplish some action or response. Third, the genre is always used by people with other people in a **social context,** and this context shapes the expectations of the form and the outcomes it may achieve. When, at the meeting I attended, the state commissioner of education said, "The research shows (or tells) us," he was invoking a genre, saying that research is a *form* of fact, knowledge, and truth. His *purpose* was, among others, to convince, impress, and persuade us, the audience, that what he was saying was true and, in so doing, to establish his authority and expertise. If successful, this strategy worked in part because of the *social context.* We were a group of parents and teachers who had come to the meeting to hear their views on education and school reform. We were probably not at ease arguing about research, nor were we familiar with the particular research he cited. Thus we appeared to accept the form at face value. This genre, "The research says," which we could call "social claims about research," is part of the social interaction by which the speakers establish who they are, their authority, and their case. The social context, which included who the commissioner and superintendent of schools were as professional men in politically important positions, and who we the audience were as women and men from a variety of socioeconom-

Genre: purpose, form, and social context

ic backgrounds with a common interest in our schools, allowed and supported the speakers in making their claims. Together the *form,* the *purpose,* and the *social context* made up the genre in this event.

7.2 *ANALYZING GENRES IN EVERYDAY LIFE*

This Investigation asks you to analyze various instances according to the three dimensions of genre. The aim is to see how dynamic these dimensions are in actual experience.

1. Look at your notes from the **thought experiment** in Investigation 7.1. For each scenario, identify three dimensions of genre—**form, purpose,** and **social context**—of the gift-giving. You may find it helpful to make a 4 x 3 matrix, listing the four scenarios down the side axis and the three dimensions of genre across the top axis.

   If you are working with others, it may be helpful to work through your own matrix first and then compare notes.

   Hint: The **purpose,** gift-giving, is the same in all four scenarios; the **forms** and the **social contexts** differ in two (as compared to the other two).

2. Now create a new 4 x 3 matrix. Choose four examples from among the situations listed below and on the matrix define the three dimensions (purpose, form, and social context) of genre for the situations you have selected. Since there is only very basic information given for each situation, you will need to fill out some of the details from your imagination and experience in order to work out the three dimensions of genre in each situation. You may also prefer to augment the list by imagining situations of your own.

   - A holiday pageant, held in the lunchroom of an elementary school
   - A parent-teacher conference, held in the teacher's classroom
   - A letter of complaint to a store about a defective purchase sent by a regular customer
   - A xeroxed Christmas or holiday letter sent annually to friends and family
   - A drive-in movie which you attend with someone you have just met
   - A wedding invitation from people you barely know
   - An e-mail inquiry for professional information to someone you do not know
   - Showing photos of a family vacation to close acquaintances

   If you are working with others, you may want to choose the situations and do the task together.

What do genres have to do with teacher-research? Several things. Broadly speaking, as I argued in Chapter 1, teacher-research has not yet been established as a genre. Its purposes, although the same at the core, vary a good deal among practitioners and across settings. Teacher-researchers seek to learn about, better understand, and thus possibly influence, phenomena through inquiry. Because they research their own settings, teacher-researchers learn both in and from the processes of disciplined examination of teaching and learning; they learn *in* doing the research and *from* its outcomes. However, teacher-researchers differ in their interest in making public their work, and thus in their commitment to influencing the practices of colleagues, the policies that shape their work lives, and their wider profession. For some practitioners, teacher-research is largely an individual practice that serves them in better understanding their own teaching and work situations. They are less concerned with pushing its implications or applications beyond the realm of the teaching and learning they can influence directly. In language teaching, action research has been a clear example. Although it was introduced as a means of participatory social change, in education and in language teaching action research has generally been interpreted as a teacher-led approach to problem-solving and improvement in classroom practice (Freeman and Richards, 1995).

For other practitioners, teacher-research can be the key to pushing for changes in educational policy and practices at the building and school-system levels and beyond (Cochran-Smith and Lytle, 1993). By documenting their understandings of successful learning and effective teaching, proponents believe they will be better positioned to argue for the changes that will improve their work and their students' learning (e.g., Gallas, 1994). They also believe they are more likely to be able to make such changes when their courses of action are based on inquiry rather than simply on opinion or what is fashionable. These positions—teacher-research as a means to evolving your own teaching practice versus as a way to effect educational change—mark two ends of a continuum. For most people, the actual practice of teacher-research is hardly as clear-cut as these extremes. In fact, its purposes often overlap and shift both within a particular project and over time. For many classroom practitioners, however, teacher-research is a function that waxes and wanes over the course of a professional work life, due to circumstances of personal time and energy, other professional commitments, and, perhaps most fundamentally, the lack of systematic support for research in the work lives of teachers.

For all of these reasons, there is no simple answer to this issue of making the work of teacher-research public. Teaching is not generally a collaborative activity; it is, as educational sociologist Dan Lortie (1975, pp. 13–17) put it, "an egg-crate profession." The inherent autonomy and isolation in teachers' work can make sharing of the processes of research, much less the findings, a challenging and sometimes divisive experience for many teachers, although it does not have to be. Because teacher-research pushes the boundaries of teachers' work in new directions, peers can often respond suspiciously or even with hostility to it as something out of the ordinary. The Japanese proverb, that the nail that sticks up gets pounded down, is quite apt. As teaching is currently structured and compensated in most settings, there is little support for teachers who want to

On action research, see Stringer (1996); also Nunan (1992).

engage, in serious and sustained ways, in thinking about—as contrasted with doing—their work in the classroom. Thus, in addition to not having a firmly established common purpose, teacher-research lacks an established and normative social context. Lacking this as a dimension of genre also slows its growth.

There are various ways to look at the ambiguity of purpose and social context that surround teacher-research as a genre. It certainly weakens the current impact of the work, and makes it tougher for serious practitioners to establish what they do. It is also true that the ambiguity is part of the larger issue of how teachers' work is viewed in society at large, as we discussed in Chapter 1. But where there is confusion, there is often also opportunity. It seems to me that the flux of genre in which teacher-research is currently caught is largely a function of its newness. Here the work of Charles Bazerman, the historian of writing discussed in Chapter 1, is instructive. He pointed out that the genre of the scientific experiment was extremely fluid when it first came to public attention in the early seventeenth century, and it evolved over time to what we now take as a well-established form. The same could well be said of teacher-research, which then suggests that defining its multiple forms is a key part of the process of establishing the genre. For this reason, some people argue that teacher-research should "look" and "sound" like other forms of educational research. If teachers use the existing forms of discourse analysis, statistical reporting, ethnography, and so on to make public their inquiries, they can draw on those genres.

This approach has definite advantages. It establishes the purpose of teacher-research as part of these particular research communities and it can create an entry into the more established social contexts in which these types of research are presented and debated. These advantages can also create shortcomings, however. If teacher-researchers only adopt existing forms, they will not create a new genre (Freeman, 1996). Their work becomes subsidiary to existing work in these established forums, rather than a genre in its own right. Given the conditions of time and effort under which teacher-researchers work, because teacher-research is work at the hyphen, as we have said, I believe it needs, and indeed it deserves, to evolve its own genre. But what would the genre of teacher-research look like? This is the focus of the remainder of the chapter.

CHOICES IN REPRESENTATION

The American Educational Research Association is a well-established community for educational research that draws practitioners from North America and around the world. It is thus, arguably, the leading social context for educational research. At a recent annual meeting there was a session titled "Alternative Forms of Representation in Research." The program announcement, reproduced on the next page, outlines the session. The session was actually two events: a presentation, and, later a moderated discussion. For the presentation of data analyses, the organizer had provided the same set of data to several different artists—including a dancer, a musician, a visual artist, a poet, and an actor—beforehand. Each artist, who was also trained as an educational researcher, was to represent the data set, using his or her artistic skills. At the first session, the various alternative forms were presented. The interpretations included a mural, a readers' theater, a dance, a musical composition, and so on. Some presentations involved the audience members as active participants, while in others they were observers. But it was clear from the whole session that the audience of a research effort had much to do with how research results are received. In terms of genre, the social context helps to create recognizable forms.

31.18	Alternative (Re)presentations of Data: Presentations of Interpretations of Data
6:15–7:45	Hyatt Regency C, West Tower, Ballroom Level

POSTER 1 Musical Representation.

POSTER 2 Photographic Representation.

POSTER 3 Graphic Representation.

POSTER 4 Artistic Representation.

POSTER 5 Spiritual Representation.

POSTER 6 Narrative Representation.

POSTER 7 Poetic Representation.

POSTER 8 Dramatic Representation.

POSTER 9 Multimedia Representation.

POSTER 10 Dance Representation.

The second part of the session, held the next day, involved an active discussion of the processes of representation and whether what had been presented were, or were not, research findings. Did these various forms so alter the nature of the endeavor that it was no longer recognized by the community as "research"?

One of the panelists referred to the work of philosopher Nelson Goodman on defining truth. Goodman proposed that in place of the conventional idea of absolute truth, we use the notion of "rightness of fit" to determine whether something is accurate and appropriate to what it represents. Goodman described three types of "fit": of the medium with its message, of the medium with how it is used, and of the medium with its audience. Thus the idea is that truth or "fit" is a matter of correspondence among what is being said, how it is said, and how it is received by the audience. Goodman's three dimensions of the fit of representation to the content are similar to the three aspects of genre: Medium with message addresses form; medium with use addresses purpose; and medium with audience addresses social context. This tripartite tension means that there cannot be an absolute determination of truth, but rather there is a constant judgment of standard and how the representation fits with the content, given our perceptions and experience. As I argued in Chapter 1, the "discipline" of the research inquiry depends both on its internal organization, or the "discipline" of its method, and on the "disciplines" or fields in which the research intends to take part. These latter disciplines have standards, or "warrants of truth,"

On disciplined inquiry, see Chapter 1, pp. 8–13.

against which the "rightness of fit," or the genre, of the research is assessed. Thus, presenting data becomes a question of the best fit in its representation, which in turn is a question of genre, and ultimately of voice and social impact. Choices in how you present research data are decisions about what you say, how you say it, to whom, and who may be willing to listen to or read what you present.

Public presentations of teacher-research: four formats

Because it is not yet a firmly established genre, and because the overall architecture of educational research is shifting, teacher-research can offer multiple choices in representation. While you may not wish to engage in the range of options used in the presentation at the American Educational Research Association meeting, it is nevertheless worth considering the variety potentially available. I want to outline four kinds of research presentations, keeping in mind that there are many others and that the rightness of the fit between the understandings and their presentation is a judgment made by the teacher-researcher and responded to by his or her audience. The four kinds are **interactive presentation, virtual presentation, performed presentation,** and **written presentation.**

Interactive presentation involves displaying research findings in ways in which the audience can publicly interact with them. Common forms of interactive presentation include poster sessions, panel or individual oral presentations, and teacher-research conferences. These formats bring the presentation and the audience together in a spontaneous and unscripted way. In choosing this format the teacher-researcher is encouraging interaction and discussion with his or her audience. Because the teacher-researcher must be there in person, these presentations can be exploratory and open-ended, allowing both presenter and public to probe the understandings that are put forward. The displays are usually spontaneous and engaging, but can generally reach only limited audiences. The emphasis is on making public the process of the research and its results, and thus creating entry to the whole inquiry. Since the interaction between teacher-researcher and audience can become a means to explore and expand the work itself, interactive presentations can also offer a way to comment, on multiple levels, on the process of research and the resulting understandings.

In contrast, **virtual presentation** does not allow for such direct interaction between the research process, findings, and the audience. Virtual presentations, such as videotape or multimedia, capture portions of data as they are, and allow the audience to hear and see learners and learning processes more directly. Students talking about or showing their work, for example, can convey learning in ways that secondhand reports may not. Virtual presentations can thus be quite powerful precisely because they bring the participants and the site of the research directly to the audience. They can reach large audiences simultaneously and can easily be repeated. However, these presentations are circumscribed by their virtual—and often technological—nature. Given the media used, it can be difficult to comment on the process of research and understandings simultaneously. Thus virtual presentations generally put less emphasis on how the research was done and more on particular aspects of the results.

In a way, **performed presentation** blends the strengths of interactive and virtual formats. Performed presentations can include readers' theater, narrative or poetry read aloud, and other types of staged events. They bring the presentation and the audience together in an organized or orchestrated manner. Like interactive presentations, this format is live, human, and interpersonal. Like virtual presentations, however, it is scripted and structured in advance. These displays can be powerfully engaging and can reach large audiences simultaneously; because they are planned in advance, they are more easily repeated. They can also comment on the research process and the understandings within the same format. However, the formality of performance can make it difficult to engage interactively with the audience, and thus to pursue the exploration and expansion of ideas.

The fourth format, **written presentation,** is probably the most common and the most self-evident. It is also highly codified: Take a look at the number of articles, books, and style manuals on how to write up research. Like any form of writing, it involves many subtle decisions and choices. Given the level of norms and definitions that surround it, written presentation of research is also arguably the most complex and the most widely accessible. Perhaps because it is the most classic and permanent form of representation, the written format involves significant decisions and choices in which genre is most clearly evident. With any presentation of understandings, but particularly in writing, there are choices to make of *purpose,* of *audience* or social context, and of *form.* In determining the purpose you are asking the question: Why am I saying what I am saying? What do I want to accomplish? Closely linked to these answers about your purpose are questions of audience and social setting: To whom do I want to address my findings? Where do I want them to "land"? How would I like my understandings to be understood? The latter two questions examine the possible impact of your work on those who may see or read it. If, for example, you want to convince school or district administrators of a finding, you may want to use a style of presentation that echoes conventional research writing. But if you want to reach parents or colleagues, it may well be that a case study narrative will carry more impact. The point is that there is no one way of writing up your research; written presentation always involves a potential choice of form.

On what sounds "scientific," see Investigations 1.3 and 1.4 (pp. 13, 15).

Choosing a form to make public your work is a way of connecting to certain audiences and being heard in certain contexts. It can be a strategic choice, or it can be a default option. Recall that forms of public expression gain credence and authority in large measure from social norms. Some forms carry with them the cachet of "scientific research"; they are what we expect to read or hear as science. Other forms exist, but have not been widely harnessed to express research findings. Because we do not yet have established norms for reporting teacher-research, we have the option of drawing on the recognized forms and/or the possibility of using new forms to express our understandings. This point was brought home to me by the following poem. The author, Ann Carlson, is an ESL teacher in southeastern Alaska. Some years ago I visited Carlson's classroom as part of her graduate training. We spent time talking about her students, their homes and classroom experiences, and the dynamics of pull-out ESL teaching which creates a private, sometimes safe, sometimes isolating, venue in which

Ann Carlson

teacher and student sort through school life while working on the English language. At some point in our discussions, Carlson told me of the poetry she wrote and how sometimes it seemed the most appropriate way to voice these experiences.

Account 7.2: Ann Carlson
"The Card Game"

I shuffle the game cards again as
the small brown face
across the table crumples,
shameful tears sliding down his chin.

More shuffling, more
tears. I wait, calculating the time
I have for this
latest international
crisis.

What happened?, I ask,
Cards slap the table.
He stares as from a dream.

I know he has no English
words for one more Anglo face today.

We are both shuffling now.

I trade another five minutes
for a smile,
a familiar joke.
There is so little time.

I can't fix it for him or
any of them but
I can shuffle the cards.

I have no gifts for this
child but a smile,
a joke, a language
that will never speak to his heart.
Such gifts!

While Carlson's poem was not written as an account of teacher-research, I would argue that it could certainly be one. The poem is a case study of an interaction with one student that crystallizes the dynamics of teaching and learning in that instance. In so doing, the account illustrates writer Eudora Welty's statement about all effective prose, that "the general resides in the particular." Carlson's poem also shows how in the choice of form lies the seeds of public impact.

7.3 *"The Card Game": Comparing Two Modes of Presentation*

In this Investigation, you compare two modes of presentation—written and performed—of teacher-research. The aim is to explore genre, and specifically how these two different forms of presentation of the same account interact with social context. The Investigation has two parts, marked (1A)/(1B) and (2A)/(2B); each part should be done with two different audiences.

If you are working with colleagues, do the Investigation alone and then compare notes.

Written presentation

1A. *As a poem:* Give Ann Carlson's poem, "The Card Game," to someone to read. Choose the reader(s) thoughtfully, making note of background, experience in schools, and experience teaching (if applicable).

Introduce "The Card Game" as "a poem about teaching."

After the reader(s) finish, probe the reaction by asking:

- What did you learn about the particular teaching situation?

- What is the author trying to accomplish? What is her purpose?

- Would you call this poem a "research account"? Why or why not?

1B. *As a research report:* Now give "The Card Game" to a different audience. Again, be aware of who you choose as reader(s); note background, experience in schools, and experience teaching (if applicable).

Introduce "The Card Game" as "a teacher-research report from an ESL classroom."

After the reader(s) finish, probe the reactions by asking:

- What did you learn about the particular teaching situation?

- How would you summarize the researcher's findings?

- What is the author as a teacher-researcher aiming to accomplish? What is her purpose?

- Would you describe this as a "research account"? Why or why not?

In your discussion, be careful and consistent in referring to "The Card Game" as a "teacher-research report" or "account."

Performed presentation:

2A. *As a poem:* Read "The Card Game" aloud to one (or more) people who have not read it before. The aim is to see how an audience responds to the poem when it is performed.

Introduce "The Card Game" as "a poem about teaching."

After you have performed it, ask the audience members how they respond to the poem and why.

- Does the poem trigger new understandings of this teaching situation? If so, how and why? If not, why not?

- What is the author trying to accomplish? What is her purpose?

- Would you call this poem a "research account"? Why or why not?

2B. *As a research report:* Find a different audience. This time introduce the reading as "a teacher-research report from an ESL classroom." After reading the poem aloud to them, ask members of this audience how they respond to it and why.

- What did you learn about the particular research situation?

- How would you summarize the researcher's findings.

- What is the author as a teacher-researcher aiming to accomplish? What is her purpose?

- Would you describe this as a "research account"? Why or why not?

In your discussion, be careful and consistent in referring to "The Card Game" as a "teacher-research report" or "account."

DESCRIPTION-ANALYSIS-INTERPRETATION

Frameworks

Written presentations of teacher-research: Options and choices

For example, Fryling, "Chico's Story" (Account 7.1 A and 7.1 B, pp. 148–149.)

Writing up your research is a bit like dining at an elaborate buffet. There are multiple choices available, guided primarily by your purpose, or appetite, and influenced by your audience and who you are dining with. Harry Wolcott, an anthropologist who has worked extensively in educational settings, has written a good deal about the choices one can make in preparing written presentations of research. In *Transforming Qualitative Data* (1994) Wolcott draws on his decades of experience with qualitative research to lay out the processes by which one can "do something with data," or move from the data to making them public. Wolcott (1994) sketches a series of circles that expand through three distinct and thoroughly interconnected layers of making sense of the data. He calls the first layer, **description,** or letting "the data speak for themselves":

> One way of doing something with data in rendering an account is to stay close to the data as originally recorded. The final account may draw long excerpts from one's field notes, or repeat informants' words so that informants themselves seem to tell their stories. The strategy of this approach is to treat descriptive data as fact . . . [so] that the data speak for themselves. (p. 10)

Wolcott contrasts description with **analysis,** "a second way of organizing and reporting data that builds upon [description] . . . to expand and extend . . . the purely descriptive account . . . to identify key factors and relationships" (p. 10). Analysis operates, he notes, in a "careful and systematic way" to create a meta-level around the data that attempts to show why things are as they are. The third way of dealing with data, which Wolcott labels **interpretation,** takes analysis to a broader frame by connecting the data to the wider world of purposes and reasons. To work on this layer, however, the researcher must sometimes "fill in the gaps." Wolcott (1994) says that interpretation

Description

↓

Analysis

↓

Interpretation

does not claim to be as convincingly or compulsively "scientific" as [analysis]. . . . [It is] neither as loyal to nor as restricted by observational data [as description]. The goal is to make sense of what goes on, to reach out for understanding or explanation beyond the limits of what can be explained with the degree of certainty usually associated with analysis. (pp. 10–11).

Wolcott's tripartite framework can be useful in locating your primary focus in making the data public: What do you need to do to "do something with data"? Do you need to **describe** them? To "build connections" among the data through **analysis**? Or do you need to **interpret the findings** in terms of broader issues and questions? All of these functions are critical, but you need to be clear on your purpose. Wolcott (pp. 17–23) goes on to outline ten ways to organize and present **descriptions of data.** These are ways of locating the plot line in your data so that you can tell the story effectively.

Ways of describing data; Wolcott (1994)

1. *Chronological order* draws on the order of events in time to tell the story.

2. *Researcher or narrator order* relates the account in "the way the story has been revealed to the researcher."

3. *Progressive focusing* uses the analogy of a movie camera to relate the immediate data and the larger context. In a study built around a specific problem or situation, this account "slowly zooms from broad context to the particulars of the case, or starts with a close-in view and gradually backs away to include more context."

4. A *"day-in-the-life"* of uses "some customary sequence of events," such as an activity period, a school day, or a week, to tell the story. It takes the reader into the action and description in the data, using an established time frame as the structure.

5. A *critical or key event* creates a story-within-a-story by focusing on one or two events or situations that are microcosms of the larger account. The full story is told through the lens of these events.

6. *Plot and characters* tells the story through its main characters and their interactions, allowing them to drive the account. Like (4) and (5), this device has a telescopic quality that brings the story into focus via a particular set of characters and events.

7. *Groups in interaction* is similar to (6), but uses groups, as opposed to individuals, to focus the account. In this approach, it is worth considering how the groups are portrayed, especially if you may be contrasting a group that is "successful" with one that is not.

8. *Following an analytical framework* uses the framework of the research as a structure into which to fit the description. This can be a delicate task in that the trick is to not let the framework drive the descriptive evidence. Rather, the aim is to assemble the data according to the framework. Wolcott likens this approach to using the instruction sheet to assemble a wheelbarrow: You need to "make sure all parts are

properly in place before tightening." Otherwise, you may distort the descriptive evidence to fit into the stronger analytical framework.

9. *The "Rashomon" effect* uses the points of view of various participants to tell he story. Like Akira Kurosawa's classic film, *Rashomon,* this approach describes the same situation or events through the eyes and perspectives of several different participants, with the net effect that no one version is seen as definitive. See also Fanselow (1977).

10. *Write a mystery* lays out an unfolding problem that the data resolve. The approach lets the problem or issue drive the telling of the account, like a good mystery, so that the story unfolds toward some type of resolution.

You can read Wolcott's suggestions in a number of ways. They lay out possibilities for how you might approach describing what you find and, in so doing, may stimulate you to go beyond the obvious or familiar ways of constructing your account. They also suggest that different inquiries and the data they produce will lend themselves to different forms of telling. This is, as I have said, a key decision in the whole issue of genre. But beyond these points, I think Wolcott's suggestions point to the creativity than can be involved in making a public account of your work. Description makes public the landscape of your research; often that is exactly all you want to do. However, depending on your inquiry and your purpose, you may want or need to go beneath the surface, which then brings in analysis as a way of telling your data.

Turning to analysis, Wolcott also has suggestions based on his experience, as he discusses how to construct an analysis based in findings. Here again Wolcott (1994, pp. 31–36) offers his thinking in ten suggestions:

1. *Highlight your findings:* Stay close to the basic themes and relationships that you have found in data analysis and use data to tell them convincingly.

2. *Display your findings:* Use data displays to orient the analysis toward the visual dimensions of your data, both concretely (for example, photos, students' work, or videos) and abstractly, as you represent patterns in clear ways. This refers to the work on data displays in Chapter 5, p. 108–112, 118–119.

3. *Follow and report "systematic" procedures:* At times, the procedure of the inquiry is what you have to report, because the findings are disparate or inconclusive. This means that you tell the story of *how* you did the research, as opposed to *what* you found. This can be a critical undertaking because, by doing so, you are opening up teaching and learning through the teacher-research process.

4. *Flesh out the analytical framework that guided data collection:* Like (3), you are telling the research process. In this case, you focus on the framework that drives your inquiry and tell its story by linking data to the framework. (See 8, "Following an analytical framework," in ways of describing data, p. 161.)

5. *Identify patterned regularities in the data:* Discussing "what-goes-with-what," Wolcott notes, helps to extend the study of a single case to understanding things beyond it. This opens up the specifics to the broader patterns it may capture or reflect. Since teacher-research is often based in case studies and small samples, this approach can allow you to broaden your analysis.

6. *Compare with another case:* In (5) you seek similarities in patterns; here you look at differences through comparison. These can be comparisons within the data or study, or beyond it. You can, for instance, compare what you are studying with what is usual in your or colleagues' teaching experience.

7. *Evaluate by comparing to a standard:* By explicit comparison to a relevant or agreed-upon external standard, you can show how what you are finding differs positively or negatively. Unlike an evaluation study, which aims to measure the particular instance—e.g., students' performances—in terms of a standard, here you are using the standard as a way to position the specifics of your data within a broader context.

8. *Contextualize your findings in a broader analytical framework:* Here you draw connections between your findings and some external authority, through reference to a recognized body of literature or theory in the relevant field. This is often accomplished through a review of relevant literature to position your work. An experienced researcher once explained this approach to me as being like "conversation management." The aim is to take a turn in the conversation about the topic. When you quote others, you show who preceded your input in the conversation and in that way you allow others to place your contribution in a context. Another way to connect to external authority is to draw on the norms of human and/or professional experience, thus allowing your readers to connect what you say to their lives.

9. *Critique the research process:* This entails making public the limitations of the processes you have used, as one way to contextualize what you have found. By not doing so, there can be the risk that your findings will appear absolute. By stating up front the limitations of the process, you in effect forestall that criticism and, more importantly, you look closely at how the research process itself generated the results.

10. *Propose a redesign of the study:* This carries (9) a step further by specifically discussing how the study could be done differently. By showing the shortcomings of your work and by talking about how to address them, you make public the evolving nature of the research process and of teacher-research in particular. However, even if most things go "right," research rarely—if ever—comes to closure. It can be very valuable to talk about what you would do in further research to pursue the loose ends and unanswered issues in what you have found.

7.4 *TRYING WOLCOTT'S SUGGESTIONS*

This Investigation connects Wolcott's ten suggestions for organizing descriptions and structuring analyses to your work and/or that of other teacher-researchers.

1. Description: Wolcott and your work

Look at the data and 0the displays that you have developed for them in Chapter 6. Review the list of suggested ways to approach describing data (pp. 161-162). Sort the ten suggestions into three groups:

A. Suggestions that would *not* work for your study and data

B. Suggestions that *might* work for your study and data

C. Suggestions that *do not seem to fit* your study and data

For (A) and (B), think through why the suggestion would not or might work.

If you are working with others, you can do this part by yourself and then compare notes. Or you can take one person's data/displays (providing you are all adequately familiar with them), and use this material as a basis for reviewing Wolcott's suggestions.

2. Analysis: Wolcott and your work

Repeat the above process, now using the list of suggested ways to approach analyzing data (pp. 162-163).

3. Description: Wolcott and other people's work

Review the various accounts of teacher-research in this book and refer to the List of Accounts (p. 195) and Appendix E. Choose one account to focus on and review it using the process outlined in (1) above.

You may also want to find examples in the various teacher-research accounts in this book and elsewhere of the different styles of describing data that Wolcott outlines.

Validity

VALIDITY

Wolcott outlines a series of choices that can guide you in "doing something with data." These choices are shaped both by what you have to say and who you intend your audience to be. How you represent your work and the understandings that result from it are circumscribed, as we said in discussing genre, by questions of purpose, form, and audience or social context. Underlying these choices of representation is the issue of how believable your research will be. This is the basic demand of **validity.** Validity asks the questions "How could I be wrong?" and "How might I have misconstrued the evidence?" Questioning the validity of your work pushes you to reexamine both your understandings and the research processes that produced them. Thus judgments of validity lie at the intersection of the inquiry and the disciplined way in which you have conducted it. As Lee Shulman (1988) points out in discussing research as disciplined inquiry, people argue about two basic things in research: whether the findings are valid and whether they have been arrived at in a valid manner. When people argue the validity of a research account, they are questioning the credibility of its findings based either on the reasonableness of the inquiry— Does it make sense to ask such questions?—or on the care and methodicalness of the research processes—How was the research conducted? Was it carried out in a disciplined manner?

Validity is about establishing credibility in research. Credibility is central to creating worthwhile knowledge: You want other people to believe the understandings you have arrived at. The validity of a research project speaks to the question of how this credibility is established. By what standards is the research to be believed? Validity is of regular concern in educational research for a number of reasons. First, educational research is generally "applied," as opposed to "pure," which means it is intimately tied to action. If, for example, a large-scale research project demonstrates the effectiveness of a certain reading program, it is more than likely that that program will be adopted in other school systems based on the research findings. Thus, if the research is valid, if others find it credible, it may well trigger actions that have an impact on other people. Second, education is a field in which everyone has some experience, based on having been a student. Therefore, people often have opinions and claim some expertise. To counteract this common knowledge, educational research has to be credible.

The research on retention in grade provides a clear example of this phenomenon (e.g. Smith and Shepard, 1987). Holding students back for a year, or retention in grade, is a widespread practice that dates back, in the United States, to the establishment of age-graded schools early in this century. There has been an abiding belief that if students are not "ready" to be promoted, they should not be moved on to the next grade. This readiness has several dimensions: There is academic readiness, the ability to handle the grade-level content; there is social readiness, the ability to interact successfully with peers; and there is intellectual readiness, which is connected to general mental ability and maturation. Retention in grade is a common practice in American schools; it is also one of the most widely studied aspects of schooling in the United States. Each year thousands of children are held back in U.S. classrooms, and researchers have sought to find out whether the practice does, indeed, make a difference to their learning. Overall, the research has been quite conclusive that retention in grade does not have a significant positive academic or social impact on students. Yet despite the validity of the research, parents, teachers, administrators, and school boards continue to believe that retention is solid educational policy and practice. It seems to be common knowledge, based on common experience, that staying back and repeating a grade "works," and research has not been able to challenge that belief.

Because research in education links to actions, and actions have consequences for others beyond the research, and because educational research often has to challenge popular beliefs founded in common experience, validity takes on a different importance. These factors are doubly applicable in teacher-research, since

On education
as a disciplinary
community,
see Chapter 1,
pp. 10–13.

it can have immediate implications for actions taken in the classroom, and it can challenge common, status-quo assumptions in teaching and learning. Teacher-research has to be credible; it has to be valid. The need is present and it is real. But the question is, by what standards should this validity be assessed? Because, as we said in Chapter 1, educational research in general, and teacher-research in particular, still lack a coherent disciplinary community, the standards of validity are open to much discussion and debate. Further, given the consequences in action that such research can trigger, as well as the bases in common experience that it often must challenge, standards of validity must respond to the broadest common perceptions of what make the research worth believing. Normative ideas of common standards for validity are based on generalized truth, that a finding will be "universally" true, and on replicability, that it can be applied in many, or even all, comparable situations. These are notions that spring from a positivist perspective on the world however. As a philosophical orientation, positivism seeks universal statements and general rules of causality. The intent is to be able to say (and believe) that X makes Y happen: "Germs cause disease," "the orientation of the earth to the sun causes the seasons," "access to oxygen makes a fire burn," and so on. In a positivist orientation, the aim of research is to show what causes certain things to happen under certain circumstances.

On positivism
and research
design, see
Freeman (1996);
also Moss
(1994).

In designing educational research, positivism was translated into the process-product paradigm in which educational processes, like teaching, are studied through the products, such as amounts of learning, they generate. Thus the "causes" of these products can be traced to elements in the processes. Positivism has provided the philosophical foundation for much of experimental science (Bazerman, 1988). Because of its pervasive nature in the public mind, the positivist view of science has often cast shadows on other forms of inquiry. To be "good," the belief holds, research must be "scientific," which, in turn, means it must generate objective facts about causes and effects. These facts are reliable if they produce the same results in different situations; thus the facts can be generalized beyond the immediate research context to other situations. These notions of reliability and generalizability are the staples of validity in a positivist view. They establish the value and believability of the research undertaking.

The problem is, however, that positivism is difficult to apply to teaching and learning. In the messy complexity of the classroom, it is very hard to isolate particular processes so as to attribute particular products or results to them. To paraphrase a well-known former congressman from Massachusetts, Tip O'Neill, "All classrooms—like politics—are local." As social environments, classrooms and schools differ tremendously according to who is in them, the wider social communities in which they are located and serve, the history that participants have with one another, the backgrounds, and so on down to the particular time of day—whether something occurs before or after lunch. Social interactions and environments are inherently less uniform, regular, and stable than physical phenomena. Thus, it is incompatible with the realities of teaching and learning to think of validity exclusively in terms of absolute truths and whether findings can be reliably generalized from one classroom or school to all others.

In place of this positivist view of validity, researchers in qualitative research have sought another standard, one that connects research to reasons and action. Meaning and meaningfulness are seen as the bridge between acting and the thinking that motivates the actions. Within the **hermeneutic paradigm, meaning** is what people understand in a given situation; meaningfulness is how they act or react given what they understand. A very simple example: When I first arrived in Japan I was shown the apartment where I would be living. Excited to see my new home, I walked into the cement entryway, or *genkan,* and without stopping I stepped up onto the wooden floor in the kitchen area, and then continued onto the *tatami* sleeping area. My Japanese colleague quickly called me back to the entryway and told me to take off my shoes. We then stepped into slippers to walk on the wooden floor. At the sill of the sleeping room, we left our slippers and walked in our socks on the *tatami.* From my fresh-from-North America perspective, I saw one floor, all of which I could walk on wearing my shoes. I brought this **meaning** to the situation from my experience. I acted **meaningfully,** according to my limited and culturally inappropriate understanding of Japanese interior space, by walking throughout the apartment in my shoes. My Japanese colleague made a tripartite distinction in meaning where I had had one. There were three types of flooring: the cement entryway, the wooden floor, and the tatami. To act meaningfully, each flooring required a different form of footware: shoes, slippers, and socks, respectively. By using the correct footware, you showed you understood the distinctions in the flooring. In other words, by acting meaningfully, you show you know the meanings in the situation.

This story also illustrates the connection between the hermeneutic view of meaning and Marton's distinction between first- and second-order orientations to the world, discussed in Chapter 4. Distinctions in meaning, like the different kinds of flooring in the apartment, are second-order because they hinge on how people perceive their worlds. Initially, I saw one floor where my Japanese colleague saw three. Perceptions depend on context. I wasn't wrong in what I saw, but I was mistaken in the Japanese context. Acting on perceptions brings meanings into the first-order realm where they can be seen and experienced. My Japanese colleague was able to see my second-order, perceptual confusion only when I acted inappropriately, as I did by walking through the apartment with my shoes still on. Because I did not act meaningfully in a Japanese sense, my colleague recognized that I did not know the appropriate meanings in this Japanese context. Thus my *first-order* actions revealed my *second-order* misperceptions. To unpack the event, one could ask the first-order question, "What did he do when he arrived at the apartment?" This would generate a first-order description of my (inappropriate) actions. To get at the reasoning underlying my actions, one would have to ask, "What happened when he arrived at the apartment? Why did he act as he did?" Thus a valid explanation for what happened depends on a second-order orientation to probe the meanings that triggered my actions when I first arrived at my new apartment.

By studying how people make, give, and respond to meanings, research seeks to understand the basis for their actions. In classrooms, this perspective covers a lot of ground and it takes into account the human complexity and messiness of teaching and learning. The standards of validity change when one studies mean-

Frameworks

The hermeneutic paradigm: Meaning and meaningfulness

On first- and second-order orientations, see Chapter 4, p. 65.

ings, as opposed to behaviors, however. In contrast to the process-product paradigm, which traces learning as a product generated by the processes of teaching, the hermeneutic paradigm focuses on how participants understand their worlds and the actions they take. Within this paradigm, validity is tied to understanding, or meaning, which is tied to action, or meaningfulness. Elliot Mishler (1990), a researcher who studies narrative, says of validity in this context:

> The essential criterion for such judgments is the degree to which we can rely on the concepts, methods, and inferences, of a study, or a tradition of inquiry, as the basis of our own theorizing and empirical research. *If our overall assessment of a study's trustworthiness is high enough for us to act on it, we are granting the findings a sufficient degree of validity to invest our own time and energy.* (emphasis added, p. 419)

TYPES OF VALIDITY

Mishler frames the overall question of validity in teacher-research: Are the understandings that have come from this study adequate for me to take action on them? To use Mishler's words, am I willing to "invest my own time and energy" on changing what I do, on rethinking my beliefs, on pursuing a further inquiry in this area? Think about the teachers who questioned the connection between attendance and motivation in Chapter 1. When they discovered a connection among students' tardiness, where those students lived, and the irregularity of the school transportation system, they may have been stimulated to do something. Perhaps they understood the complexity of tardiness and these students' lives in a different way. Or perhaps they would advocate for them in new ways, or argue for improved transportation. In any case, however, the basic validity of their findings would lie in what they did about them. They might ask themselves "How could we be wrong about our findings?" And if after reviewing their data and how they had analyzed them, they remained convinced of their accuracy, they would have a basis for action.

On valuing, see Chapter 8, pp. 188–191.

Within validity are several subareas; you can think of these as areas in which findings "could be wrong." Validity is classically divided into internal and external validity. The former refers to issues within the research process itself; the latter to how the research findings square with the world. **External validity** is a matter of testing and retesting explanations until you arrive at an understanding that fits with the phenomenon you are studying. It is a matter of saying "If this is true, then this should follow." In teacher-research, external validity is a central concern because it links the research work to the world of classroom and school in which it takes place.

External
Validity

The following is an example of one researcher's process of examining external validity. Arlie Hochschild (1997) is a sociologist who has examined the lives of working families. In an article titled "There's no place like work," she explains how she probed the question of why workers, who can spend more time at home with their families, often choose not to. Hochschild's data came from two sources: extensive interviews she conducted with workers in a major corporation, which she calls Americo, and a study of worker satisfaction conducted by the U.S. Bureau of Labor Statistics. This study found that 62 percent of workers surveyed "preferred their present schedule"; 28 percent "would have preferred longer hours." Fewer than 10 percent said they wanted a cut in hours. Of these data, Hochschild asked the obvious question: "Why? Given the hours parents are working these days, why aren't they taking advantage of an opportunity to reduce their time at work?"

Hochschild then reviewed the three alternative explanations for why working parents might choose not to reduce their hours when that possibility was available to them. She posited that (1) working less might cause financial problems; (2) parents might fear losing their jobs if they took more leave; or (3) they might not know the leave options that existed for them. Each explanation tests the external validity of the findings against common assumptions about why parents work, and therefore why they may not take available leave to spend more time with their families.

> *Explanation #1—Money:* "The most widely held explanation is that working parents cannot afford to work shorter hours."

> Noting that this is true for many working parents, Hochschild also offered some counterevidence: "If money is the whole explanation, why would it be that at corporations like Americo, the best-paid employees—upper-level managers and professionals—were the least interested in part-time work or job sharing, while clerical workers who earned less were more interested?"

> She continued, "Similarly, if money were the answer, we would expect poorer new mothers to return to work more quickly after giving birth than rich mothers." Here again, there is counterevidence: "Among working women nationwide, well-to-do new mothers are not much more likely to stay home after 13 weeks with a new baby than low-income new mothers.

> So, regarding the validity of explanation #1, Hochschild concluded: *"Money is important, but by itself does not explain why many people don't want to cut back hours at work."*

> *Explanation #2—"Working scared":* "Workers don't dare ask for time off because they are afraid it would make them vulnerable to layoffs. With recent downsizings at many large corporations, and with well-paying, secure jobs being replaced by lower-paying, insecure ones, it occurred to me," wrote Hochschild, "that perhaps employees are 'working scared.'"

> To examine the validity of this explanation, Hochschild returned to her data: "When I asked Americo employees whether they worked long hours for fear of getting on a layoff list, virtually everyone said, "No." Even among a particularly vulnerable group—factory workers who had been laid off in the downturn of the early 1980's and were later rehired—most did not cite fear of their jobs as the only, or main, reason they worked overtime." So, *"working scared" as an explanation did not adequately cover the situation.*

> *Explanation #3—Lack of information/support:* Hochschild wondered: "Were workers uninformed about the company's family-friendly policies?"

Developing alternative explanations, Hochschild (1997)

She concluded not. Many workers mentioned being proud of such enlightened company policies. "Were rigid middle managers standing in the way of workers using these policies?" "Sometimes," she found. Nonetheless, Hochschild noted, "When I compared Americo employees who worked for flexible managers with those who worked for rigid managers, I found that the flexible managers reported only a few more applicants [for reduced work time] than the rigid ones." So *it seemed that lack of information and support was not an adequate explanation for employees declining to take advantage of increased leave.*

Hochschild developed these three possible explanations for the status quo that workers tended not to take advantage of increased leave time available to them. Each explanation is a potential threat to the external validity of her study in that, if it were true, there would be a way to explain why U.S. workers were spending more time on the job. As none of these three explanations held up against the data, Hochschild concluded that there was a paradox: "Workers weren't protesting the time bind. They were accommodating to it." She thus needed to explain why this paradox might be. Her fourth explanation, below, accounts for the data in what Hochschild calls a "counterintuitive way." She thus addresses the threats to the external validity of her findings raised by the first three possible explanations: lack of money, fear of being laid off, and lack of knowledge and support.

> *Explanation #4—Work as home/Home as work:* "The worlds of home and work have begun to reverse places," Hochschild argues. "We are used to thinking that home is where most people feel the most appreciated, the most truly 'themselves,' the most secure, the most relaxed. We are used to thinking that work is where most people feel like [they are] 'just a number' or 'a cog in a machine.'"

> She points out that "new management techniques so pervasive in corporate life have helped transform the workplace into a more appreciative, personal sort of social world." At the same time, the "emotional demands" of home have become more "baffling and complex." "*Work has become a form of 'home' and home has become 'work,'*" Hochschild concludes. Therefore, faced with the choice, it seems that many workers are loath to cut back time at work, which they find comfortable and personable, in favor of more time at home, which is stressful and demanding.

7.5 *Examining External Validity Using Meaning and Meaningfulness as a Frame*

In this Investigation, you examine Hochschild's alternative explanations from the standpoint of external validity.

> Using Hochschild's research as detailed in Explanations 1 through 4, list the potential threats to the external validity of her findings and how she addresses them. Use the distinction between *meaning* and *meaningfulness* as a tool. How does Hochschild define the *meaning*

that might lead to an explanation ("Perhaps employees are . . ."), and then what does she look for as *meaningful* actions to corroborate it ("If this meaning were true, then . . .")?

Create two columns and for each explanation, list the *meaning* Hochschild proposes, in one column, and, in the other column, the *meaningful* actions that would follow if that meaning were true.

INTERNAL VALIDITY

Internal
Validity

While external validity is what most of the world worries about in assessing the credibility of research findings, it is not the only concern. External validity is about the implications of the research; internal validity is about the design and the research process itself. **Internal validity** is generally divided into four areas: **descriptive validity,** also called apparent or content validity; **ecological validity,** which is also sometimes called instrumental or criterion validity; **interpretive validity,** sometimes called concurrent or predictive validity; and **theoretical** or **construct validity** (Kirk and Miller, 1986; Selinger and Shohamy, 1989). While the terms may seem off-putting, the concepts are basic and sensible. **Descriptive validity** is about whether what you say or write reflects what you studied. For example, if you say your study included seventh and eighth graders, and in fact there were no actual data from the seventh graders, then this is an error of description or content that should be readily apparent. **Ecological validity** addresses whether the means of data collection and analysis capture the information that you need to address the research question. In this sense, does the ecology of the study—its research questions, setting, data collection, and analyses—all fit together coherently? Are there problems with the instruments used in data collection or the criteria used in analysis? If, for instance, you want to investigate students' views of writing and you only look at what they write, but you do not have them keep reflective journals or write about their writing, or you do not interview them or give them a survey, you will have created issues of ecological validity. You will be looking at first-order data—their writing samples—for evidence of a second-order question—what they think about writing.

Interpretive validity has to do with findings. In his typology for analyzing data, Wolcott distinguishes among description, analysis, and interpretation. As you move from one to the next, you move farther from the immediate data to build a larger view of what is happening. At this point, issues of interpretive validity may enter in. If the elements of your findings do not fit together analytically or if you are making jumps in logic or interpretation and prediction, your findings can be weakened by these problems. Similarly, if the theory or ideas out of which it is constructed are flawed, the whole research project may be built on shaky ground; these issues are called **theoretical** or **construct validity.** These issues are illustrated in the account that follows, a newspaper column written by the late Albert Shanker, then president of the American Federation of Teachers.

In his column, Shanker discusses two contradictory research studies on the use of tuition vouchers. In a tuition voucher program, the state or municipal government pays the school tuition, in the form of vouchers, directly to parents so that they can select the schools that they want their children to attend. The aim of such programs is to create a "buyers' market" in which parents can choose the kind of schooling—public, parochial, or private—they want for their children. Proponents of vouchers argue that introducing economic competition will improve public education; this is not a position shared by the national teachers' unions however. Shanker discusses two major studies on the use of tuition vouchers in Milwaukee, Wisconsin, a city that pioneered this approach. In these studies, and in the general debate over vouchers, success—or lack of it—is generally framed in terms of improvements in students' test scores. The two studies, it turns out, used the same data set, but they reached different—indeed, opposite—conclusions. The first study, by John Witte, showed no appreciable benefit of vouchers, while the second study, by Paul E. Peterson, reanalyzed Witte's data to show that students who attended private schools on vouchers did benefit. Since both researchers used the same data, the difference in the studies had to be found in the analysis and interpretation of those data. Challenging these aspects of the research involves raising questions of at least internal, and possibly external validity, which is what Shanker, as teachers' union president, did in his column.

FROM "WHERE WE STAND"
New York Times, September 1, 1996
By Albert Shanker—President, American Federation of Teachers

An Important Question

We're in the midst of a national debate about school vouchers. Voucher supporters argue that all students, and particularly poor, minority students in inner-city schools, should be given a chance to go to private schools at public expense. Permitting students to do this, voucher supporters say, will greatly improve their academic performance.

In Milwaukee, Wisconsin, there has actually been a voucher experiment to see whether there is anything to voucher supporters' claims. Since 1990, a small number of poor youngsters have been given public money to go to private, non-religious schools. The Wisconsin Department of Public Instruction commissioned John Witte, a distinguished researcher and professor at the University of Wisconsin, to gather and interpret data, and for five years, Witte has been publishing reports about the experiment. He has looked at such questions as how many students elected to enter the voucher program, how many were selected by the private schools, how many subsequently dropped out, and, of course, how well the private school students have done in comparison with public school students from similar backgrounds. His conclusion? Even though many parents like the voucher schools, there is no difference, so far, between the math and reading scores of voucher students and comparable youngsters who have remained in public school.

This would seem to provide us with an answer as to whether students who go to private schools do better than public school students. (Of course the experiment could be continued because it may take longer than four or five years to achieve an academic turnaround.) But several weeks ago, a group of researchers led by Harvard University professor Paul E. Peterson published a study of the Milwaukee voucher program that came up with totally different conclusions from Witte's.

Peterson, assisted by Jay P. Greene of the University of Houston and Jiangtao Du of Harvard, took the data Witte used but employed different methods in analyzing them. According to their findings, by the time choice youngsters had been in their private schools for three and four years, their reading and math scores were markedly better than those of comparable students who had remained in public schools.

Of course, contradictory findings about student achievement are nothing new. After Education Alternatives, Inc. (EAI) had been running a group of Baltimore schools for two years, the media reported that student test scores were down. EAI then hired its own experts who said, "No, indeed! Test scores are up," In the end, pushed by the mayor, the school district asked a group of independent evaluators to assess EAI's performance. The evaluators found that students in EAI schools were doing no better than comparable students in non-EAI schools. Parents and members of the public in situations like those in Baltimore and Milwaukee are always likely to face conflicting evaluations about the success of a program.

The question is, how can we tell whether a researcher has reached sound conclusions? The average person can't. The media can't either. Most reporters are not knowledgeable in the field of statistics. In writing about a technical study, they are likely to pick up what researchers claim to have proved and report it as fact—which is like a jury's accepting a lawyer's closing argument as proof. Perhaps the time will come when an impartial organization will evaluate reports of research the way Consumers Union evaluates products. In the meantime, there are certain clues that ordinary people can use to evaluate a piece of research. For example, what do other knowledgeable people think about it?

In education and other academic fields, researchers submit their work to professional journals and undergo a peer review process. Witte's work has been peer-reviewed, and interested experts have had five years to examine and critique his findings. Peterson et al., on the other hand, did not submit their research to peer review. They went directly to voucher advocacy groups and the media with their report. This is something that consumers should consider when they ask themselves whether Witte's finding or those by Peterson et al. are more likely to hold water. And there are things in the report itself. For example,

- The table that contains Peterson et al.'s main analysis—the one on which they base their conclusions—fails to take account of family background. This violates one of the basic rules of research on student achievement because accounting for family background is the only way researchers can distinguish between the advantages a student brings from home and the value added by the school. When researchers take account of family background, they can compare, for example, scores of students whose parents have had a high school education with those of students whose parents have had a college education. One of Peterson et al.'s later tables does take account of family background. Their results are then identical to Witte's: There is no difference in achievement between voucher students and their public school peers. But Peterson et al. slough off this table in their discussion, and no newspaper story that I've seen has picked up on it.

- Peterson et al. also stack the deck by using a statistical standard that is much lower than researchers ordinarily use or accept. When researchers employ statistics to show that a program works, they look for results that are "statistically significant." This means there is little likelihood of error in their findings. Peterson et al. do not talk much about "statistical significance" because their findings are not statistically significant. They talk, instead, about results that are "substantially significant" or "substantially important." These are made-up terms that have no meaning among researchers. But they do deceive the public into thinking that Peterson et al. have proven their case.

The question of which schools do the best job of improving student achievement is not going to be easy. How can lay people decide when the bases for their decisions are highly technical reports that are likely to come to conflicting conclusions and when the media are not in a position to shed light on the question? If those who support vouchers expect us to make the kind of radical change that a voucher system will involve, they will have to come up with an answer to this problem.

7.6 *EXAMINING INTERNAL VALIDITY*

In this Investigation, you examine Shanker's column, "An Important Question," on conflicting research on school vouchers. The aim is to use the four categories of internal validity—descriptive, ecological, interpretive, and theoretical—to examine his arguments.

Read through Shanker's column, making note of the criticisms he makes. Then, using your notes and the column itself as reference, organize his criticisms according to the four categories of threats to the internal validity: **descriptive, ecological, interpretive,** and **theoretical validity** (see page 171).

List Shanker's issues. Then use that list to draw a mind-map. Put "school vouchers" at the center, and then link his criticisms to it, labeling each one by the type of validity threat (descriptive, ecological, interpretive, theoretical) it represents. Alternatively, you can make a matrix, with Shanker's issues down the left side and the four threats to validity across the top. Fill in each cell according to Shanker's criticisms and/or your own ideas.

If you are working with others, read the column alone and make your initial determinations by yourself, then work with others to complete the task.

Validity is essentially an argument over who and what to believe. Shanker's discussion shows the political nature that such debates can have. Shanker and his union say that school vouchers will siphon off much-needed resources from public schools. Proponents of vouchers, like the governor of Wisconsin, the state in which the Witte study was done, support vouchers as a means to improve schooling for students who do not have the financial means to choose their schools. Thus the research findings have important implications for action on both sides of the question. The question Shanker asks—"How can we tell whether a researcher has reached sound conclusions?"—is a central one, not only in this instance, but in all research. It is a question that generally points to the internal validity of the work. To defend your research, then, you have to think carefully about how you have addressed each of these four areas, the descriptive, the ecological, the interpretive, and the theoretical.

THE RESPONSIBILITIES AND CHALLENGES OF NEW WAYS OF SEEING

Issues of external and internal validity notwithstanding, the challenge of going public with teacher-research is one of pushing the limits of convention. To accurately represent what teachers find in researching their teaching will no doubt require using new, as well as conventional, forms. The art historian E. H. Gombrich is supposed to have said, "Artists don't paint what they see; they see what they know how to paint." This chapter has been about that statement, and how we represent what we see. I strongly believe that in doing teacher-research lies the capacity to see new things in classrooms that have, heretofore, gone unnoticed, unremarked, and untold. This is both a challenge and a responsibility. To see these things and not to make them known publicly is not responsible. To make them public in ways that are accurate or fair to what you have found is the challenge. Elliot Eisner (1997), who writes about the interaction of art and research in a form of educational research he calls "connoisseurship," describes the challenge and responsibility in the following way:

> As the use of alternative forms of data representation increases, we can
> expect new ways of seeing things, new settings for their display, and
> new problems to tackle. The invention of time-lapse and slow-motion
> photography has enabled us to see what is otherwise invisible to the
> naked eye. The invention of the telescope and the microscope has
> made possible the formation of questions that were unaskable before
> their presence. Put another way: Our capacity to wonder is stimulated
> by the possibilities that new forms of representation suggest. (p. 8)

Suggested Readings

There is a great deal written on genre, both in writing and in research. On the former, I'd suggest Sunny Hyon's fine 1996 summary "Genre in three traditions: Implications for ESL"(*TESOL Quarterly* 30 (4): pp. 693–722). On the latter, Clifford Geertz's 1980 article, "Blurred genres: The reconfiguration of social thought" (*American Scholar,* 49) is a classic introduction to widening research paradigms in social science. The last chapter, "Afterword: The passion of portraiture" of Sara Lawrence-Lightfoot's book *The Good High School: Portraits in Character and Culture* (New York: Basic Books, pp. 369–378, 1983) puts Geertz's discussion of "blurred genres" in the context of her research in schools; it is extremely readable.

On questions of validity in teacher-research and in educational research more generally, Yvonna Lincoln's article "Emerging criteria for quality in qualitative and interpretative research" (*Qualitative Inquiry* 1 (3): pp. 275–289, 1995) provides a very good overview of the issues. Elliot Eisner's article "The promise and the perils of alternative forms of data representation" (*Educational Researcher* 26 (6): pp. 4–9, 1997) broadens the discussion to examine the boundaries of what is considered data in such work. My chapter, "Redefining the relationship between research and what teachers know," in Kathleen Bailey and David Nunan's edited volume *Voices from the Language Classroom.* (New York: Cambridge University Press, pp. 88–115, 1995) looks at how teaching is represented in various research traditions.

8

BEYOND THE CYCLE: CHARTING THE DIMENSIONS OF TEACHER-RESEARCH

My interest in the relationship between classroom teaching and research is both personal and professional. When I started out teaching, I saw little—if any—connection between my own practice as a classroom language teacher and what I understood to be the work of research. In part, my skepticism was borne out of ignorance. My concern at the time lay in surviving, and in getting the job of teaching, as I understood it, done in a respectable manner. So I had little time for information that did not serve my immediate ends. The skepticism stemmed partly from an intuitive recognition of the gulf that generally exists between the worlds of teacher and researcher. I believe that the gulf, which is variously described as "theory versus practice" and "research versus application," certainly exists in the experience of many teachers, as it did in mine.

Later, in my work as a teacher educator and a researcher in teacher education, I continued to wonder about what impact that research knowledge might have on what teachers know and what they do in their classrooms and professional lives (Freeman, 1996; Freeman and Richards, 1996). What I found is hardly a foregone conclusion. In fact, research and curricular knowledge do not appear to translate into classrooms in the seamless, logical fashion in which we might hope or expect they would (Clark and Peterson, 1986). Changing people's ideas about teaching and learning is not as straightforward as building the proverbial better mousetrap; "improved" solutions in education are often more a matter of belief than a question of reason or evidence. Because people do not necessarily share the same definitions of the "problems," their approaches to addressing these problems reflect their positions and values. Thus there are many competing views of how to improve teaching. In this flux of competing perceptions, definitions, and responses, what teachers know is often not voiced or heard. Because teachers do not often present their understandings of teaching and learning, or they present their views as matters of opinion without disciplined evidence to support them, teacher input does not have the impact on understanding teaching and learning that it could or should.

It is also fair to say that the relationship between teaching and research is changing. The old hierarchical, unidirectional relationship is under challenge. That view held research as concerned with documenting, describing, measuring, correlating, and generally scrutinizing classrooms, while teaching focuses on what goes on in those classrooms: what and how students do—or, at times—

On work at the hyphen, see Chapter 1, pp. 5–8.

don't learn, and what and how teachers teach them. Thus, while teaching and research both engage what is happening in classrooms, and so they share to a degree a common purpose, there has been a great difference in their relative status and prestige. Efforts to reframe a nonhierarchical relationship have generally concentrated on making teaching more like research. With some notable exceptions, such as exploratory teaching (Allwright and Lenzuen, 1997), action research (e.g., Stringer, 1996), or teacher-as-researcher (e.g., Cochran-Smith and Lytle, 1993), the general approach has been to argue that teachers need to adopt the perspective of research in order to bridge the gap. But moving from lesson plans, activities, and students to research-oriented questions, data analysis, and findings can transform both the teacher and the classroom. Thus it is possible that the daily, ordinary activity of teaching will be sacrificed in order to document and understand it. I have argued that combining teaching and researching by working at the hyphen actually transforms both functions and the activities one does to carry them out.

Four dimensions of teacher-research

In this chapter, I want to return to teacher-research as the work at the hyphen, to examine the basic orientations that underlie it. These orientations are attitudes or perspectives which I believe go to the heart of doing teacher-research. Each orientation captures a **dimension** of the process, so I have called them dimensions of the relationship between teaching and research. In Figure 8.1 below, the four dimensions are superimposed on the map of the teacher-research cycle from which we have worked throughout the book.

Figure 8.1: Orienting the teacher-research cycle

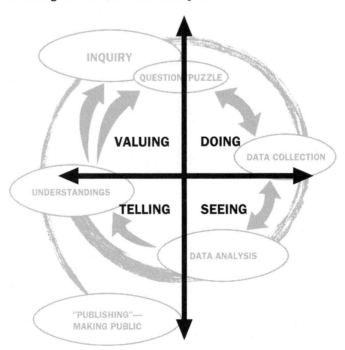

I have called these dimensions **doing, seeing, telling,** and **valuing.** In a sense, they serve as points of a compass that orient the underlying attitude and work in that quadrant of the cycle. In another sense, each dimension (and its attitude) calls on the teacher-researcher to play a different role: as **activist, anthropologist, storyteller,** or **theoretician,** respectively. These roles frame the four underlying orientations that are shared by teaching and research. In elaborating them and in tracing their connections, I want to sketch out the territory in which teaching and research coexist and suggest how they may better be brought together.

Ken Heile

To anchor discussion of these four dimensions, I want to refer to some teaching knowledge, which I will call a "story of teaching practice." Using the label "story" creates a certain expectation of genre. However, it should not mislead you into thinking that what follows is only anecdotal or illustrative, a point to which we will return in examining telling as a dimension of teacher-research. This story of teaching practice intrigued me for a number of reasons, not the least of which was because I did not grasp it when I first heard Ken Heile tell it. Heile was a foreign language teacher who taught Spanish and Latin at the local high school for more than 20 years before his retirement. In addition to his teaching duties, he also worked as a teacher educator in a professional development school that links the local schools to the graduate program in which I teach, (Levine, 1997). In this capacity, Heile would mentor graduate student teachers learning to teach, offering close guidance, support, and critique as they worked with him throughout the school year.

Account #8.1: Ken Heile's story, "It all starts in the parking lot."

Ken Heile came to present to graduate student teachers in their regular teacher-education seminar. The topic that week was structuring practice in the language classroom, how to organize and manage effective practice activities with senior and junior high school students. To start off the session, the graduate student teachers had generated several questions, the first of which was "What factors do you take into consideration in structuring practice activities?" Someone posed the question to Heile and he began talking about a workshop on choral music that he had recently attended in connection with his work as a church deacon. The workshop had been led by a man who was well known for successfully integrating music into the service and for generating widespread and active participation among the members of the congregation. Someone had asked the workshop leader, Heile said, how he got people to sing in church. The workshop leader replied, "It all starts in the parking lot, before they even get into church. It even starts on the way to church." He meant, Heile told the seminar, that it's all part of an attitude, an attitude of feeling welcome and feeling free to participate in the church service, that you belong and have a reason to be there.

"That's how I think about practice," Heile continued. "It starts with how students feel about the class, and that starts with how you interact with them in the hall, on the stairs, in class, and so on. That is the foundation on which practice is built."

He went on to talk about how he had learned not to limit how he thought about teaching simply to the classroom. He recognized, over the course of his career, that the bells and the closed doors that separated the 42 minutes of his Spanish class from the rest of the school day were artificial boundaries. He also acknowledged that early in his teaching career, the challenge was to get through class unscathed. From that perspective, planning practice activities was a matter of creativity, and managing them was a matter of stamina. Over time, however, as he looked at what did and didn't work in his teaching, Heile was drawn inexorably into the wider picture. "But that makes you a teacher all the time you're at school," one student teacher reacted, "You're on all the time from 7:15 in the morning to 3:30 in the afternoon . . . even when you run into the kids around town."

DOING AND THE ACTIVIST

Doing as an orientation

Eleanor Duckworth is a psychologist who has spent her professional life "understanding children's understandings." In an essay titled "The virtues of not knowing," Duckworth (1987) examines the idea that "in most classrooms, it is the quick right answer that is appreciated. Knowledge of the answer ahead of time is, on the whole, more valued than ways of figuring it out" (p. 64). In concluding the essay, she then makes the observation, which I have quoted previously, that "What you do about what you don't know is, in the final analysis, what determines what you will ultimately know" (p. 68). Duckworth's statement is about doing; it captures an attitude of engagement and risk-taking that is fundamental to the orientation of the activist. In Chapter 1, I argued that unfortunately most teaching is not oriented toward "not knowing"; students and teachers are not, by and large, encouraged to take risks, to speculate, and to probe things they are unsure of. The pressures of accountability, as measured by covering curriculum, successful performance on standardized assessments, and of maintaining classroom order and authority, leave many teachers with little space to explore what does not make sense, what they do not understand, or what they do not have answers for.

There are many factors and norms that underlie this drive for right answers in teaching. Joe MacDonald (1992), a teacher-researcher who now works closely with a U.S. national school reform project, the Coalition of Essential Schools (Sizer, 1983; 1992), describes this norm as a "conspiracy of certainty" (p. 2) in which questioning, doubting, speculating, or wondering about teaching is viewed as a sign of weakness or inability to do the job. This social norm in schools can create an attitude of conservatism among teachers; there is little to be gained in taking risks, asking questions, and focusing on what you don't know. Thus the first challenge in doing teacher-research lies in orienting yourself away from pat answers and tried-and-true activities and toward the risk of exploring the unknown. The challenge is, in the words of teacher-researcher Peggy Tiffany, "to lift the shawl of shame" from what is not known, misunderstood, or confusing in teaching, and thus to make those things more public so they can be improved.

While these norms of conservatism, and the conspiracy of certainty that stems from them, can work against exploration, engaging in a wider and deeper view of teaching is well worth the risk. Carol Brooks, a high school Spanish teacher, explains the shift from certainty to not-knowing in this way:

> I realize what used to make me tense in the classroom. It was always trying to beat the clock and always feeling like someone was telling me, "You have to fit this, this, and this into this lesson." It was me that was doing it to myself, but nobody ever stopped to tell me, "That's okay. Maybe if you listen to these kids or watch these kids a little more closely, you'd see that what they are doing is plenty." To take the questions they ask more seriously as a guide to where they are with the material.

Carol Brooks

In questioning what she didn't know about her students, Brooks created a climate of inquiry in her work and became a potential investigator of her own world. Her statement captures two distinct types of doing: One involves getting the job done and the other, engaging more fully in what is happening as you do it. Brooks expresses this first type of doing, on which the functioning of schools is built, as "beating the clock . . . [trying] to fit this, this, and this into this lesson." She talks about the second as "listening and watching kids a little more closely," and "taking the questions they ask as a guide to where they are with the material."

Doing as action; doing as engagement

The doing of teacher-research has both meanings. But it is not so much a matter of replacing the first type of doing with the second as it is recasting or transforming how you go about getting the work done so that it includes—or even requires—the engagement of not-knowing, which is the second type of doing. Subsuming the doing of action within the doing of engagement in that action is what articulating an inquiry is all about. Speculating, wondering, puzzling, and forming questions can all carry teaching beyond itself, toward the attitude of not-knowing Duckworth talks about. But this engaged form of doing must be supported by another orientation of looking closely, gathering information, and probing what you see. As Brooks puts it, "If you listen to these kids or watch these kids a little more closely, you'd see that what they are doing is plenty."

SEEING AND THE ANTHROPOLOGIST

In his pioneering work early in this century, anthropologist Franz Boas argued that his contemporaries had gotten the process backwards. Boas said that an anthropologist could not understand a group of people, a community, or indeed an entire culture only by looking from the outside in. He wrote "If it is our serious purpose to understand the thoughts of a people, the whole analysis of experience must be based on their concepts, not ours" (1943, p. 314). Nowhere is this statement more true than in understanding the culture of teaching and learning in classrooms and schools. The aspects that non-teachers see and choose to tell about teaching are interesting, but they are told from the outside in, which anthropologists and ethnographers call the etic perspective. In contrast, "understanding the thoughts of a people based on their concepts," to paraphrase Boas,

Seeing as an orientation

On emic and etic, see Chapter 4, pp. 69–70

is an emic undertaking. Simply put, it is their distinctions, their meanings and values, and their interpretations that matter in understanding their work.

Here Ken Heile's story of practice is instructive. As I listened to him talk in the seminar, I could not figure out what Heile was getting at. I was an outsider to his reasoning. I wondered where his presentation was heading, why he was telling us this story, and what church choral workshops had to do with structuring practice activities in the language classroom. I brought all of my etic concerns to what he was saying. However, when he finished the story of practice, his emic view made sense to me. I could see a newly articulated set of connections that weave classroom teaching into the wider social world in which it takes place. Heile's story of practice asserts that, as a teacher, what you do—or don't do—in hallways is as much a part of successful teaching as what you do in the classroom. From his emic perspective, the divisions in time and space that make up the egg-crate life of schools are largely a mirage. While class periods and classrooms may enable schools to function as institutions, Heile argued that they do not serve teachers, or student teachers learning to teach, as ways of learning to think about the basic job of teaching. He contended, in essence, that you need to see students in the entire experience of their lives, not simply through the lens of your subject matter.

This is a central issue in **seeing** as the second dimension of teacher-research. What you see depends on who you are and where you stand; or, put another way, it is difficult to separate doing from seeing. To grasp the emic perspective, we must either do the work ourselves or hear and see it as the insiders do. If we are outsiders to the classroom, we will not see the same things, in the same ways, as the teacher and students who learn there. This issue dissolves as teachers research their teaching, or at least it becomes less of an obstacle. Emic and etic, as noted in Chapter 4, are always relative. In doing teacher-research, teacher-researchers are more insiders to their settings than researchers whose work lives are elsewhere. However, within an inquiry, especially a second-order study of students' experiences and perceptions, it may be the teacher-researcher who has the etic perspective. Thus a strength of teacher-research is political in that it positions teachers, as insiders, to investigate and "not-know" in their own workplaces. Its strength is also functional: seeing classrooms from the inside-out, as it were, should generate new understandings and knowledge.

This point is made quite wonderfully by preschool teacher Vivian Paley. Although she is not usually thought of as an anthropologist, Paley has devoted considerable energy and talent to understanding teaching and particularly her own students as they go about learning. As a teacher-researcher telling her own work, Paley (1986) writes of this endeavor:

On seeing in teaching, see Paley (1986) and Carini (1979).

> The classroom has all the elements of theater, and the observant, self-examining teacher will not need a drama critic to uncover character, plot, and meaning. We are, all of us, the actors trying to find the meaning of the scenes in which we find ourselves. (p. 131)

How to relate emic and etic perspectives—how the insider actor and the outsider drama critic see things—is the central challenge of integrating teaching and research to do the work at the hyphen. Paley makes the point that teachers, as insiders, can see their work very fully, and that the drive to observe and make sense of the phenomena one is involved in is an essential human undertaking. In this sense, teacher-research is about seeing what you do in your teaching and how it impacts on your students' learning.

There is a second sense of seeing involved in teacher-research. It is embedded in the idea of disciplining the inquiry by being methodical about how you investigate, see, and listen to the teaching and learning around you. This second sense we might call **seeing differently**, to distinguish it from the seeing Paley talks about. In an interview, choreographer and filmmaker Meredith Monk and choreographer Merce Cummingham talk about this second kind of seeing, and how it is essential to the energy and perception needed to portray the world through dance. In discussing ways in which they "keep going and creatively renew" themselves, the two agree that going to the movies can be very valuable.

Seeing
and seeing
differently

> **Cunningham:** . . . Not just if the movie is good, but the way the camera works. It's different from the stage. When I started working with a camera, I was absolutely amazed.
>
> **Monk:** It's a different syntax, a different language.
>
> **Cunningham:** And it gives you new ideas about what to put in the [dance] technique, about speed, about sudden changes of angles. You need [these things] for camera work, I think, because a small shift is so visible, but on the stage it would not be visible.
>
> When I first worked with a camera, I kept seeing something that didn't look right. Then, I'd look at [the same movement] on stage, and it seemed fine. I'd go back, and finally I realized one of the dancers had her foot this way while the others were that way. At first you can't figure out what you're seeing. So you look again. It makes you rethink, open your mind.
>
> **Monk:** Do you read at all?
>
> **Cunningham:** Yes, but mostly I draw. I love drawing. I draw animals, flowers, anything I can look at. It's the most extraordinary way to get out of yourself, because you suddenly realize how stupid you are, how you *don't* see. (Monk, 1997)

Cunningham is talking about seeing differently, and about how working with a different form of discipline—in his case, filming or drawing instead of dancing—"makes you rethink, open your mind, [and] suddenly realize how stupid you are, how you *don't* see." As a choreographer, Cunningham is familiar with the world of movement in one way; by doing something differently, using a camera or drawing, he forces himself to engage with this familiarity in a new way. The same is true, I think, of researching your own teaching. You, as the teacher, are quite familiar with the world of classroom, your students, and your subject matter. Doing teacher-research pushes you to engage with these things differently, and thus, potentially, to see them differently. As Carol Brooks says, "If you listen to these kids or watch these kids a little more closely, you'd see that what they are doing is plenty." You need to see your own work for your-self, as Paley says. It is discipline, in the sense of method and structure, that enables you to engage in seeing differently that which is familiar. Taking some-one else's word for things will probably not transform your own point of view.

These are the two senses of seeing involved in teacher-research: Seeing for yourself, as Paley talks about, and seeing differently, as Cunningham describes. They are intertwined aspects of the same process. Just as you must *do,* in the sense of activity, in order to *do,* in the sense of engagement, you must *see* for yourself in order to *see* what is going on in your classroom in a different light. The public face of these processes of doing and seeing lie in how they are told.

Telling as an orientation

TELLING AND THE STORYTELLER

Telling teaching is, to use Paley's phrase, a way "to find the meaning of the scenes in which teachers and students find themselves." When teachers talk about their work, they often do so in stories; they portray the storied nature of what they know, and how they see and interact with their world. Ken Heile's story (Account 8.1) about the choral workshop and how singing in church starts in the parking lot is a case in point. His story can be heard in a number of ways: as a personal anecdote, as one teacher's perspective on an aspect of his work, or even as a truism with a moral—if you treat students decently, they will want to participate in class. To its listeners, the story may bring new or reconfirmed insights into teaching, or they may question whether it says anything they didn't already know. All of these are responses to this particular narrative as a story of one teacher's practice. Beneath these reactions, however, lie qualities of stories in general, particularly when they are understood as expressing what someone knows about a complex activity like teaching.

In accepting the Nobel prize for literature, the writer Toni Morrison (1994) began with the following statement: "Narrative has never been merely enter-tainment for me. It is, I believe, one of the principal ways in which we absorb knowledge" (p. 7). Morrison observes that telling stories is a way of creating and sustaining knowledge; by telling stories about the world, we come to know it in certain ways. We weave values and meanings into a cloth of perception, absorbing knowledge both by telling and by listening to stories. This is particu-larly true of teaching, where teachers' understandings often take the form of narratives. Freema Elbaz is an Israeli researcher who has studied teachers' nar-ratives as manifestations of personal and professional knowledge. Elbaz (1992) explains stories as knowledge in this way:

> Initially, a "story" seems to be a personal matter: There is concern for the individual narrative of a teacher and what the teacher herself, and what a colleague or researcher, as privileged eavesdroppers, might learn from it. In the course of engaging with stories however, we are beginning to discover that the process is a social one: The story may be told for personal reasons but it has an impact on its audience which reverberates out in many directions at once. (p. 423)

On genre, see Chapter 7, pp. 150–154. Elbaz and Morrison distill some of the critical qualities of stories: That they express knowledge, although they may appear as simply entertainment, and that stories depend on, and indeed, create their audiences. Stories have plots; they unfold in ways that are surprising and that sometimes defy expected or conventional logic. In reading Heile's story, your first reaction might have been, "But what does singing in church have to do with practice activities in the high school foreign language classroom?" Perhaps you then saw the link he was making; a link that you may or may not have accepted as valid, but a link that evidently made sense to Heile as the storyteller. In this way, stories are uniquely coherent; they begin by making sense to their tellers, and usually end up making sense to their listeners or readers. In this way, stories are, as Elbaz points out, fundamentally social. As they are read or told, stories engage other people in webs of understanding. They thus exist in and through a social context. This social dimension of stories may reflect the fact that much of teachers' knowledge is built on interpersonal relationships with students, colleagues, parents, administrators, and so on (e.g., Ben-Peretz, 1995). Like others who work in what are known as the "helping professions," medical personnel or child-care workers, for example, teachers are primarily concerned with the worlds of others. Thus, when what teachers know about teaching is publicly told, it makes sense that it is framed in the social, interactive form of a story, expressing the unique logic of a specific teaching situation and through it the broad coherence of shared professional knowledge (Carter, 1993).

On narrative and personal theories, see Johnson, *Teachers Understanding Teaching* (1998).

How does telling as an orientation connect teaching with research? To answer that question we need to refer back to the orientations of doing and seeing. Doing, as activity or as engagement, does not by itself create public knowledge; it is concerned with individual action. As Duckworth says, "what *you* do about what *you* don't know determines what *you* will ultimately know"; acting on not-knowing is a private affair. Similarly, seeing is individual. Teachers see what they are doing and what goes on in their classrooms, but they rarely tell it publicly. What they do say publicly about teaching is put in genres that have limited social impact. The narratives teachers use are often labeled negatively as "war stories" or "gossip," or they may be categorized as opinion or self-interested positioning, as when teachers argue that increasing class size makes a difference to student learning.

By calling Ken Heile's story a "story of practice," then, I have meant to introduce a neutral term. However, Heile's story of practice is not a teacher-research account per se; it lacks the necessary element of discipline. He does not show how he gathered information through experience to support his understanding that "It all happens in the parking lot." In contrast, for example, Wagner Veillard's account of how he began to study his students' responses to different styles of correction in their written work incorporates the discipline of how he conducted his investigation with the understandings that emerged. Although Veillard's and Heile's accounts were prepared for different purposes and audiences, their contrast illustrates different types of telling. Heile's is a story of practice; it captures in a narrative the knowledge he has established through his work. Veillard's is a teacher-research account; the intent is to make public his understanding of how a group of students respond to the correction of their writing.

Contrast Chapter 6, Wagner Veillard, and Account 8.1, Ken Heile.

Herein lies the distinction I would draw between **teaching reflectively** and **researching teaching**. Teaching reflectively, examining your practice to better understand what you do and its impact, depends on *doing*, in Duckworth's sense of engagement, and on *seeing*, as Paley used the term. However, teaching reflectively does not require that the practitioner use a particular form of discipline or methodicalness to see what is going on, in Merce Cunningham's sense of seeing differently. Nor does it suggest that by telling the results of their work, reflective practitioners will necessarily contribute to knowledge of teaching and learning. That is to not say that reflective teachers are not disciplined in their thinking and analyses of what they do; they certainly are and can be. Nor is it to say that reflective teaching cannot be interactive and collaborative; it certainly can. However, at its core reflective teaching is individual; it focuses on the practitioner developing a clearer and deeper understanding of learners, the learning process, and how teaching can support it.

Teacher educators Kenneth Zeichner and Daniel Liston write about the American philosopher John Dewey, whose work in the early part of this century launched the idea of reflection in education. Dewey, in Zeichner and Liston's words, "defines reflective action as that which involves active, persistent, and careful consideration of any belief or practice in light of reasons that support it and the further consequences to which it leads" (1996, p. 9). Like teacher-research, reflective action can be directed in many areas of education, from what is happening in classrooms, to curricula and materials, to conditions of teaching and schooling. Fundamental to reflective teaching, however, is the study of learning and learners. Dewey (1933) outlines this essential focus in his book *How We Think*:

> The teacher must have his mind free to observe the mental responses and movement of the student . . . . *The problem of the pupils is found in subject matter; the problem of teachers is what the minds of pupils are doing with the subject matter.* Unless the teacher's mind has mastered the subject matter in advance, unless it is thoroughly at home in it, using it unconsciously without need of express thought, he will not be free to give full time and attention to observation and interpretation of the pupils' intellectual reactions. (p. 275, emphasis added)

Dewey goes on to suggest the kinds of information that may show "the pupils' intellectual reactions." Interestingly enough, he describes what, in our terms, are first-order data, as possible evidence, in italics, of the students' perceptions:

> The teacher must be alive to all forms of bodily expression of mental condition—*to puzzlement, boredom, mastery, the dawn of an idea, feigned attention, tendency to show off, to dominate discussion because of egotism*, etc.—as well as sensitive to the meaning of all expression in words. He must be aware not only of their meaning, but of their meaning as indicative of the state of mind of the pupil, his degree of observation and comprehension. (p. 275, emphasis added)

Dewey outlines three attitudes that he sees as prerequisites to reflective action in teaching. They are **open-mindedness**, or what I have been calling "engagement"; **responsibility**, which means looking beyond the immediate to the wider consequences of one's work; and **whole-heartedness.** In this third attitude, he captures the depth of commitment that open-mindedness and responsibility require of practitioners. For Dewey, reflection, if it is done whole-heartedly, can be an antidote to the deadening routine of teaching as doing activity (Freeman, 1996). He says of reflection, it "emancipates us from merely impulsive and routine activity . . . to direct our actions with foresight. . . . It enables us to know what we are about when we act" (1933, p. 17). It is in this sense that reflective teaching engages teachers in directing their work, to become conscious of its implications and mindful of its processes and outcomes. To this end, the three attitudes Dewey describes are entirely consonant with the orientations of doing and seeing that underlie teacher-research.

Researching teaching differs from reflective teaching in its necessary commitment to discipline, or explicit method used in gathering and analyzing data, and to the fact that this commitment can be publicly told. Telling teacher-research supports both the findings and how they are arrived at. It raises the fundamental question of who generates knowledge about teaching and learning, and how that knowledge makes its way into the public domain. As I said in Chapter 1, the principal function of teachers is to do, not to tell. Researchers, on the other hand, are tellers; they recognize that private doing, if it is not publicly told, cannot create or influence common knowledge. For teachers to adopt a telling orientation toward their work means shifting their priorities; it can mean refashioning their ways of telling information about teaching and learning. Teachers' usual ways of telling teaching have less impact because the narrative genre they commonly use is not recognized as conveying abstract, principled knowledge. Teaching knowledge is largely storied knowledge, as in Ken Heile's story of practice, for example. This storied knowledge captures the individualism and idiosyncrasy of teachers' experiences; it carries their personal theories about what happens in teaching and why. Storied knowledge mirrors the inherently social nature of teaching, the fabric of human relationships within which the job is done. Storied knowledge occurs in natural texts that give voice to experience as it happens, from the point of view of the person who lives it; it arises out of doing the job. Stories or narratives are what teachers tell in staff rooms; they are how teachers process their work days, and how they convey what they have learned from experience to others who are learning to teach.

On narrative and personal theories, see Johnson, *Teachers Understanding Teaching* (1998).

The problem with storied knowledge is one of recognition and status. When asked what it is important to know about teaching, most teachers will cite the higher status knowledge that comes from academic disciplines. Language teachers, for instance, will refer to applied linguistics, teaching methodologies, second language acquisition, cognitive psychology, and so on. Many teachers appeal to this knowledge to provide legitimate explanations for why, what, and how teaching happens. They will not usually mention the everyday knowledge that comes from teaching itself, like Ken Heile's story of practice. For these types of understandings to become legitimate forms of knowledge about teaching, two things must happen. First, teachers' understandings must be arrived at in a disciplined manner; second, they must be valued.

Valuing as
an orientation

VALUING AND THE THEORETICIAN

Valuing teaching knowledge has two facets, the public and the private, that intersect and build on each other. In Chapter 1 we talked about the fact that teaching is not a discipline, in the sense of a field of endeavor engaged in by a community to generate knowledge. Thus teaching does not constitute a disciplinary community in the same way that, for example, biology or psychology does. Within these fields there can certainly be subcommunities, each of which may hold specific "principles of regularity and canons of evidence," to use Lee Shulman's term (1988). But the subgroups within a field have more affinity with one another than they do with groups who are not in their field. Microbiologists and marine biologists share more with each other than they do with cognitive psychologists, for example. Pluralism within a disciplinary community can reenforce its fundamental orientation toward what matters in the world. Teaching is not a disciplinary community; it has not yet developed shared ways of creating and assessing knowledge. This is the issue of power and status. Because teachers do not formally acknowledge what they know about teaching, other groups are unlikely to do so. Instead, teachers often import ways of knowing teaching from other arenas; research in general is just such a form of importation. Research, as a way of understanding teaching and learning, is appealing because it seems to offer a more organized, structured, and coherent view of the world, compared to the personal, idiosyncratic, and social ways of understanding teaching that are indigenous to teachers' lives. Research is "disciplined"; teachers' local understandings seem not to be.

On teaching as
a disciplinary
community,
see Chapter 1,
pp. 10–11.

This disciplined perspective that research can bring to teaching has clearly been attractive. It can help teachers break out of their professional isolation, and it brings a certain status. There is a cachet to research findings as a form of knowledge that stories of practice have yet to achieve. As noted in Chapter 1, however, research itself has not always been the highly structured approach to investigating and understanding the world that we think of today. Indeed, what we characterize as research knowledge is a relatively recent phenomenon that has been emerging since the mid-seventeenth century. It may well be that teaching in general, and language teaching in particular, are on the cusp of a transition as they move to defining their own disciplinary forms of knowledge. In this transition, there will continue to be vying forms of telling what teaching is, and more critically there will be differing views of what can and should be seen in the classroom and by whom.

It would be naive to think that teaching is somehow insulated from the attempts of other disciplines to define what is important and worth knowing about schools, classrooms, subject matter, and learning. Teaching is such a central social enterprise that many people outside the classroom will try to define what it should or shouldn't be. Because we are in the midst of the highly political landscape of education reform and social policy, teachers need to move consciously to articulate their ways of understanding the classroom, and thus to defining their own forms of knowledge. This first aspect of valuing is its social facet.

Valuing, in a social sense, refers to a group who entertain common views on what is important and believable; in terms of research, we have called such groups "disciplinary communities." However, communities do not act; individuals do.

How, then, does valuing become individual? In his work on narrative and how people talk about their experiences, medical researcher Elliot Mishler has grappled with questions of how narratives can be evaluated within the broader frame of scientific research. In so doing he has tackled the problem of why we should believe in nonconventional forms, such as stories, as knowledge. Mishler (1990), who was mentioned in the last chapter (p. 168), argues that validity is a judgment of trustworthiness that leads to action. He thus makes two important points relevant to this discussion about how we value what is seen and told. If validity is a judgment about trustworthiness, then the basic question is: Can I rely on the particular study as the basis of my own work? An essential measure of trustworthiness, and hence of validity, is action: Do I trust this study's findings enough to act on them? When cast in this frame, the basic challenge to teacher-research is who will see its understandings as legitimate bases for action? This second aspect of valuing is its individual or personal facet.

On trustworthiness, see Chapter 7 pp. 164–175.

When valuing is cast in terms of trustworthiness, it often collides with the issue of generalizability in research. While the findings of teacher-research may be deemed trustworthy enough to trigger individual actions, can they be extended to other teaching contexts? Are they generalizable? Here the comments of a statistician are interesting. In a classic article titled "Beyond the Two Disciplines of Scientific Psychology," statistician Lee Cronbach talked about the convergence of quantitative and hermeneutic approaches in psychology. On the issue of generalizability, Cronbach (1975), noted "When we give proper weight to local conditions, any generalization is a working hypothesis, not a conclusion" (p. 125). Teacher-research is inherently local. The work generally investigates a particular aspect of teaching and learning through the examination of a specific classroom and group of students, within one teacher's experience. Thus the findings that result cannot presume to be universal. This is not a weakness, but a strength. Teacher-research simply "gives proper weight to local conditions." Its findings are, to borrow from Cronbach, "working hypotheses, not conclusions."

This is the central dilemma in valuing teacher-research. On the one hand, individual understandings may well lead to different ways of doing things and to more effective actions. This valuing I would call **valuing in experience**. As you read this book, for example, as a practicing teacher you will evaluate the various teacher-research accounts here against your experience. If, then, you do something differently in your teaching because of an account—perhaps you rethink the success or failure of an activity, or you approach a situation with a new or different perspective— you will be making a judgment of validity, as Mishler defined it. You will have found something in the account trustworthy enough to base an action on it. When you make such judgments, whether positive or not, you grant these accounts by teacher-researchers the status of research findings. As you value them as ways of telling teaching, they become part of your individual knowledge of teaching.

Valuing in experience; valuing in community

These understandings do not create generally recognized forms of knowledge that can shape the policies and practices that make for effective education, however. They cannot create this form of knowledge unless and until they are valued by the teaching community. This valuing I would call **valuing in community**. When student teachers and fellow teachers in the graduate seminar value Ken Heile's story of practice as a basis for action, they create a teaching community around that knowledge. Because the community is small, however, the impact is limited. This raises the question of how local knowledge can garner the support and action of those beyond the immediacy of its setting. The teaching knowledge of individual practitioners is so deeply contexted, so strongly influenced by social norms at the building and community levels, so predicated on their beliefs about what works for students in their classrooms, that generating from it a wider professional knowledge base is very difficult. I believe that these orientations of telling and valuing are critical in transforming the dilemma of this private-public dynamic.

Figure 8.2: Individual and community: The cycling of teacher-research

The four orientations of teacher-research, doing, seeing, telling, and valuing, chart a dynamic relationship between individual practitioners and the community of which they are a part. Experience, and acting on it, is an individual matter. However, experience is defined and articulated within communities. These communities create values through what they recognize. We create terms for our experience out of what is around us, in communities. As Figure 8.2 suggests, there is a dynamic relationship between the doing and seeing which create our experiences and the telling and valuing which place those experiences in the social world. What is valued socially by the community finds its way into our individual experience. In the teacher-research cycle, inquiries arise from the social setting, from individual experience, and most fundamentally from the individual experience of teaching within the social setting of the school and the classroom. The value of each is thus individual and, potentially, social.

Wagner Veillard's work is an example. His interest in writing is at once individual—he loves to write himself—and it is based in the school community where he was teaching and his concern for the development of his students' writing. The impetus of his first attempt at researching this teaching phenomenon, in Chapter 3, arose largely out of individual interest, although the interest was framed by the social context of the teacher development group he had joined. The initial work then carried him to further questions, in Chapter 6, that probed more deeply the issues of teaching writing in his school context. Thus an individual interest is refracted through the various social environments of school and professional life, much as a ray of light is refracted through a prism. As a prism articulates the light into a spectrum of colors, so do these communities present ways of telling and valuing that articulate the doing and seeing of individual interest. And like refraction through the prism which focuses the light, this process of refracting the individual's interest through the values of the community can strengthen and focus the understandings that result.

The accounts of Wagner Veillard's work are in Chapters 3 and 6.

BEYOND THE CYCLE OF TEACHER-RESEARCH

There is an old Shaker hymn, the chorus of which is:

> When true simplicity is gained,
> To bow and to bend we shan't be ashamed!
> But to turn and to turn will be our delight,
> Till by turning and turning we come 'round right.

The hymn speaks of the Shakers' love of dancing and the trance-like turning that brought believers joy and enlightenment. It also captures the sense that by moving in cycles, or "turning," we can see things differently. In turning we see the same things again, and we see new things for the first time, and thus we come to new and different understandings. Most of our images of progress, learning, and understanding are not like these Shaker turnings, however. Progress and development are generally seen as linear; growing older, following a career path, mastering a language, or even professional development are generally couched in the linear terms of steps, stages, or phases, and of cumulative development. Learning moves to mastery, on which new learning is built, and so on. Research and the generation of knowledge is no different. It generally draws on the same set of sequential and linear metaphors. Knowledge and understanding are supposed to build, through time, in a more or less cumulative fashion such that past knowledge provides the basis for current and new insights.

Teaching, classrooms, and schools are hardly linear, however. In fact, they are far more likely to be cyclical. Time, in the school day, the term, and the school year cycles back to begin again. Likewise content, in teaching units, skills, curricula, and so on, spirals back onto itself with greater depth and complexity. In classrooms there is a sense that you can always start again; if not immediately, you can do so over time. It is this cyclical rhythm of teaching and learning that is captured in teacher-research. Inquiry leads to questions, which lead to data collection and analysis, which lead to understandings and possibly to publishing those understandings. The process does not end there; understandings generally breed further questions and other inquiries. As Wagner Veillard shows, the work goes on and the inquiry deepens. Because teacher-researchers are constantly living their research in their classrooms, there are infinite places to begin again and again. There are also multiple opportunities to put the study on hold for a while, or even to abandon it. All of these interruptions have good reasons, but none of them make the inquiry and its questions go away. Teacher-research is work at the hyphen; once you realize that perspective, it becomes a way of thinking about and working with what is going on in the classroom.

In this way teacher-research is propelled by both its content and its process. Whatever engages you as an inquiry will continue to pull you forward as you want to understand the topic more thoroughly. But the way of thinking, the research process itself, creates its own momentum. These dual sources turn the process and carry the cycle along. Cathy Fleischer (1995), a veteran teacher-researcher, describes the momentum this way:

**Cathy Fleischer
(1995)**

> Because teacher-research is more than a method—is, in fact, a way of thinking about issues of power and representation and storytelling and much more—its very existence and development are dependent upon our understanding not only of the particular issue we are researching but also of the complexities of the research process itself. My own dynamic development as a teacher-researcher has depended not only on my interest in my students' literacy (the subject I have chosen to pursue) but also on my constant reevaluation and rethinking of what it means to conduct research in the way that I do. (p. 4)

Fleischer talks about the source of her inquiry—her students' literacy—and the fact of engaging in an inquiry on that issue—"what it means to conduct research in the way that I do"—as the two foundations of her work. These sources are clearly intertwined, as the content supports the process, and the process pushes further into the content. So her teaching and researching come together to focus on her students' learning.

Teacher-research is founded on a tension, however. As we have said, teaching is generally anchored in activity. It is seen as doing, based on an idea that you are doing the right thing with the students in these particular circumstances, at least for the time being. Research, on the other hand, is anchored in another kind of doing: To paraphrase Duckworth, "doing something about what you don't know to determine what you will know." The crux of teacher-research is to integrate these two perspectives within one person and within one complex set of activities. It is a complicated balancing act in which action is offset by investigation, certainty by speculation, assumptions by questions, and knowing by not-knowing. Mahatma Gandhi (1957) captured this notion of balance in the introduction to his autobiography, *The Story of my Experiments with Truth*. He described the actions he had taken throughout his life as "experiments" in which he tested the truth of his beliefs and perceptions. There was a permanent temporariness about this relationship between belief and action:

> Far be it from me to claim any degree of perfection with these experiments. I claim them for nothing more than does a scientist who, though he conducts his experiments with utmost accuracy, forethought, and minuteness, never claims any finality about his conclusions, but keeps an open mind regarding them. (p. x)

Gandhi goes on to lay out the balance between the certainty of action and the speculation of inquiry:

> I am far from claiming any finality or infallibility about my conclusions. One claim I do indeed make, and it is this. For me they appear to be absolutely correct and seem, for the time being, to be final. For if they were not, I should base no action on them. (p. xi)

Teacher-research opens up this notion of acting on what seems "correct and, for the time being, final." It raises the questions of how to be sure of and to question things at the same time. How to act on your assumptions as you speculate on their accuracy. How to do the things you believe at that moment to be best for your students, even as you remain open to the fact you do not know how these actions will actually turn out. To me, this is like the dizzying turning the Shaker hymn sings about. The underlying orientations of doing, seeing, telling, and valuing can serve to balance these cycles. Ultimately the work of researching teaching goes on, and as it does you make better sense of what you do and of how your students learn. You will doubtless learn from your inquiries and, if you make them public, others may learn from them as well. There remain larger social and political ramifications, but in the final analysis, doing teacher-research is an individual matter. The only thing that you can do wrong is to not start.

Suggested Readings

I encourage those who are entering into teacher-research to look at Eleanor Duckworth's great collection of essays on teaching, *The Having of Wonderful Ideas and Other Essays on Teaching and Learning* (New York: Teachers College Press, 1987). I also recommend any of Vivian Paley's work: *Mollie is Three* (Chicago: University of Chicago Press, 1986), *Wally's Stories* (Cambridge, MA: Harvard University Press, 1981), *The Boy Who Would Be a Helicopter: The Uses of Storytelling in the Classroom* (Cambridge, MA: Harvard University Press, 1990), and particularly her article "On listening to what children say" (*Harvard Educational Review* 56 (2): pp. 122–131, 1986). Another interesting example of genre and research roles is K. D. Samway and D. Taylor's chapter, "The collected letters of two collaborative researchers (in *Delicate Balances: Collaborative Research in Language Education,* edited by S. Huddleston and J. Lindfors. Urbana, IL: National Council of Teachers of English, pp. 67–92, 1993).

On story and narrative in research, Kathy Carter's article "The place of story in the study of teaching and teacher education" (*Educational Researcher* 22 (1): pp. 5–12, 18, 1993) gives an excellent summary.

There has been a tremendous amount written recently on reflective teaching, not all of it particularly good. I would suggest Kenneth Zeichner and Daniel Liston's short and readable book *Reflective Teaching: An Introduction* (Mahwah: NJ: Lawrence Erlbaum, 1996) as the best entry into this literature. Joe MacDonald's book *Teaching: Making Sense of an Uncertain Craft* (New York: Teachers College Press, 1992), while not explicitly about reflective teaching, presents an excellent case of how teachers can transform their work through self-examination.

Teacher-Research Accounts

List of Figures

CHAPTER SIX

CHAPTER SEVEN

CHAPTER EIGHT

Appendix A
LOOP WRITING AND WORKING WITH VIDEOTAPES

LOOP WRITING

Setting yourself up: Get yourself in a comfortable writing position; set a timer or plan to watch the clock. Get a clean sheet of paper and a good writing instrument or set yourself up on the computer.

1. Think about the teaching you have done recently (in the past week or two). Start writing about whatever comes to mind in this area and continue writing without stopping for three (or up to five) minutes. Keep going even while you're thinking. Don't let yourself pause. Don't read over what you have written. Just keep writing for the allotted time. What you write should be almost stream of consciousness.
2. Stop at the allotted time; shake out your writing hand. Relax a minute; stand up and stretch.
3. Reread what you have written. Underline the key ideas, words, phrases— whatever seems important and grabs you as you read.
4. Without thinking too much about it, choose one thing you've underlined in Step 3 and write this word or phrase at the top of a clean sheet of paper or in a new computer document. This now becomes the starting point for your next loop.
5. Set the timer and start writing again for three (or up to five) minutes. Again, keep yourself going even while you're thinking; don't pause and don't reread yet. The aim is to keep writing for the allotted time.

Loop writing is best done in series of threes, so you may want to repeat the process once more.

A BASIC PROCEDURE FOR WORKING WITH VIDEOTAPES

Stage 1. Global viewing: Indexing what is on the tape

Take sparse notes to index what is on the tape. Note major episodes or activities, who does what, and any transitions between them.

Stage 2. Narrowing the focus: Selecting episodes for closer analysis

Select the episodes you want to analyze in detail to copy onto a second "copy" tape. You will need to time the segments, name them in some way, and describe the context which precedes and follows each episode. These junctures between the episodes you select and the rest of the taped material are important as they mark the boundaries of the excerpted material. It is important to be explicit about why you are selecting the episodes. For example, if you are examining turn-taking, you may select episodes when girls lead off in class discussion. Or you may select episodes when several students seem to be competing for the floor. The rationale of your choices is part of the discipline of your work.

At this stage you can also ask participants to view the "copy" tape to give their emic views of the episodes. If you work in this way, it is useful to audiotape their comments about the episodes. You can thus use the voice track from the "copy" tape to cross-reference participants' comments on the audiotape. This process is known as "stimulated recall."

Stage 3. Detailing: Describing the participation structures

Describe as carefully as you can who is doing what in each episode; these are called "participation structures" (Cazden, 1988).Often you can use a matrix or table to capture these interactions, or you can write up field notes. You can also make notes on why you think things are happening as they are. These are called "observer comments," and should be clearly marked with a bracket or "OC" in the margin to distinguish them from the descriptive notes.

Stage 4. Generalizing: Getting at principles of social organization

Based on the participation structures, outline statements for why people interact as they do. What reasons seem to underlie the surface behaviors in the interactions? These are called "principles of social organization." At this stage it is critical to triangulate what you believe is happening by using other data and/or testing your ideas with participants. Keep in mind, however, that participants cannot always explain why they do what they do. Therefore, you need to look for other forms of data to support your findings.

Adapted from Erickson, F., and J. Shultz. 1981. "When is a context? Some issues and methods in the analysis of social competence." In *Ethnography and language in educational settings,* edited by J. Green and C. Wallat. Norwood, NJ: Ablex Publishers.

See also van Lier, L. 1988. *The classroom and the language learner.* London: Longman, p. 65.

Appendix B

DATA-COLLECTION MATRIX (CHAPTER 4)

DATA	COLLECTION STRATEGIES	SOURCES	SCHEDULE	FIRST-CUT ANALYSIS
What kinds of data will respond to the question?	How can/will I collect the data?	Where and from whom will I gather the data?	When and how often will I gather the data?	What will I do with the data? What is my "first-cut analysis?
(Investigation #4.5)	(Investigation #4.6)	(Investigation #4.7)	(Investigation #4.8)	(Investigation #4.9)

Appendix C
DATA COLLECTION TECHNIQUES
Prepared with the assistance of Kim Parent and Wagner Veillard

INDEX OF DATA COLLECTION TECHNIQUES

A note on format: Each of the data collection techniques listed above is explained in some detail in the following section. The format includes a description of the technique, its purpose, suggested advance preparation, the procedure, and advice gleaned from experience. There are also suggestions for where to find further information. In this regard, three books that are generally useful on data collection are:

Hopkins, D. 1993. *A teacher's guide to classroom research* (2nd ed.). Buckingham, UK: Open University Press.

Includes a good but short section on various data collection techniques, with a clear discussion of the pros and cons of each technique. The book is oriented toward teachers in general.

Hubbard, R. S., and B. M. Power. 1993. *The art of classroom inquiry,* Portsmouth, NH: Heinemann.

Includes a thorough treatment of data collection, oriented for teachers in general. The book has excellent examples, drawn from K-12 teaching in the United States, as well as a clear discussion of using the various techniques described.

McDonough, J., and S. McDonough. 1997. *Research methods for English language teachers.* London: Arnold.

Includes a discussion of the reasoning behind commonly used data collection techniques. The descriptions are less procedural. The book, which is oriented to language teachers, has a particularly good discussion of quantitative techniques and data analysis.

ANECDOTAL RECORDS

Definition:
Anecdotal records are quickly written notes about students, student behavior, interactions with students, or other aspects of the teaching and learning in the class that seem compelling and related to the inquiry. These notes are called "anecdotal" because the unit of reference is the "anecdote" or brief vignette. For some researchers, the term "anecdotal" makes such data suspect and undisciplined; however, these notes can be immensely useful in exploring and developing an inquiry. Over time, the notes can help the researcher to detect patterns or themes in learning and/or behavior.

Purpose:
- To allow the teacher-researcher to make note of everyday behavior and happenings in the classroom in an organized manner. In a sense, an anecdotal record is an extension of a grade book in which you keep track of what and how students are doing in the class.

Advance Preparation:
- You will need a quickly drawn chart (described in 1, below) to easily capture your observations.

Procedure:
1. Create a chart to record notes:
   - List students' names on the vertical axis.
   - Label the horizontal axis with the date and/or other categories that suit your research needs.
   - Write comments, quotes, or notes about what the student says or does in the appropriate space on the chart.
   - Make notes at regular intervals (e.g., after each class or each time you do a particular activity).
2. Use the chart to record such things as who read or spoke in class, or what you talked to a student about during an individual conference on homework, or written work, etc.
3. As the information accumulates, examine entries for patterns.

Advice:
- These records provide a quick, organized way of taking notes on what students say or do as it is happening.
- The chart format allows patterns to be identified easily. However, do not overload one chart with too many entries. It helps to keep one chart per day/week or activity so that patterns are easier to see and comparisons are easier to make.
- Accuracy is important. Be careful not to "jump" columns and record information in the wrong student's row.

- Have a back-up system in case you run out of room on the grid. Post-it notes are invaluable for this purpose.
- Try to be consistent in the frequency, quantity, and quality of notes as you record information.
- It also works to use index cards to record such information, using one card per student. Index cards are more difficult to analyze for patterns because it is harder to see patterns in the whole class at once.

Further References:
Samway, K. D. 1994. "But it's hard to keep fieldnotes while also teaching." *TESOL Journal* 4 (1): 47–48.

CLASSROOM DIAGRAMS AND MAPS

Definition:
Classroom diagrams and maps are visual representations of how space and movement work in the classroom. As such, they show the locations of people, desks, windows, and other relevant items. They can also show patterns of movement, which some ethnographers call "tracks and traces," as students and the teacher move around during the lesson.

Purpose:
- To observe how people and things occupy the classroom space, and thus how the physical environment affects behavior or learning.
- To create a gross record of physical movement in an activity or lesson.

Advance Preparation:
- If you are making a map of your own classroom to use while you are teaching, you will need to assign a task that students can complete on their own so you have time to sketch.
- Your paper should be big enough to make your drawing resemble a "panoramic photo."
- Use simple symbols to represent the people and things in the room. This way you can draw more quickly.

Procedure:
1. Outline a bird's eye view of the classroom space that shows the walls and other structures as if you were looking at them from above.
2. Identify everything you can see; be as detailed as you reasonably can. Include yourself in the picture. Scale is less important than accurately including as much as possible.
3. Use the same symbol for a category (e.g., circles for students and squares for desks). You can create ways of showing differences within a category (e.g., green circle is a bilingual student; red square is the teacher's desk).
4. To record students' movements, draw a line from where the student starts to where he or she ends the movement (Day, 1990, below). If the student makes the same movement more than once—perhaps he or she goes back and forth to the teacher's desk for help—you can put a check on the basic trace line to keep track of the number of trips (ASCD, below).

Advice:
- The focus is on what you see, as opposed to what you hear or think.
- To get students' views of the classroom, the teacher can ask students to create their own maps. This also allows people to compare and contrast their spatial perceptions.
- Maps can become irrelevant if not done systematically (e.g. one map every Tuesday), or confusing if the teacher is not consistent in the symbols used.

Further References:
Day, R. 1990. "Teacher observation in second language teacher education." In J. C. Richards and D. Nunan (eds.) *Second language teacher education.* New York: Cambridge University Press, 43–61.

Association for Supervision and Curriculum Development (ASCD). *Another set of eyes* (a video-training series on classroom observation). Alexandria VA: Author.

DISCUSSIONS

Definition:
Discussions are opportunities for students (and teacher) to engage in an exchange of ideas. They can also be done indirectly via computer, letters, or dialogue journals.

Purpose:
- To get information about how students are experiencing and interpreting what is going on in the class.

Advance Preparation:
- Decide on the topic; determine whether it will be student- or teacher-generated.
- Decide on the format: Will the discussion be face-to-face or conducted in written form? If it is face-to-face, will the discussion be conducted with the whole class, in small groups, or one on one? How long will it last and who will keep track of time? If it is written, what format will be used? Who will respond to whom? and so on.
- Define the parameters of the discussion and how it will operate. For instance, Who can speak? For how long? How many times? Will students be asked to express their own opinions or will they be asked to defend an assigned point of view?
- Define your role as participant, facilitator, or observer. Also determine how you will keep a record of the discussion: Will you be the note taker? If so, will you take notes during or after the discussion? Another option is to audio or videotape the discussion (see listings for those techniques).

Procedure:
1. Inform students of your decisions regarding the topic, the format, their role, and your role.
2. If you are having a face-to-face discussion, have the students arrange seats appropriately.
3. Get the activity started and bring it to a close.

Advice:

- Depending on your purpose and on how much time you allot for students to prepare, their responses will be more or less spontaneous. Sometimes it can be useful to assign the topic in advance so that students can think about what they want to say about it (e.g., How would you describe your progress this term?). In other cases, a spontaneous discussion can generate more useful data (e.g., How did this activity help your writing?)
- More so than other data collection techniques, conducting oral discussions requires careful advanced planning and good classroom management skills. This is especially true if you decide to be an observer or to operate audio or video equipment.
- Discussions become more productive when they are held regularly. Students learn the rules of the game, and therefore less energy is spent on setting up and running them.

Further References:
Cohen, E. 1986. *Designing group work: Strategies for the heterogeneous classroom.* New York: Teachers College Press.

ARCHIVAL DATA: DOCUMENTS AND STUDENT WORK

Definition:
Archival data are anything produced by the teacher, the students, the administration, or the parents in conjunction with classroom teaching and learning. This material reflects what is happening inside, and possibly outside, the classroom. Thus archival data can run the gamut from student work or test scores, to notes to or from parents or students, to minutes of teachers' meetings or administrative planning memos, and so on.

Purpose:
- To capture data from material generated through, and in conjunction with, the teaching and learning process.

Advance Preparation:
- Obtain permission, as necessary legally and ethically, to use the data you collect.
- Decide what you need beforehand.
- Obtain access to a copier; help with copying can be extremely useful.

Procedure:
1. Decide what material will be useful to your inquiry. Decide when, and in what form you want to collect it. For instance, do you want to use student work as it is turned in without teacher comments, or after you have made comments or given it a grade?
2. Collect the documents you have chosen.
3. Copy the material and identify it by student, class, date, assignment number, or whatever identification is relevant to your project.
4. Keep the copies and return the original materials.

Advice:

- The amount of archival material can quickly become overwhelming if it is not carefully managed. It helps tremendously to narrow the focus of collection to the data that support your research question.
- You also need to create a careful filing system *before* you start to collect the material; otherwise it can get lost or become easily disorganized.
- In writing up your research, documents can be tools that show students' production, demonstrate their competency, add life to the research report, and allow you to illustrate findings for parents and administrators.
- Collecting archival data is a two-edged sword. On the one hand, it does not add extra work to teaching because, by definition, you are drawing on material that already exists in the classroom or school situation. However, copying documents can be very time-consuming and difficult to do within a teacher's regular schedule. It can also be costly if you do not have institutional support.
- Because the process essentially involves examining existing information from a new perspective, archival data can allow you to see and hear students differently. For instance, approaching a written assignment to mark it can be quite different from reading it to see the kinds of errors the students are producing. This first stance requires a judgment, while the second is essentially descriptive.

FEEDBACK CARDS

Definition:

Feedback cards are a fast way of collecting data from individual students. They are usually done on the spot, just after an activity, and have a short time limit. The data that result are on 3" x 5" cards, which are easily manipulable for analysis.

Purpose:

- To collect concisely focused information (e.g., in response to yes/no questions) and factual data (e.g., students' names, ages, nationalities, etc.).
- To gather impressions after a particular lesson/activity while they are still fresh.

Advance Preparation:

- Have index cards or slips of paper available. Make sure they are big enough for students to write their answers to the question(s) you will be asking.
- Make sure your questions are specific and clear.
- Limit the number of questions. You can also limit the length of the responses (e.g., "Write two to three sentences about X").
- Allow a realistic amount of time to answer the question(s).

Procedure:

1. Provide the instructions before handing out the cards so students listen to you.
2. Model and/or write what students are to do on the blackboard. Often students will benefit from an example.
3. Pass out the index cards or slips of paper.
4. Give a time warning before collecting (e.g., "You have another minute to finish writing your comments.").

Advice:
- Feedback cards are easy to handle and fast to read. They lend themselves to tabulation, sorting, and/or easy rearrangement for comparisons.
- The small size of the card or slip of paper can help students to focus their comments (e.g., "Write the pros of an activity on one side of the card. Turn it over and write the cons on the other side.").
- Because there is little time for reflection, you can get a sense of students' immediate responses to an issue. However, too little time may result in shallow, flip, or incomplete responses.
- As with archival data, a thorough filing system helps enormously. It is easy to lose or misplace index cards or slips of paper.

MAKING AND TRANSCRIBING AUDIO RECORDINGS

Definition:
An audio recording captures spoken interactions in the activity or lesson.

Purpose:
- To capture the oral interactions in an activity or lesson between teacher and students, and among students.

Advance Preparation:
- The tape recorder and the microphone should be tested in advance. If students are to manipulate it, they may need to be taught how to use the equipment as well.

Procedure:
1. Place a microphone or tape recorder near those students you wish to record. If you are using a small machine, students can pass it from speaker to speaker, or have one individual carry it around during an activity.
2. Start the tape running to record the entire interaction.
3. After tapes are made, they will need to be transcribed.

Advice:
- Check the equipment thoroughly before class to make sure it is working.
- Audiotaping captures what people are saying during class, and it can free you to concentrate on other aspects of the interactions.
- In group work, more than one group can be recorded at the same time if you use multiple recorders. Be very sure to accurately label the tapes so you know where the data come from and when they were collected.
- Students may be nervous about being recorded and not respond as usual. You may want to "practice" with the recorder and microphone to allow people to become comfortable and familiar with them before attempting to gather crucial data.
- Transcribing tape recordings is very time-consuming. The usual ratio is 3 or 4 to 1. That is, depending on the complexity of the talk and the skill of the transcriber, it can take three or four hours to transcribe one hour of tape.
- Background noise can be very distracting and make voices inaudible. A few "practice" experiences can help you find a strategy for dealing with ambient noise.

- Using stereo recording microphones makes transcribing easier because you can turn to one channel and then another, thus eliminating some of the background noise while you transcribe.
- Don't record over tapes until the research project is completed, if then. Often, you may want or need to refer back to earlier tapes that may not have seemed relevant at the time. It is always worth saving tapes.

Further References:
van Lier, L. 1988. *The classroom and the language learner.* London: Longman.

Allwright, R., and K. Bailey. 1991. *Focus on the language classroom: An introduction to classroom research for language teachers.* Cambridge UK: Cambridge University Press. Appendices A-H, pp. 202–223.

MAKING AND TRANSCRIBING VIDEO RECORDINGS

Definition:
A video recording captures both verbal and nonverbal interactions in an activity or lesson.

Purpose:
- To capture the verbal and nonverbal behavior and interactions of an entire class, a group of students, or the teacher interacting with students.

Advance Preparation:
- You will need to locate, set up, and test the video equipment. You may also need to identify a camera person.

Procedure:
1. Locate the video equipment and learn how to use it ahead of time.
2. Test the equipment before class to make sure it is working. (Don't forget to check the battery if you are using one).
3. Decide whether you want to have a moving or stationary camera. If the camera will be moving, identify a camera person. If the camera will be stationary, decide where you want to set it up.
4. Decide whether you want to let the video run, or plan to start and stop it as needed.
5. To analyze the video, you will need to review and transcribe it.

Advice:
- Setting the camera up several days before you intend to do any recording may help the students to get used to it and thus make them less self-conscious when you actually begin taping.
- Always check the equipment thoroughly to make sure it works and to make sure the camera person knows how to operate it.
- Don't film with the camera pointed toward any strong source of light (e.g. windows) or you won't be able to see anything except shadows.
- Background noise may make the audio track difficult to hear.
- Videos are an excellent way to observe yourself interacting with students. They also allow you to see what other students are doing when you are working with an individual or a group.

- Videos allow you to document participation that is not oral, and thus to gain a fuller sense of the class or activity. However, for this reason there is the danger of collecting too much information.
- Remember that analyzing video tapes, like transcribing audiotapes, takes time. You will need a coding scheme (see Appendix A; also Allwright and Bailey, 1991, below).

Further References:

van Lier, L. 1988. *The classroom and the language learner.* London: Longman.

Allwright, R., and K. Bailey. 1991. *Focus on the language classroom: An introduction to classroom research for language teachers.* Cambridge: Cambridge University Press. Appendices A-H, pp. 202–223.

CLASS OBSERVATION / FIELD NOTES

Definition:
Class observation or field notes are notes taken by the teacher either as a participant (participant observer) or as an observer in another teacher's classroom (non-participant observer). Observations may be general or guided by a particular question or concern. Note-taking may be continual or at regular intervals, (e.g., every five minutes).

Purpose:
- To provide descriptions of teacher or student behavior with emphasis on the setting, group structures, nonverbal information, and interactions among participants.

Advance Preparation:
- Non-participant observers will need to be informed of the focus of the observation.
- You will need paper and writing utensils for notes. It is also possible to take notes on a laptop computer if you type very quickly.

Procedure:
1. Before the activity or lesson begins, describe the setting briefly. Note the layout of the classroom and provide other information about the classroom environment (e.g., noise level, temperature, lighting). You can also sketch a quick classroom diagram or map (see technique).
2. As the activity or lesson progresses, make notes about what is happening. Note interactions between participants and/or individuals' behavior.
3. If you have thoughts or ideas about why things are happening as they are, note these as well, but mark them clearly. These are called "observer's comments" and can be marked with an "OC" in the margin.

Advice:
- Observation and field notes are a useful way to gather information about classroom happenings. Notes are a low-tech alternative to videotaping and, although they are far less comprehensive, they "predigest" the information, which you would have to do as you analyzed the videotape.

- Sometimes students behave differently when there is a visitor observing, so the participant observer may be able to gather a more accurate record of a typical class than would a non-participant observer.
- Results are only as accurate as the observer is diligent. It is important to be consistent in recording information.
- It's difficult to collect accurate data while teaching; in other words, it is hard to be your own participant observer. For that reason, anecdotal records can work better if you are teaching.
- Non-participant observers can gather valuable information about observable phenomena (e.g. how many times the teacher calls on a particular student, how many times students ask questions, who the teacher calls on).

Further References:

Boglan, R. C., and S. K. Bicklan. 1982. *Qualitative research for education.* Boston: Allyn & Bacon. pp. 74–93.

Day, R. 1990. "Teacher observation in second language teacher education." In J. C. Richards and D. Nunan (eds.) *Second language teacher education.* New York: Cambridge University Press. pp. 43–61.

Samway, K. D. 1994. "But it's hard to keep fieldnotes while also teaching." *TESOL Journal* 4 (1): 47–48.

Journals Kept by Teacher or Students

Definition:

Journals record the thoughts, feelings, reflections, and observations of the writer. They may be focused on a specific lesson, activity, or student, or they can describe the writer's more general day-to-day thinking or questions. The description below is separated into teacher journals and student journals.

Teacher Journals

Purpose:
- To identify issues, puzzles, or questions in teaching.

Advance preparation:
- You'll need writing materials or a computer.

Procedure:
1. Decide on a regular schedule for writing in the journal.
2. Record your thoughts, questions, or concerns in general or as they relate to a lesson or issue you are currently focusing on.
3. It can be very useful to reread your journal periodically. Any notes you make on rereading should be kept separately, either in another section of the journal or in another color pen or computer font.

Advice:
- If your students write in journals during class, you can use that time to write in yours. Often this parallel activity can be very useful in modeling the value of journaling.

- In general, the more frequent the journaling, the more useful it is. Ideally you should find time to write in your journal every day.
- You can use the journal to anticipate reactions, writing about things before they happen. It is interesting to compare your "before" and "after" thoughts.
- If you keep your journal on a computer, it is easy to read and to code; however, if the computer is not available in the classroom, it can limit your writing time.
- Always make back-up disks of any journal kept on computer.

STUDENT JOURNALS

Definition:
Student journals record how students perceive their own learning. These journals are usually longer and more reflective than other forms of data collection.

Purpose:
- To collect data from the students' point of view.

Advance Preparation:
- You need to decide on the logistics of the journal, (e.g., Is it a section in an existing notebook, a separate notebook, on a computer disk, etc.?).
- You also need to decide on the frequency, when and where the students should make their entries, as well as the general parameters of focus, what they are to write about (e.g., Is the topic open or is it focused on a particular issue, skill, or activity?).
- Finally, you need to decide if, when, how, how often, and who will provide feedback. There are endless options here. There can be no feedback, or the feedback can be teacher-student, student-student, or whole group discussion about journals; it can happen after every entry, weekly, or monthly; it can focus on form, understanding content, reacting to content, etc.

Procedure:
1. Tell students about your decisions on logistics, frequency, and parameters.
2. Explain what will happen to the data once they finish their journal entries (Sharing with peers, conferencing with teacher). It is very important, ethically and procedurally, that students know who the audience of the journal will be before they start the process. You need to be explicit about who will read the journal, when, and for what purpose.
3. Pose a question or prompt that is open-ended so students have something to write about.
4. It is important to get students' permission to draw on their journals for data before you collect the journals.
5. Copy or take notes on relevant passages.

Advice:
- Because they are not face-to-face, student journals can be more private or personalized than interviews or discussions, for example.
- If students write on the same size paper, it will save you a great deal of time and frustration when photocopying their entries.

- Reading and responding to journals can be very time-consuming. It can be easy to fall behind, and thus not allow you to provide timely feedback. For this reason, it is important to think through the frequency of entries and the feedback strategies you plan to use *before* students start journaling.
- Students may show initial resistance if they consider journaling to be too much writing. They may also see it as an invasion of privacy if you read their journals. Some students may doubt the value of journals as a learning tool if the entries are not corrected regularly. All of these issues can be addressed if you are very clear about the parameters and the types of feedback *before* you start the process.
- You can ask students to reread their entries and to reflect on their own thinking and progress. This rereading can also allow students to begin analyzing their own journals, particularly if you enlist them in the research project. If you then take (1) the journal itself, (2) the student-writer's analysis, and (3) your analysis, you have a solid set of interpretations to triangulate.

Further References:
McDonough, J. and S. McDonough. 1997. *Research methods for English language teachers*. London: Arnold. pp. 121–136.

LESSON PLANS AND TEACHING LOGS

Definition:
Lesson plans describe the objectives of a class, the materials and processes planned to meet those objectives, and the expected roles of participants. They provide a *prospective account* of the *lesson as planned*.

Teaching logs record what happened during a lesson; they provide a *retrospective account* of the *lesson-as-taught*. Although they can be used separately, lesson plans and teaching logs are most effective when done together, as complementary forms of data collection.

Purpose:
- To allow comparison of the teacher's expectations for a class with what actually happened.

Advance preparation:
- Have paper and a writing utensil ready to take notes during and/or immediately after the lesson.

Procedure:
1. Write the lesson plans according to whatever style is most comfortable and familiar.
2. Leave room for notes that will be taken during class.
3. Teach the class.
4. During class, take notes about student behavior, timing, last minute changes, unexpected problems or outcomes, etc., in the space allotted on the lesson plan or on a separate piece of paper.

5. Review the notes and lesson plans after the lesson. Write up a teaching log entry that summarizes all the salient points from your notes. Reference the log to your lesson plan so you can see what you planned, what you did, and what happened.

Advice:
- The basic questions for the teaching log are: What did you plan? What did you actually do? What happened? It can help to keep them in mind as you are making notes during the lesson.
- If you write directly on the lesson plan in a different color ink, your notes will be easy to see. However, this practice can also deface the plan itself, so it is best done on a copy of the lesson plan so that you have the original as a separate record.
- Other options include inserting the lesson plan in a loose-leaf notebook and making notes on interleaved sheets of paper; dividing the paper into two columns and making the lesson plan in the left column and the notes in the right column; using large Post-it notes (although this can easily get messy as the notes can separate from the plan and get lost).
- If you have access to a laptop computer, you can enter your lesson plan and then enter notes directly in the lesson plan in a different font. You can also enter your teaching log in the lesson at appropriate points, again in a different font.

SOCIOGRAMS
Definition:
Sociograms are maps of how participants in a class or activity see one another as measured by given criteria. Sociograms collect second-order data of participants' perceptions, (e.g., Who is best writer in the class? Who has the best pronunciation? Who would I like to work on X project with the most?). A sociogram can thus capture participants' views of the "chemistry" of the group. Each participant is an "element," and these elements are connected by arrows indicating preferences, to compose a "social product."

For an example of a sociogram, see Chapter 6, p. 140.

Purpose:
- To have students compare and contrast their views of themselves and their work to those of others, in relation to the group.

Advance Preparation:
- Decide what you want to find out in the sociogram. Decide why you want to find it out: How does the sociogram relate to the research question and design? It is important to make the focus simple.
- Have materials (index cards or slips of paper) ready.
- Do the sociogram task yourself (e.g., Name the three top writers in this class). Assign numeric values or a different type of line to each response (e.g., All #1 selections will get 5 points or are connected by dotted lines); otherwise, your sociogram will become unreadable.

Procedure:

1. Explain the task and why you are doing it. This context is necessary so students know what is going to happen with the information. For example, "We have been studying vocabulary a lot in this class, and I am interested in your ideas about who seems to have the easiest time learning new words and why. On this slip of paper, I'd like you to write down the names of three people in the class who seem to have the easiest time learning new vocabulary. You can list yourself. Number your choices from 1 to 3. Then, next to each name, write why you think that person is good at learning vocabulary. This information will help me in deciding how to group you in activities next week."

2. To help students be aware of all the choices, it is useful to list everyone's name on the blackboard. You should also emphasize that students can list themselves if they choose.

3. Hand out the cards or slips of paper. Do not allow students to talk or consult with other classmates while making their choices. They are to work silently and independently.

4. Collect the cards. At this point, you may choose to have a discussion about the task.

5. Afterwards build a sociogram with the results. There are two ways to do so (see Chapter 6, p. 139 for examples).

Numerical analysis: To calculate the total score for each participant, multiply the total number of times the individual is given a ranking by his or her classmates by the number of rankings you asked for. For example, in the sociogram on vocabulary, above, in which students were asked to rank the three best vocabulary learners, you would take the number of times the person is chosen "best vocabulary learner" and multiply it by three (since you asked them to list the three best vocabulary learners in the class); then the number of times that student is chosen "second-best vocabulary learner" and multiply that number by two; and then the number of times he or she was chosen "third-best vocabulary learner" and multiply that number by one. Add these scores together to get a total score for that student (see Chapter 6, p. 139, for an example of a sociogram chart).

Diagrammatic analysis: To draw the sociogram results, write the names of the students in a random pattern on a large sheet of paper, leaving ample space around them. Then draw an arrow from Student X to the person he or she ranked as first for the task. Draw a different type of arrow (color or dotted) from Student X to his or her second choice, and so on. The map that results will show visually how students perceive themselves and their peers in relation to the task. For instance, the student with the greatest number of lines to him or her is perceived by peers as the best or strongest at the task (see Chapter 6, p. 139, for a discussion of a sociogram diagram in a research report).

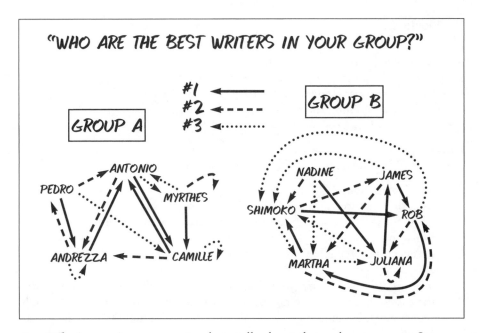

"WHO ARE THE BEST WRITERS IN YOUR GROUP?"

In analyzing sociograms, researchers talk about three phenomenons. **Stars** are the participants who are selected the most often by their peers. An **isolate** is a person who is not selected by any other member. **Mutual choices** are two individuals who select each other. Sociograms also look at patterns of selection. A **cleavage** is when the group divides itself into two or more subgroups that fail to nominate anyone from the other subgroup. For example, in a sociogram among fourth graders on who wants to work with whom on a project, girls might only pick other girls, while boys would pick only boys. **Cliques** are subgroups or individuals who select each other and tend to avoid other participants. Cliques are generally less dramatic than cleavages; they are patterns in and among subgroups whereas cleavages are patterns of the whole group. (See Hubbard and Power, 1993, p. 41.)

Advice:
- It can be very useful to ask students to explain their choices in order to understand *why* they perceive their peers as they do.
- Sociograms are quick, visual tools that can challenge your perceptions of how individual students see themselves and are seen by other members of the group in relation to a task or issue. The diagram can allow you to see stars, isolates, cleavages, cliques, and mutual choices.

Further References:
Hopkins, D. 1993. *A teacher's guide to classroom research.* (2nd ed.). Buckingham, UK: Open University Press. pp. 137–140.

Hubbard, R. and B. Power 1993. *The art of classroom inquiry.* Portsmouth, NH: Heinemann.

INTERVIEWS

Definition:

An interview is a structured oral (or possibly written) exchange with someone . It aims to gather information. There are two basic types of research interviews: **unstructured** or **open-ended,** and **structured**. The former allow participants more latitude in guiding the exchange, while the latter generally follow a predetermined set of questions (see Patton, 1990).

Purpose:

- To gather information and/or perceptions from participants in the study

Advance Preparation:

- In both structured and open-ended interviews, it is important to prepare a guide for the interview in advance. The **interview guide** outlines the questions and probes that will make up the exchange (see below). (For an excellent and readable discussion of interviewing, see Patton, 1990, pp. 277–368.)
- You need to decide how participants' responses will be captured. Clearly, the easiest and most common way is to audiotape the interview, although researchers also take notes. (See also the two-minute interview, described below.)
- If you are audiotaping the interview, always check the tape recorder and microphone thoroughly in advance. You will need to test the recording level to make sure responses are audible and to check the machine so you know how to operate it.
- If you are interviewing people under age 18 (in the United States) or in a school setting, it is generally necessary to get written permission from their parents or guardians. Interviewing people without proper permission may result in complications later. As a teacher, speaking to your students about their work is well within your job, however, decisions about permission may depend more on if and how you plan to use the data beyond your teaching responsibilities.

Developing an interview guide:

The following list, abbreviated from Patton (1990), outlines six general types of interview questions. While an interview need not include questions of all six types, the overview is helpful in developing the interview guide according to your inquiry and the function of the interview in your data collection.

CATEGORIES OF INTERVIEW QUESTIONS

1. Behavior/experience: *What a person does/has done.*

2. Opinion/values: *What a person thinks or believes.*

3. Feelings: *How a person feels, his or her emotional responses and reactions.*

4. Knowledge: *The "facts" as viewed/known by the person.*

5. Sensory information: *The person's sensory world—smell, sound, sight, touch, taste.*

6. Demographics/background: *Information about the person that helps to situate the person in relation to others.*

Procedure:

1. Start the interview by saying who you are talking to and when (date and time) so you have that information. You may also want to introduce the purpose and general structure of the interview, and how long you expect it to last. These details can help to relax the person being interviewed.

2. Ask your questions in the form and order on your interview guide. In open-ended interviews you may vary the order of the questions and you may use probes to elicit further information or clarifications (see Patton, 1990). In structured interviews you generally follow the sequence and wording of the questions very closely.

3. When you have finished the questions on the interview guide, close the interview. Be aware that it is human nature that people often mention fascinating and critical information as the interview is winding up and you are packing away the equipment. In this case, you can either remember their comments and write them down, or you can ask the person to restate the comment on tape.

4. After the interview, the tape will need to be transcribed.

THE TWO-MINUTE INTERVIEW

The **two-minute interview** is a useful variant on the basic interview and is particularly adapted to teachers who are researching in their own classrooms when time is a major factor. In the two-minute interview, you limit yourself to one or at most two short questions. You choose an individual student to interview, according to the research plan, and you do so during a break or group activity. Instead of recording the response, you recall the student's answers and write them down immediately afterwards. Because of the brevity of the interview and the fact that nothing is being taped, two-minute interviews are rather unremarkable from the students' point of view and are quite easy to weave into the fabric of class activity. They can seem like a question-answer exchange. For these reasons, I recommend them as a way to easily sample students' thinking.

Advice:

■ The advice given for audiotaping (pp. 207-208) also applies to interviewing, as the vast majority of interviews use a tape recorder. It is well worth rereading

■ Even if you are taping the interview, it is worth your time to make rough notes of the person's answers for several reasons. Tapes do fail, and they generally seem to do so just when the most crucial or interesting information is at stake. These notes can help you quickly locate passages of the interview as you need them. Transcripts are lengthy and tapes take time to listen to, so the notes can serve as a rough table of contents. To this end, it is worth using a tape recorder equipped with a digital counter so that you can note the counter number as the person starts a new topic or answers a major question.

- Transcribing tape recordings is very time-consuming. The usual ratio is 3 or 4 to 1; that is, depending on the complexity of the talk and the skill of the transcriber, it can take three or four hours to transcribe one hour of tape.
- Don't record over tapes until the research project is completed, if then. Often, you may want or need to refer back to earlier tapes that may not have seemed relevant at the time. It is always worth saving tapes.

Further References:

McDonough, J., and S. McDonough. 1997. *Research methods for English language teachers*. London: Arnold. pp. 171–188.

Patton, M. Q. 1990. *Qualitative evaluation and research methods* (2nd ed.). Thousand Oaks, CA: Sage Publications.

Mishler, E. 1986. *Research interviewing*. Cambridge, MA: Harvard University Press.

Appendix D

LETTERS ON BECOMING UNEMPLOYED

The following letters were taken from the *New York Times*, in an article titled "Downsizing: How it feels to be fired" (March 17, 1996). They are divided into two data sets. The first four letters, which make up **Set A**, are used in *Investigation 5.5*, on "Grounded" data analysis. The second five letters, which make up **Set B**, are used in *Investigation 5.6*, on "A priori" data analysis. The entire set, A and B, are used in Investigation 5.7, on quantification within an a priori approach.

SET A: GROUNDED DATA ANALYSIS

(See Investigation 5.5, page 101)

Letter #1

In early 1990, my husband accepted a job offer in Orange County, Calif. We sold our home in northern New Jersey, packed up our three children and went off into the Pacific sunset.

We were convinced this would be a better life of more money and greater opportunity. We bought a beautiful home. I found a great job. Our kids were beginning to call this place with palm trees "home."

In January 1993, the horror that is now our life began. My husband's job was eliminated; the company that relocated us was relocating itself to Colorado. This wasn't supposed to happen to professional people like us. Out of work for seven months, my husband again relocated—back to New Jersey—the only offer he'd had.

The children and I remained in California for one year as we attempted (unsuccessfully) to sell our home in a dying economy. Eventually, once again, I sacrificed my career and uprooted three happy kids to the either cold or humid, albeit familiar, Northeast.

Although the new employer generously funded the moving, no resources were available to us upon our arrival that would allow us to stock up empty cupboards or sign up little boys for the fall soccer season. Because we were unable to recoup our previous salary levels, we have fallen into financial ruin.

No longer yuppies, now we work and work and yet are barely solvent. My marriage is on hold.

Shelly Kaplan
Succasunna, N.J.

Letter #2

My wife and I joined the army of the downsized two years ago, and it has been a mixed blessing. Yes, we have experienced a loss in income; we moved to a smaller house; we scaled down dramatically; we experienced feelings of self-doubt and uncertainty.

On the other hand, as executives in a large corporation, we had become used to an unhealthy lifestyle—one that placed material ahead of spiritual well-being. We assumed that our places in the corporation were assured, and took for granted everything that went with that—eating out every other night, postponement of savings and a consumerist outlook. Our family pulled together out of our crisis. We completely changed careers, and although we make less money now, we like what we are doing and do not miss for a moment the corporate politics we used to wade through every day.

Our children don't beg to go out every night anymore. They know the prices of their clothing, since they buy their own clothes from their chore money. We think long and hard about the real need of each purchase, rather than just the want behind it. As a consultant, I know now what many full-time workers around me are just beginning to realize. I know that employment with a client can end the next hour.

At the very least, the short term vision of today's corporate chieftains is creating a generation of people who will never again view the latest company campaign as anything more than a ruse to boost short-term bottom-line performance. "Teamwork," "Empowerment," "Total Quality Control"—I used to spout these out right along with the best of them. No more. Even if I could believe them, I know no one else would. Five years ago, I thought Deming could be the voice of the corporate world. Now I know it is really Dilbert.

Tom Scott
Encinitas, Calif.

Letter #3
Recently, I saw a political cartoon depicting an affluent older man making a speech at a banquet. He was saying, "Last year, thousands of new jobs were created in this country." The thought balloon over the waiter's head said, "Yeah, and I've got three of them." I didn't know whether to laugh or cry.

You see, for the past year, I've had two jobs instead of the one job I used to have. Together, those two jobs pay approximately 10 percent of what my one job used to pay. I have a Ph.D. in chemistry from a larger university with a well-respected chemistry program.

I had entered graduate school with a dream of working for an I.B.M. or an AT&T, doing research that would make a positive difference in people's lives. It took me five years after graduation to land that first industry job. I took great pride in the knowledge that I was working to decrease pollution and produce a useful product. I took my $20,000 sign-on bonus and bought a condominium.

After 2 1/2 years, I was downsized out of the company. I spent eight months writing hundreds of letters, making hundreds of phone calls and networking at conferences. I got one job offer—800 miles away. I bid tearful good-byes and put my condo on the market. The market wasn't very good—everyone else was downsizing, too. My $20,000 became $10,000 overnight.

Just before Christmas 1993, I started work at the central research facility of a "good, stable company, heavily committed to research." After one year, things appeared to be going well, so I bought a house. I paid my taxes, bought company stock and planned for my future.

In 1995, I received a pink slip for Valentine's Day. My new job had lasted all of 15 months. That was almost a year ago, and I'm still looking for full-time work.

Nancy K. McGuire
Bay City, Michigan

Letter #4

I have been downsized by the World Bank, after more than 15 years working as an economist. Both my wife and I were made redundant the same month (last August). I am 57, my wife 53.

Fortunately, we have no mortgage on a large old townhouse in D.C. The World Bank has given me a more than adequate severance package, we have managed to save quite a bit since arriving in the U.S. some 16 years ago, and I can cash in a large part of my pension.

We now look at this unexpected situation as a unique chance to change life styles, spend more time together, structure our working day differently and do new things. The first thing we did last year after being made redundant was to buy an old sailboat! In the short run, we'll go sailing, do a lot of writing and happily get by on about $3,000 a month pre-tax, compared with close to $10,000 post-tax before. People shouldn't only look at the negative side.

Eugene Versluysen
Washington, D.C.

Set B: A Priori Data Analysis

(See Investigation 5.6, page 103)

Letter #5

I was downsized for the first time in my life in November of 1991. Being a fairly sharp guy with an extensive background in electronics and computer programming, I didn't think it would be all that difficult to find a new job. I was somewhat concerned about my eight-month-old baby at home, but optimism was the word of the day.

My first real shock came three months after being laid off: It would cost $598 a month to continue my medical benefits. Due to the fact that we were now living on unemployment compensation of $300 a week, this was impossible. I could also no longer afford my blood pressure medication either, but I thought that my first obligation was to give my son as good a start in life as I could. I applied for Medicaid when I lost my insurance. The social worker thought it was pretty funny that someone collecting the princely sum of $300 a week should think he was eligible for Medicaid.

Eventually my unemployment ran out and we suffered the indignity of welfare for a month. The one good thing I can say about welfare is it gave me access to a very good career counselor who helped me land a job with a computer consulting firm in the summer of 1993. They kept me for six months, then laid me off. I collected unemployment again for nearly six months, and in the nick of time I got my present job, which seems to be as secure as anything is today.

The reason I mentioned the blood pressure medicine is this. The high blood pressure which I could not treat destroyed my kidneys. I am now on dialysis and trying to get a transplant. If I lose my job again it will destroy me. My dialysis costs my insurance company $5,000 a month. When I get a transplant, I will have to take anti-rejection drugs for the rest of my life. I cannot change jobs due to this pre-existing condition.

Michael McGinn
Monroe, N.Y.

Letter #6
I worked for the U.S. General Accounting Office, a Congressional agency that exposes fraud, waste, abuse and mismanagement of Federal funds. The agency got a 25 percent budget cutback from the Republicans. But no one in my office expected the New York field office to close.

We received the bad news on Aug. 7. At the time, I was 8 1/2 months pregnant. I was unable to look for a job because no one was interested in interviewing someone in that condition. I appealed to upper management for an extended time with the employment counseling services, but was denied. The exact quote from the Washington lawyer was, "G.A.O. didn't get you pregnant."

The office closed on Nov. 10. I have been looking for a job since then. My husband has taken on a second job, often working 90 hours a week. I am having a hard time looking for work while caring for my daughter. I can't hire a sitter until I have income coming in.

Diana Erani
Riverdale, NY

Letter #7
In the 19 years since receiving my Ph.D., I have worked full-time for seven colleges and universities in three states. The longest I was able to stay at a single institution was six years, and I stayed at several institutions for periods as brief as one year. I have drawn unemployment compensation five, yes five, times. I have currently been unemployed for two years. I have applied for close to 2,000 jobs.

At age 45, I have little hope that I will have any more of a career as an academic psychologist. The standard cliché is that we need a better educated workforce. Well, from where I am sitting, having an education is no guarantee that one won't be left behind.

James C. Megas
St. Paul, Minn.

Letter #8
Bell Atlantic, soon to merge with NYNEX, has not had massive layoffs, as yet, but many have retired with incentives to leave the payroll. These jobs have not been filled. My story concerns the employees who are left. Many have been suspended for minor violations of safety which would have evoked only a warning

in the past. Vacation, even though we have earned it, is getting more difficult to schedule. Forced overtime is on the horizon, as well as punishment for sickness.

Downsizing is a catastrophe for those who lose their jobs, and I would not presume to say that the irritations I suffer compare to that. However, downsizing makes life very stressful for the ones who hang on to their jobs a little longer, as well. Mostly, we are living in fear that we are next. We are!

Phillip Ruby
St. Albans, W. Va.

Letter #9
My husband was, until little over a year ago, a senior executive with an international organization. He had been in his field for over 25 years. I was an executive secretary with a worldwide company for 20 years until I was "outplaced" and he was "downsized." My husband decided to start his own company—a job search firm.

Within my own group of friends, out of four women known as the "Lunchbunch" at the office, only one is employed at present. The job market for mature secretaries is bleak and we are getting by, or trying to, by temping, searching for alternative careers and, in my case, assisting my husband in his new venture.

Mary Berne
Franklin Lakes, N.J.

SET C:
(Use all nine letters for Investigation 5.7, p. 105, quantification within an a priori approach.)

Appendix E

LIPT CASE STUDIES

The following five case studies are taken from the Languages Inservice Program for Teachers (LIPT), a teacher-centered professional development program. It is a collaborative project of the South Australian Education Department, the Catholic Education Office, and the Independent Schools Board.

Aims of LIPT are to:

- Provide teachers with up-to-date information about the theory and practice of teaching and learning languages

- Develop teachers' skills in analyzing and improving their teaching practices

- Widen teachers' range of classroom strategies and programming skills

- Support teachers in the process of curriculum renewal through membership of Languages Other Than English (LOTE) networks.

Using More Indonesian in the Classroom

Maree Nicholson

Maree Nicholson teaches Indonesian 8-12 at Loxton High School. She has previously taught Indonesian in New South Wales for three years and in the Northern Territory for 13 years.

Maree was dissatisfied with the amount of Indonesian both she and her students were using. She wanted to encourage her students to speak Indonesian more often and to use it for more than just set work. Here she describes the effects that using Indonesian for routine classroom communication had on their motivation, risk-taking and cooperative learning skills.

Introduction

Loxton High School in the Riverland is a school of 550 students of mainly Anglo-Saxon or German background. Two languages are taught, German and Indonesian, with enrolments in German about double that in Indonesian. Indonesian has been taught there since the early 1970's and this year there is one class at each year level, ranging in size from about 25 students in Year 8 to two or three in Years 11 and 12.

Why I Joined LIPT

I joined the Languages Inservice Program for Teachers (LIPT) Stage 3 with some knowledge of the Australian Language Levels (ALL) guidelines and related changes to the direction of my language teaching, such as more communicative activities and less emphasis on formal grammar. However, I wanted to examine my teaching more closely to test whether the aims and objectives of ALL were being achieved.

My teaching approach during my two years at Loxton has been one of using selected modules based on topics or themes in Year 8. I introduce vocabulary and expressions through brainstorming, then use visual stimuli reinforced with role-play and written exercises. By Year 10 students do more reading, writing, extension conversation and a closer study of structures.

My concerns were how much vocabulary and structures my students were retaining, and how much they were able to exend themselves independently through their understanding (intuitive or otherwise) of the language patterns being used. However the focus of LIPT 3 (language use in the classroom) made me aware of another area which provided an opportunity for my students and I to extend our use of Indonesian beyond the language relating to classwork: that is, through using Indonesian for everyday classroom instructions and expressions.

Why I Chose My Topic

As part of the initial two-day LIPT conference, I taped a lesson with my Year 10 Indonesian class (a lesson based on introducing a new structural concept through studying a passage previously read). A transcript of the tape revealed that:

- 80 - 90 % of the lesson involved teacher-dominated talk

- The proportion of Indonesian used was very small and related only to the specific passage being studied.

The students only used Indonesian when I questioned or prompted them in Indonesian. I was also using mainly English, not only to explain the concept, but also in routine instructions such as *"All right"*, *"Just a minute"*, *"How would you say...?"*. I therefore decided on my research topic:

> *How can I extend the use of Indonesian in my lessons through using it for routine classroom expressions?*

The Student Group

Initially I had decided to work with my Year 9 Indonesian class, a group of 16 lively, talented, highly motivated students who had already shown the ability to extend themelves in independent language use.

However, on reflection, I decided to work with my Year 10 class, mainly because they were a smaller group. They were nine very intelligent but less motivated students, who furthermore were a very disparate and often conflicting group of personalities. Year 10 lessons were a challenge in maintaining student attention and, more importantly, in encouraging this small group to work together cooperatively. A highly competitive streak in the more dominant half of the students led not only to often acerbic competition between themselves, but also to instilling a lack of confidence in the more passive students.

How I Set Up The Project

I introduced the Year 10 group to the idea of the project and what the plan would be. Surprisingly the response was excellent and the students were keen to be involved.

We began by taping a "normal" lesson, which featured lots of English. In the next lesson we listened to the tape and individually listed the expressions which related to the classroom and classroom procedures. We then produced a composite list which was later rationalised to 50 commonly-used expressions (see Appendix 1). As the taped lesson had been a reading comprehension, naturally many of the expressions were to do with reading and answering questions. At the end of the lesson I asked the students to note down their responses to the tape and their expectations of how the lessons would change with the implementation of the program.

The response was encouraging with comments like *"We should speak only Indonesian in the classroom but first we would need to know more words"*, *"We should tape ourselves every five weeks to see how much more Indonesian we are using"* as well as *"I would like to be able to say "Shut up..., you're thick!"* (Note my original comments about the nature of the class.)

The Program in Progress

I introduced the list of 50 expressions gradually, ten expressions at a time. Originally I intended to introduce ten per week, but this proved too ambitious and I amended the number to ten per fortnight or every three weeks. I gave the students a sheet with 50 expressions listed in English on which they had the option to write the Indonesian equivalents as they were introduced (most chose to do so). One strategy I used was to display the Indonesian expressions around the classroom. With each new set of expressions the class would focus on these and use them as much as possible.

Initial Results

Within the first two weeks, students were using and responding to the expressions regularly in class. Some students were beginning to make connections and extend the basic expressions for example, changing *"Bolehkah saya membaca?"* (May I read?) to *"Bolehkah saya ke kamar kecil?"* (May I go to the toilet?).

It soon become clear however that 70 - 80 % of the expressions were ones I, rather than the students, used more regularly. The challenge was to obtain the appropriate response from the students. In response to the initial enthusiasm, I introduced more Indonesian expressions which were not on the list or which were further down in the list. After I provided a simultaneous English translation a few times, the students quickly picked up some of the expressions, such as *"Coba lagi"* (Try again).

Further Developments

By the time the second and third sets of expressions were introduced, the initial success of the project had begun to diminish. The students acquired some of the expressions quickly, others required much more concentration and repetition, possibly because they did not arise as frequently in class. Originally I had intended to remove the previous set of ten expressions from the wall as each new set was put up. However the students resisted this idea very strongly, so I acquiesced and left all the expressions on the wall.

I also noticed that this approach required maximum impetus from me. If I was feeling tired and lapsed into English, the students immediately did the same. I was reminded of how much effort is required for second language learners to sustain this level of target language use.

Some Side Effects

One of the more surprising and positive side effects of the project was the extent to which the class began to operate as a much more cohesive group. Rather than ridiculing those who could not remember or who failed to use Indonesian, the more able members of the class would prompt and encourage them to do so. This in turn gave the less able students the confidence to use more Indonesian, generally with some pleasing improvements.

One of the more disappointing outcomes was that, in spite of the prominently displayed expressions around the classroom, other classes, especially the Year 9 group, showed little curiosity or interest in learning any of them. The implications seem clear: everything depends on the teacher initiating action in the classroom! Until I consciously use those expressions with other classes, they will not begin to acquire them.

Changing Direction

In an attempt to redress the imbalance of "teacher" expressions to "student" expressions, and particularly to improve the use of the expressions in the latter part of the list, we decided as a class to:

- conduct some lessons where the students took the part of the teacher, thus having the opportunity to use "teacher" expressions

- spend at least part of one lesson a week reinforcing and revising the expressions in a more structured way.

We used these strategies before the third and final taping of a lesson.

The Results

The students being "teacher" met with limited success. Most found it quite a frustrating experience, given the still limited number of expressions they could use. While they were able to use such expressions as *"Diam"* (Be quiet), *"Sudah cukup"* (That's enough), *"Siapa ingin membaca?"* (Who would like to read?) quite confidently, they wanted to be able to extend this to such expressions as "Be quiet or go outside.", "Finish these questions for homework" and "I'm the teacher, not you". Needless to say, their "students" were not entirely cooperative.

Evaluation

The project had a very beneficial effect on the Year 10 class in that it:

- increased the amount of Indonesian they spoke in class (in the first taped lesson, we used English for 80 % of our talk. By the second taped lesson, about 42 % of the total talk was in Indonesian)

- heightened their awareness of and their enthusiasm for using Indonesian in everyday communication

- improved the cooperative learning atmosphere in the class.

The project did however have its limitations in that:

- the students could use only a few of the expressions introduced without some initiation from me

- the rigid structure of the project imposed some artificial barriers to the spontaneous language acquisition which occurred while we were learning and in the process of using the expressions

- despite the wall charts, there was little flow-on to other classes.

Implications for My Future Teaching

The list of expressions for use in the classroom is an ever-expanding one. I would like to promote its use in all my Indonesian classes in the future. However, I would like the process to occur in a more spontaneous way, with a longer time frame, that is, through a gradual acquisition of expressions as they naturally arise out of a lesson. Two strategies seem necessary for this to succeed:

- I will need to taken the initiative at all times in using as much Indonesian in the classroom as the students can absorb until it becomes a routine.

- I need to encourage the students to develop an enquiring and cooperative approach to learning language, for example by compiling their own resource list of useful expressions in Indonesian.

Appendix 1

List of 50 Common Classroom Expressions
THE THINGS WE SAY
Marilah Kita Berbahasa Indonesia

Can I read?	*Bolehkah saya membaca?*
What page?	*Halaman berapa?*
Have you got your book?	*Sudah membawa buku anda?*
Have you got your book open?	*Sudah membuka buku anda?*
I left my book at home.	*Buku saya tertinggal di rumah.*
Are we ready to start?	*Sudah siap mulai?*
Excuse me.	*Maaf.*
Who would like to do question...?	*Siapa ingin menjawab pertanyaan nomor?*
How else could you answer?	*Ada jawab lain?*
Anything else?	*Ada lagi?*
What's the correct answer?	*Jawab apa yang betul?*
That's a good answer.	*Jawabnya baik.*
Did anyone have anything different?	*Ada yang jawabnya lain?*
I don't know the answer.	*Saya tidak tahu jawabnya.*
I didn't understand.	*Saya tidak mengerti.*
Who remembers?	*Siapa ingat?*
Who can help?	*Siapa bisa menolong?*
Can you say...?	*Bisa dikatakan...?*
That's good.	*Itulah baik.*
What does ... tell us?	*Apa yang bisa kita ketahui dari...?*
What does ... mean?	*Apa artinya...?*
I'll do the next one.	*Saya ingin menjawab yang berikut.*
Is that what you had?	*Apakah jawab anda sama?*
Who hasn't done their homework?	*Siapa yang tidak membuat pekerjaan rumah?*
I did my homework.	*Saya sudah membuat pekerjaan rumah.*
I didn't do it.	*Saya tidak membuatnya.*
Why didn't you do it?	*Mengapa anda tidak membuatnya.*
Which ones did you answer?	*Yang mana sudah anda jawab?*
That's not acceptable.	*Saya tak senang pada hal itu.*
Write out three times.	*Harus ditulis tiga kali.*
Who's done number...?	*Siapa sudah menjawab nomor...?*
Sshh!	*Diamlah!*
It doesn't matter.	*Tidak apa-apa.*
Wait a minute.	*Sebentar saja.*
Could we settle down please?	*Harap tenanglah.*
Pay attention.	*Perhatikan.*

Have you finished?	*Sudah selesai?*
We haven't finished.	*Belum selesai.*
Settle down!	*Tenanglah!*
Keep your mind on what we are doing!	*Tetap perhatikan!*
All right.	*Baiklah!*
Try again.	*Coba lagi.*
... wants to say something.	*... ingin berbicara.*
Not quite.	*Hampir betul.*
You're wasting your time.	*Anda membuang waktu.*
Don't forget.	*Jangan lupa.*
That will be your homework.	*Harus diselesaikan di rumah.*
Note that down.	*Harus dicatat.*
Nobody will miss out.	*Semua orang akan ada giliran.*
Bless you!	*Sayang!*

Suggested additions during course of project:

We are getting off the track.	There are still ... minutes.
Who else would like to read?	We are going to read about...
We are going to talk about...	Anybody?
Give him/her a chance...	
Wrong one!	
Can you tell us about...?	
Let it go!	

It's Too Hard!

Margaret Surguy

Margaret Surguy teaches Spanish R-7 at McRitchie Crescent Primary School, Whyalla. She has been teaching a variety of subjects, including French, for the best part of twenty years from Junior Primary to Secondary level. This is her first primary Languages Other Than English (LOTE) position, and the first time she has taught Spanish.

In this article Margaret describes her attempts to encourage a more positive attitude to writing in Spanish in a Year 3/4 class, and to have children make use of the available resources for their writing.

The School

McRitchie Crescent Primary School has appromixately 250 students and is situated in the west of Whyalla. It has a significant number of Aboriginal children and children from transient families. In 1989 the number of transfers in and out of the school exceeded 200. During the course of this project several children in the class left and others enrolled. Most children are of English-speaking background.

Why Spanish?

When we began the Spanish program in the first term of 1989, there were several Spanish-speaking families in the school. It appears the request that Spanish be offered in Whyalla had originated from the Spanish-speaking community. There had been a Spanish Ethnic School operating but this had been discontinued. Unfortunately in the second term of 1990 the last mother tongue students left.

Highs and Lows

I began planning the Spanish program in October 1988 and classes started for all levels from Reception to Year 7 at the beginning of 1989. I was impressed and encouraged by the enthusiasm of the younger children but found that many of those in Upper Primary were unwilling to attempt activities or even, in some cases, to cooperate at all. This was something new in my experience and I at once wondered where I was going wrong. My self-confidence was somewhat restored when the Principal and other colleagues assured me that this reluctance to take risks or accept the new or different was a common reaction among this school's students. In the end we decided to remove Spanish from the Year 6/7 curriculum. There was no opportunity for the children to continue it at high school so we felt we were not disadvantaging them.

Despite this set-back I felt the first year of Spanish had been relatively successful. All classes had a minimum of two 40 or 50 minute lessons per week, one of which was attended by the classroom teacher. This meant that very useful follow-up work was done in the classrooms and the class teachers were interested and involved.

Things changed in 1990 when LOTE positions were used to provide class teachers' Non-Instructional Time (NIT) and LOTE time was reduced. Class teachers no longer attended lessons. Who could blame them? It was their non-contact time. I began to feel like a Jack-of-all-trades, teaching Spanish, Science and some Current Affairs. I needed help!

LIPT to the Rescue

I had wanted to join the Languages Inservice Program for Teachers (LIPT) the previous year but had been unable to do so. Being not only a LOTE teacher, but also the only Spanish teacher in the area, I felt about as much a part of things as a shag on a rock! My morale was flagging badly and I hoped the LIPT program and the contact with other language teachers would give me a much-needed boost. They did!

What to Investigate?

Choosing a focus for my research proved difficult, though I did want to concentrate on reading and writing, as I was concerned about the chldren's general lack of progress in those areas since the previous year.

In this "Year of Literacy" the school had made literacy in English its much-needed major focus, with the emphasis on writing. It seemed appropriate to work on the same area in Spanish.

Although I knew the children's reluctance to write in Spanish reflected a similar reluctance to do so in English, I was not prepared to sit back and accept it. It was neither feasible nor satisfactory to restrict two 40 or 50 minute lessons per week to oral and aural work and worksheets, especially once the children reached middle primary level. I felt I must do something to encourage the children to write in the target language, but what?

The Class of 1990

Despite my vagueness about the topic I decided to work with one of the two Year 3/4 classes. I rashly chose the one in which a small group of children were becoming very reluctant Spanish learners. Was their response a fear of failure? Boredom? Parental views about LOTE? All or none of the above? I didn't know.

Up and... Tottering

I decided to begin by asking the children in this class one question: *"How do you feel when I ask you to write in Spanish?"* To keep it non-theatening I said they didn't have to answer and if they did they could say whatever they felt. They could also tell me, rather than write down their comments. The answers were depressing but, doubtless, honest. Of the 21 responses, 17 were negative (see Appendix 1).

Where to start?

Futile Efforts?

One of the most popular activities of the previous year had been the making of *Me Gusta* (I like) books. These were simple picture books. Each page began with the words *Me gusta...* The children then drew or pasted pictures of things they liked and the older ones wrote the Spanish for each object. The more adventurous versions included *No me gusta* (I don't like) pages. I had displayed the completed books in the reading corner until the end of the term when the children took them home. I hoped for a high-interest, low fear-inducing start by making *Tengo* (I've got) books along the same lines (see Appendix 2).

I made the process as clear as I could. We'd already worked orally and completed worksheets using the vocabulary. Each child would make his/her own book and could include real possessions or ones they wanted. I included a *No tengo* (I haven't got) option for the negative-minded.

I found the results disappointing. Of the 18 books I received only two (with a maximum of six pages) were completed with three-word Spanish sentences, such as *"Tengo una espada"* (I've got a sword) and two students only got as far as their front covers. The rest were in between. The majority only managed to complete the sentence with an English noun, for example *"Tengo un* boat" and *"Tengo* lota cars". There were one or two encouraging signs, such as *"Tengo cinco* fingers" (I have five fingers), but overall it had been heavy-going. This was obviously not the way to attack the problem.

Defining the Topic Further

After considerable cogitation I came up with the question: *"Will the consistent use of written texts on permanent display, or permanently available in the classroom, make children more confident about writing in Spanish?"*

It was soon pointed out to me by other LIPT members that measuring any increase in confidence, let alone the reasons for it, would be very difficult if not impossible. It was suggested the question become: *"What use do students make of the resources available in the classroom when writing?"* This sounded good to me!

Gathering Data

I decided on a simple checklist of the various resources available in the classroom (see Appendix 3), and to limit my observations to three children, at least to start with. I chose two girls and one boy at random. A colleague who was already doing some work with me in this class volunteered to observe the children while we wrote.

Problems arose in the first lesson. Bill decided to sulk and spend most of the lesson with a book in the reading corner, while the two girls worked together using the backborad exclusively. We'd obviously have to observe the whole class to gather any useful amount of information. And the following week my volunteer observer couldn't come to the lesson!

Back to the Drawing Board

Desperate measures were called for. Neither the book writing nor the data collection was working. I needed to take things in easier stages and do more modelling of the writing. I also had to re-define my research question. What about: *"How can I develop more positive attitudes to writing in my classroom?"*

We had already been working on the topic *"Yo"* (Me). I made extra wall charts with pictures of brown eyes, curly hair and so on and confined the writing on them to Spanish (*los ojos castaños, el pelo rizado* etc.)

I hadn't been able to find a simple English/Spanish dictionary although quite good ones were available in Spanish/English. All I had were vocabulary picture books which listed words under headings such as "Sport" and "The Weather". Although fun to look at, as reference books they required much patience and stamina from these children and were very frustrating.

So I tried to put together any books and pictures relating to personal appearance and had them ready and waiting. Finally I wrote a selection of useful verbs and noun/adjective combinations on the board, all colour-coded. I had already found this strategy useful. Although they might be unfamiliar with grammatical or simpler terms for the parts of speech, the children still found it helpful to know that you needed a green, a yellow and a blue word, in that order, to make a sentence, for example *Tengo* (I have) *el pelo* (the hair) *rubio* (blond) - I have blond hair.

In the first lessons we went through the vocabulary on the board and I pointed out the wall-charts which listed the same words and phrases. We then played a game using the language orally in which we guessed the identity of a child in the class from a description gleaned from the word lists. I was pleasantly surprised at how quickly and eagerly the children took over from me in leading the game.

One Step Forward...

The next step was for each child to draw him/herself or a friend and write three descriptive sentences to accompany it (see Appendix 4). At this point we added two more verbs and some handy adjectives such as *gracioso* (funny), *tonto* (silly), *inteligente* (clever) and *pasota* (cool). I was thrilled with the results. Every child had written at least one sentence by the end of the lesson. Most had three and two had four! We even had a touch of humour: *Soy calvo!* (I'm bald!) So far, so good.

A new term arrived with a new topic: *"Animales"*. Building on from last term's success the children were to choose an animal, bird or other living creature and feature it in a poster. Again, I asked them to write a minimum of three sentences about it. This time they could work either alone or with a partner and were to use words found in the appropriate books and charts.

I was pleased to note that a few children immediately homed in on the bookshelves. Jim, in particular, not only used them himself but also directed others to the most appropriate one. Success!

And Another

But not for all. I had again made too great a jump for some, so I devised another game to help the children practise their use of the resources in the classroom. I made a list of 20 Spanish words which I placed around the room, either with their English equivalents or explanatory drawings. The children had to race the clock to find as many as they could within a set time. It was a noisy but successful activity. However I was surprised and enlightened to find that a small number of children had difficulty finding the appropriate charts for numbers, colours and so on, indicating considerable English literacy problems.

The Proof

In the first week of Term 4 I asked the class the same question I'd posed in the beginning: *"How do you feel when I ask you to write in Spanish?"* Once again they were not obliged to respond.

What a relief! Of the 24 responses 15 were positive. I was also interested to see that although two of the children still found it difficult, they were now able to either enjoy or find value in writing. I also asked the children themselves to assess the value of the various resources available. I asked them to rate each one under the following categories: "very useful", "useful", "sometimes useful" and "not at all useful". Some children rated each resource, some only one or two. This made it more difficult to assess results, but the fact that most children responded to the question regarding the blackboard and charts in itself indicated how useful they found these two resources (see Appendix 6).

Onward, Ever Upward

Perhaps I can sum up the answer to my final research question about how I could develop more positive attitudes to writing in my classroom in two parts:

- by making resources available
- by constantly monitoring my classroom practices.

The project showed me that my expectations had been too high. I had left processes too open-ended, and even half-way through my research, I was still making leaps that were too great for many of the students. I am now trying to lower my expectations and to allow as long as the children need, rather than the time I want to spend, on a process or skill so that the children can feel confident and be successful. I now believe what I suspected before, that students need to be guided slowly in short steps to overcome fear of failure. I am convinced that this "step-by-step" approach, which in some ways contradicts much of present practice in writing in the primary school, can bring results, especially for children who can't or won't take risks.

Last, but definitely not least, as their own comments show, these children have started to make better use of the resources available and are more confident about tackling their writing in Spanish.

Appendix 1

Student Comments on Writing in Spanish

"I feel worried cause I don't know how to do it."
"I don't want to do it."
"It's boring."
"Fun."
"I'm afraid that it's going to be too hard."
"I hate it."
"I hate it."
"I like it."
"It's hard filling in Spanish words."
"It's bad, it's too easy."
"It's a nightmare."

"I feel embarrassed."
"I don't feel like doing it."
"I hate it."
"I'm scared that I'll do mistakes."
"I'd be too scared to write - I might make a mistake."
"I'm scared."
"My hands will shake. (It's good)??"
"There's too many Spanish books and you can't read them."
"It's really excellent."
"It is fun."

Appendix 2

Examples of *Tengo* Books

tengo pencil.
lapiz

Tengo
un cohete

Appendix 3

Using Resources - Checklist

Child's Name	Black-board	Charts Posters	Books	Diction-aries	Teacher	Other Children

Examples of *Yo Books*

Appendix 5

Students' Comments on Writing in Spanish

Good	(2)	Terrific	(1)
O.K.	(5)	Don't like it	(3)
Hate it	(1)	I like it	(2)
Difficult	(2)	Not good	(1)
Excellent	(1)		

"I feel normal (it's very good)."
"You can say anything you want to say. Sometimes I haven't a clue - it's hard"
"Sometimes it's hard e.g. putting the little lines on top in the right places e.g. ñ."
"I think it's very useful because some children have Spanish cousins etc."
"Sometimes it's complicated for some people."
"It's OK - You have to concentrate on different things - sometimes it's hard."

Appendix 6

Usefulness of Resources

Resource	Very Useful	Useful	Sometimes Useful	Not Useful at All
Blackboard	3	15	1	-
Wall-Charts	7	4	4	-
Books	1	9	3	1
Teacher	8	6	-	-
Another Person	4	2	2	2

Maria Vithoulkas has been teaching for three years. This is her second year at Berri Primary School, where she teaches Modern Greek to Years R-7.

Maria wanted to find out how she corrected errors in her students' spoken Greek, and how her students responded to her correction techniques.

Introduction

Picture this...

You're a student in a Year 3/4 class and it's Monday morning. Your first Greek lesson for the week has begun. You've strategically chosen to sit towards the back of the room near someone bigger and smarter, where hopefully you'll be out of the teacher's direct view. Somewhere "safe".

Only occasionally do you want the teacher to know you're there. That's when your arm shoots up in the air and you're frantically waving it back and forth. You're just dying to give the right answer. Of course the teacher chooses the person next to you. Well, that's it for you, until, sure enough, the next question has been kindly directed to you. You think back to the time when you once thought you had made a mistake. What embarrassment, anger and disappointment! But wait, you remember that you hadn't made a mistake after all?!? With a sense of relief you give your answer.

When you hear your neighbour giggle all you want to do is crawl under the desk and disappear. Just then, to your surprise, you hear your teacher say *"Good try, but not quite right. Do you want to have another go?"* You think it must surely be a trap, but then again teachers say mistakes are for learning and this teacher actually means it! Here you go again.

My Topic

I could only assume the same mixed emotions I once experienced when answering questions in class were shared by my own students. I wanted to create the most supportive learning environment that I could, and I felt that correcting errors positively was an important part of this. So now, as a teacher, I asked myself: *"What language do I use to correct errors in students' oral language?"* and *"How do my students respond to these correction techniques?'*.

My Motives

I could appreciate my students' anxieties and frustrations when learning a second language and making mistakes. I therefore wanted to create an environment that would:

- be non-threatening
- increase the students' level of confidence
- encourage risk-taking
- encourage self-correction and second attempts
- help children accept mistakes as part of their learning
- promote a positive attitude towards learning a second language at an early year level.

My Methods

I decided to work with my Year 3/4 class, as they were a responsive and manageable group.

Taping a Lesson

I first tried to record a lesson so that I could analyse the language I was using and the students' responses. However, this proved to be technically unsuccessful. I found that my moving around the room from group to group made it difficult for any language to be clearly recorded.

Student Survey

I then decided to devise a questionnaire for the students (see Appendix 1). This gave me the most useful and concrete data of all that I collected.

1. Attitudes to Making Mistakes

    All 22 students believed that it was all right to make mistakes.

★ Why do you feel this way?

1. because no One is perfit

2. beacuse mistakes are apart of Learning.

2. Feelings About Making a Mistake

Seven students felt *"embarrassed"*, four felt *"sad"*, one felt *"angry"*, and 14 chose other descriptions such as *"puzzled"*, *"normal"* and *"hopeless"*. Some children gave more than one answer.

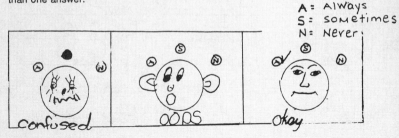

A: Always
S: sometimes
N: Never

confused   OOPS   okay

3. Rating Language Used for Corrections

I asked the children to rate seven expressions I used when correcting errors on a scale from 1-10, with 10 being for the most preferred expression.

Expression	% of class giving highest rating
"Good try, but not quite right."	71.4
"Ask your neighbour."	61.4
"This is how you say it."	50.3
"Can someone else say it?"	45.4
"No, try again."	44.5
"That's wrong."	11.8
"This is how you say it."	50.3

4. Preferred Language for Corrections

I asked the children to indicate what they would like me to say when correcting their errors. Most simply copied the expressions from the previous question and put them in the same order of preference. Some children gave slight variations:

Sorry you got it wrong I hope you do better next time.

you say it arfter me.

5. Need for Error Correction

All but two students thought I should correct their errors and could give reasons for this opinion:

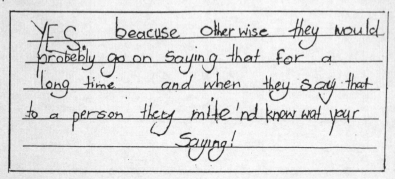

YES beacuse otherwise they would probebly go on saying that for a long time. and when they say that to a person they mite'nd know wat your Saying!

It seemed that the children welcomed corrections and understood the need for them, but also recognised that making mistakes could be embarrassing if the teacher did not respond sensitively. They preferred me to indicate errors positively in ways that acknowledged their efforts and encouraged a further attempt. They also liked to be able to work on error correction with their peers. I would now like to devise some sort of checklist for students to use regularly to see if I am continuing to use positive language to correct errors, and how often.

Recording a Lesson by Video

I recorded a game that was played towards the end of a lesson. I had planned to use less positive language during one round and more positive the next, and then compare the students' responses during the two rounds.

During the first round one student physically stepped back from the circle we were in after I had said *"No"*. She seemed to be embarrassed, yet interestingly enough, I maintained eye contact and she then made another attempt to answer correctly. I used less positive comments in Greek as well, and at times some students would self-correct without my prompting them. Others were given a few seconds to answer and if they could not, I moved to the next person.

During the second round the student who had stepped back before happened to be corrected again. This time I said *"Not quite right, have another go."*. She remained still, smiled and tried again. Most students followed this pattern. From what I could observe, they seemed discouraged when I responded less positively to their errors, but if I maintained eye contact, would attempt another answer. If I used a more positive expression to correct, they seemed quite willing to try again immediately.

Observing a Lesson

I asked my Language Inservice Program for Teachers (LIPT) Facilitator to note how the children responded to my corrections. We found that they generally seemed comfortable when given a choice about having another attempt to answer correctly. Some would try again, others would ask a friend and be happy to pass on the answer to me, and some would decline but still have a smile.

Having focused on **how** I correct I would like at some stage to investigate **when** I correct and **what** I correct. I'd also like to look at the effects of correcting students publicly and privately.

Conclusion

I believe that my project was useful. I now have a list of possible correction phrases that I can continue to use in the future, phrases that don't make the children want to crawl under their desks and disappear. Action research makes you step back and look closely at what you're doing in the classroom, and consider how you could change it and why. I believe that at the moment you recognise a concern or issue in your teaching practice, and begin to act on it, you have already made progress. With continual effort, reflection and support, regardless of any survey results, you've actually made progress.

What I liked most about being involved in this action research project was that I could determine my own aims, objectives and methods, and whatever the outcomes, it was my choice as to what I was going to do about it. As teachers we are all concerned about our students' learning, but what about our own learning? Being involved in LIPT 3 was one of <u>my</u> greatest and most valuable learning experiences.

Did You Say Something?

OOPS...I made a mistake!!

① Is it allright to make mistakes?

(YES)   (NO)

★ Why do you feel this way?

_____

_____

② How do you feel when you make a mistake?

A: Always
S: Sometimes
N: Never

sad   embarassed   angry   _____

③ Give these sayings a score.

"Thats wrong" /10   "Good try but..." /10
                      "not quite right"

"No, try again" /10

"Have another go" /10   "Ask your neighbour" /10

"This is how you say it" ./10   "can someone else say it" /10

④ What would you like the teacher to say if you make a mistake.

_____
_____
_____
_____

⑤ Do you think the teacher must let you know that you have made a mistake? Why?

_____
_____
_____
_____

Thank-you!!

Towards
a Positive
Classroom

Athena Frangos

Athena Frangos is a Year 4 teacher at Smithfield Plains Primary School. Previous to this she spent six years teaching Greek to second language learners from Years R-7.

Athena wanted to give the children in her class some exposure to Greek language and culture, in a way that would encourage them to want to learn more. In this article she describes how she worked to create a more positive learning environment through greater use of praise.

School Background

The school population is basically of English-speaking background with only a handful of ethnic children. There are many children from socially and economically disadvantaged backgrounds.

My school introduced a language program for the first time this year, offering German to only a few classes. For most children this is their first exposure to a language other than English (LOTE).

Background to the Project

Since most of my teaching career was spent in the LOTE area, it seemed only natural to introduce a language into my classroom when I finally became a class teacher. I decided to teach Greek, which is not offered in the school.

I wanted to make it a pleasant, positive learning experience, so that the children would wish to continue Greek next year. Hopefully the children's enthusiasm for Greek would lead to it being offered throughout the school along with German.

Planning My Project

I wanted the children not only to enjoy the language lessons but also to learn some Greek language and culture. I was limited in the amount of time I could put towards this as it wasn't an official part of my class curriculum.

My project was based on two questions:

- *Was my teaching style positive and encouraging?*

- *What knowledge did the children already have about Greece?*

Plan of Action

1. Observation

To answer the first question I taped a lesson and analysed it. Something that became obvious by the end of the tape was my flair for negative comments! In a 40 minute lesson I made nearly 20 negative remarks. To make sure this wasn't just the result of an "off" day I had another teacher observe a lesson. She noted down all the positive and negative comments I made. The results were similar. I was using far more negatives than positives.

2. Questionnaire

To answer the second question I handed out a questionnaire to the children asking a variety of general knowledge questions about Greece. The results showed that the children believed Greeks were dark-skinned, dark-haired, wore flowing robes, spoke Egyptian and ate snails on a regular basis! Obviously these children had little knowledge of Greece.

3. Action

I worked out a series of lessons to be presented over a ten-week period. The focus would be on culture, with an introduction to language. There would be two 40 minute lessons per week. I planned activities to teach greetings, numbers, directions, colours etc., and organised group work assignments dealing with Greek food, lifestyle and mythology. My aim was to praise each child twice by the end of each lesson, thus promoting a positive atmosphere.

Outcomes

Within the first two weeks the children's response was amazing. They eagerly awaited each Greek lesson and participated enthusiastically. At the end of the ten-week program I taped a lesson. I tried to be as natural as possible and not let the tape influence my actions. Listening to the tape later I still heard some negative comments about children's behaviour, but these were far outweighed by the positive comments. What was even more interesting was hearing some of the children praising and encouraging each other!

I gave the questionnaire to the children again at the end of the program. They still described Greek people as dark-haired and olive-skinned, but at least they now knew that Greeks spoke Greek and ate *souvlakia* ! I also asked the children whether they would prefer to do German or Greek next year. Only one out of the 25 opted for German, which I felt showed that they had enjoyed the exposure course and had a positive attitude towards the Greek language and culture.

Conclusion

Being able to sit down and plan how to tackle the problem of motivating the children was very useful. To put the plan into action and watch the results gave me a sense of accomplishment. Praising the children helped create a more positive atmosphere and increased the children's desire to learn a language. However, being positive all the time was very difficult for me and it was farily easy to slip back into making negative remarks. The benefits from this classroom research flowed into other teaching areas. I found I was using more positive responses in other curriculum areas. Praising children's efforts was coming to me more naturally and the children were certainly "lapping it up". This doesn't mean there were no problems. There were still children who needed to be disciplined and who weren't as interested in learning as others, but even with these children the situation improved. For this school community, where many children have an *"I don't care"* attitude, it was quite heartening to see them taking such an interest in learning another language.

In French Please!

Roger Kennett

Roger Kennett teaches Science and French at Balaklava High School. He set up the school's French program seven years ago, and has been responsible for designing curriculum and running all the French courses across Years 8-12.

Roger wanted to find out how beginning students would respond to lessons conducted entirely in French. In this article he reports on his work with two introductory Year 8 classes.

Setting the Scene

Balaklava High works on a module system, whereby all students select courses in ten-week units. There are no compulsory subjects or units, with the exception of introductory units in Year 8. By staff decision, French is not one of these compulsory units, although most other subjects are. Students choose their modules based on interest and need, allowing for prerequisites. For example, students must have done background work at Year 8 to proceed to Science, French, Maths etc. at Year 9.

Initial Stages

When it came to choosing my action research topic and which class to work with, fate seemed to lend a hand. I had been interested in following up the material on target language use supplied at our initial Languages Inservice Program For Teachers (LIPT) Stage 3 conference in April. Articles presented there seemed to suggest that wonderful results could be achieved by immersing students almost totally in the target language, even with limited lesson time. Common sense told me that it should certainly improve their vocabulary, fluency, grasp of the language, and confidence in using it. For my own part, I had always tried to provide as much lesson work as possible in French, including written instructions on assignments and tests, but a close look at some of the lessons which I taped for our preliminary LIPT exercise had shown me just how much was conducted in English on an oral level. If I made a conscious effort to attempt to use 100 % French in the classroom, would I notice any improvement in my students' language use?

As it happened, a fluke of the timetable had given me two classes of L115 (our introductory ten-week French unit at Year 8) in Term 2. 26 students had elected to take the module, but it had been offered on two separate lines and had generated one class of 15 and another of 11 students. None had any background experience in French. It was too awkward to change the students' individual timetables to combine them into one class. They would be left as they were.

Fate having given me the opportunity, how could I resist? I decided to try teaching one class entirely in French (well, as close as possible anyway) and one in the mixture of

French and English that seemed to have become my norm, particularly at Year 8. The classes would cover essentially the same work, in essentially the same manner, and I could compare their performance through various common exercises and tests.

Reservations

To be fair, I had one large reservation about the project. Since our French modules are elective, and the students involved did not have to continue with the language, it would be easy for them to pull out if they felt uncomfortable with my approach. In order to ensure that we had enough students for the next ten-week module, and each module thereafter, I could not afford to alienate anyone. In fact, I would be aiming to convince most of those who hadn't elected to take the follow-up units to do so. As a safety net, I therefore decided to attempt the program in fortnightly blocks, checking our progress and the students' feelings about the project as we went along.

We Begin...

I began by explaining the LIPT project to the students involved. To avoid the implication that one class was "better" than the other, I told them that I would choose which one would be the "French only" class by flipping a coin. We discussed the possible advantages of working in 100 % French, and the possible difficulties. Many students were concerned that it would be too hard, or that they wouldn't cope. I respected their fears, and assured them that we would keep a check on their progress. If they felt too uncomfortable or I could see that one group was being disadvantaged by the program, then we would rethink the whole project.

The Course

The L115 course is a hybrid of various resources, designed as an introductory unit to French language, culture and customs. We cover basic greetings, identifying oneself and others, asking for food and following directions: the basic survival stuff! *Tour de France* is there as a text, but because I don't greatly like its approach and many students find it boring, I really only use it as a resource, alongside other exercises, games and hand-made booklets. The students talk, read and write with the emphasis being on developing a grasp of basic vocabulary and word recognition. My approach is similar to *Festina Lente*, and introductory Italian course that I stumbled across years ago.

And the First Lesson

By the time we started the project, we had covered basic greetings and were getting into the *"Where do you live?"*, *"How old are you?"*, *"What is his or her name?"* aspects. During our first few lessons we used French almost totally for about 35 of the 45 minutes allocated. Time had to be allowed for the students to arrive and settle in, and for me to get into gear! After an initial reluctance (*"Oh, this is too hard!"*) the class began to enjoy it. Most thought it was fun - and realised it was harder for me too.

It wasn't easy for me to swap from thinking in Year 12 Physics-ese to Year 8 French at the drop of a hat, particularly at the end of the day or if I was tired. I would often only teach two lessons a day in the Language Room, and had to accept the fact that time would be spent at the beginning and end of the lesson in getting out equipment, putting it away and/or cleaning up after other classes that had been using the room.

...With Good Results

We all felt pretty impressed after our first attempts. The students were happy that we had managed to speak so much French, and that they had been able to follow my instructions (hand signals are wonderful aids to understanding when you're stuck for words!). They were quick to point out that I slipped into English to tell Gary not to swat the flies with his ruler, but accepted that I did, at times, have to back up my instructions with a few words in English to a particular student with learning difficulties. Other than that, all seemed rosy.

There was an immediate need for extra vocabulary. We had covered simple instructions such as *"Le lavabo/les toilettes, s'il vous plaît"* , in the first few weeks, but now we needed additional words such as *"prêt"* (ready), *"commencez"* (begin) and *"allez"* (go), not to mention *"Ne frappez pas les mouches!"* (don't swat the flies!). Some of the class began to complain about the number of extra words they had to cope with, but we persevered.

But After the Sunshine...

Within a few days, however, the shine began to wear off. Two of the boys in the French only class (class A), were not participating much at all. They were reluctant to present their conversational skits on stage. In contrast, the mixed language class (class B) were much more cooperative. This distinction became more apparent when we tried a song. The song *"Je suis étranger"* ("I am a foreigner" - music pilfered from "She'll Be Coming 'round The Mountain") was a real flop with the French only class. There was no interest amongst the students, I sang alone. No such problems in class B. Why the difference? I asked myself. Both classes had been fairly similar in the first few weeks: willing to learn, cooperative, seeming to enjoy themselves. Now there was far more fidgeting and disruptive behaviour in class A than in class B.

We discussed the program, and the commitment that they and I had made. Several students were feeling threatened, because they didn't know enough French to say a lot. That provoked a good discussion about what it was like to live in a country where your language wasn't spoken and we agreed to keep trying. I tried to expect a little less, and work a little more slowly, even if it meant that the two classes diverged content-wise.

After a day's break for Religious Education, which used up both Year 8 lessons, class A seemed to be happier. Lessons were more productive, less disruptive. In fact, both classes were back on a par. It was becoming obvious to me, however, that the course wasn't lending itself to an all-French approach. For a start, translations require the use of English, and when we tried one together it seemed out of kilter with our approach thus far in class A. I also realised that the "Food and Customs" section which was coming up would be difficult to run entirely in French. The resource book itself was in English, and I wouldn't have time to rewrite it. By the same token, I was loathe to scrap the course, because it had been constructed through years of trial and error. It had been successful in developing communication skills and an understanding of aspects of another culture. Was I throwing out my natural, intuitive flow here for the sake of the research project? That was really beginning to worry me.

As we continued through the next few weeks, I found that conversational work was fine conducted in French only. But then, really, that was how I'd always run it. Aside perhaps from greater emphasis on instructions in French for class A, which meant that we took more time starting lessons, there was little difference in my approach with either class. In other areas, however, such as discussion of French customs and culture, the need to work almost completely in French was hindering learning. Should I change the course? Did I want to retain the class discussions that, to me, were as vital in developing an understanding of another culture as the language itself?

The Results Come In...

To top it off, the students' results for exercises and tests after a fortnight indicated no difference between the classes in their fluency or basic language skills. I realised that I could not really expect to observe any significant differences in language development between the two groups after such a short time. However, if the results test-wise were the same, were we gaining anything from our efforts? The first Section Test covering vocabulary grasp, comprehension and ability to hold a simple conversation gave the folllowing average marks out of 35:

CLASS A   24.7
CLASS B   24.2

If there was to be any significant gain from the increased use of French, I had expected it to be in oral fluency and grasp of vocabulary. The results of an oral homework exercise (see Appendix 2) should have been enlightening in this regard. I had given the students a week to tape and translate a passage based on the work we had been doing in class. The results, out of a possible total of 30 marks, were as follows.

	AVERAGE FOR THOSE PRESENTED	MARK AS AVERAGE FOR WHOLE CLASS
CLASS A	19.8	15.8
CLASS B	19.4	17.4

How Did I Feel?

The results were disappointing, to say the least. Although the highest marks for the exercise had been for students in class A, so had the lowest. Although on average students in class A had scored marginally higher, the number of students who didn't bother to hand in the exercise was also higher.

In fact, there was a definite difference in attitude emerging between the two classes. Repeating the survey carried out at the start of the course after about three weeks showed that the students in class A felt less comfortable and were turning off (I had noticed that without the survey!). Several had informed me that they had decided not to continue with French, and were pulling out of the next module. In class B, the situation was reversed. Several students who hadn't originally chosen to continue with the next module now felt they would like to.

There could have been many other factors contributing to the negative attitude of some students in class A, such as the dynamics of the group, individual personalities, or my own behaviour, which may unconsciously have been different. However, using French only in lessons was definitely not motivating the group. The numbers enrolled for the next module were borderline. If too many students pulled out, there would not be a French course.

By the end of the fourth week, we were reaching decision time. I didn't feel comfortable with what was happening in class A, and class B seemed to be learning just as much and just as effectively. What were we to gain if I turned students off French all in the name of my LIPT project? Thus it was at this point that we all sat down together, discussed what was happening, and agreed to end the project.

On Reflection

Perhaps our situation at Balaklava High is unique, in that our students can opt out the French course every ten weeks. This makes their feeling of security and sef-confidence paramount. The students clearly felt much more comfortable with a mixture of French and English in the classroom. They felt more in control, and I felt happier with that. My instincts had always led me use such a mixture, with the aim of increasing the use of French for instructions and so forth as time progressed.

What, then, did I learn from all this? I guess, overall, I learnt once again that I should trust my instincts, my own judgement and my experience to determine what works for me in the classroom. I have always felt that, as a partner in the learning exercise, I need to be sensitive to the group's needs and feelings. Hopefully, as a successful teacher, I harness that empathy, and use it to match course content and teaching methodology to the learners' needs and interests. What works for one teacher with one class in one school does not work for others in other situations, nor does it work in the same school for different classes, from year to year.

For me, with these classes, in this year, a mixture of French and English was the most effective way for them to learn. I will continue to aim to increase the use of French with those students who continue to progress through the course, but only by instinct. I will continue to try different things, remembering what works and what doesn't, and add them to my repertoire... but, overall, I have to ensure that the students feel secure and happy. If I don't achieve that, there will be no course, and no learning.

The Future

It may be interesting to note that, as always, the project generated other changes to my teaching, changes that were not part of the original plan. As I came to realise once again that I have to fully trust my own judgement in teaching, I gained the confidence to attempt something I've wanted to do for years. I HATE the *Tour de France* course and always felt it needed too much supplementation to keep students motivated. So, taking the bull by the horns, I offered both my Year 8 and Year 9/10 combination classes the opportunity to throw away the text book and choose themes for study by negotiation. It means a lot more work for me, and time spent finding material and preparing new worksheets, but it's paying off in enthusiasm. Both classes say they are enjoying lessons more, and an increased number would like to continue with French next year. For the survival of the subject, that seems vital. Now, if I could just convince the staff to make the first ten weeks of French compulsory, so that I could access a greater number of students to begin with...

References

Festina Lente, South Australian Education Department.

Tour de France, 1982, Scottish Central Committee on Modern Languages, Heinemann Educational Books, London.

Appendix 1

Survey

1. Le français, c'est ....

   horrible / ennuyeux / ça va / bien / extra / inutile / utile

2. La meilleure partie du français, c'est ....

   la conversation / les exercices / la vocab. / la musique /

   les romans / les journaux / l'ambience / autre _____

3. Je parle le français ....

   mal / ça va / bien / extra

4. Je sais .....

   rien / un peu / ça va / bien / beaucoup ... de vocab.

5. Mon abilité en français, c'est ....

   pas existent / pas bien / ça va / bien / extra

6. Je voudrais continuer le français après ce module ...

   oui / peut-être / non.   Merci

Appendix 2

L115

Devoirs   *A rendre mardi au plus tard*

Tâche un: Enregistrez sur la bande

Bonjour. Je m'appelle André(e). J'ai treize ans. J'habite à Pinery en Australie. Je suis australien(ne). Où habitez-vous? Vous êtes français, non? Voici mon ami Michel. Il a douze ans. Il est canadien. Il habite à Toronto au Canada. Voilà mon amie Suzi. Quel âge a-t-elle? Elle a treize ans. Elle est allemande. Vous aimez le poulet? Vous préférez le poulet ou les hamburgers? Le coca ou l'orangina? Moi, j'aime le pizza!   /20

Tâche deux: Traduisez en anglais.   /10

L115

Homework   *By Tuesday 21/5*

Task one: Record on the tape

Bonjour. Je m'appelle André(e). J'ai treize ans. J'habite à Pinery en Australie. Je suis australien(ne). Où habitez-vous? Vous êtes français, non? Voici mon ami Michel. Il a douze ans. Il est canadien. Il habite à Toronto au Canada. Voilà mon amie Suzi. Quel âge a-t-elle? Elle a treize ans. Elle est allemande. Vous aimez le poulet? Vous préférez le poulet ou les hamburgers? Le coca ou l'orangina? Moi, j'aime le pizza!   /20

Task two: Translate into English   /10

References

Allwright, D., and R. Lenzuen. 1997. Exploratory practice: Work at the Cultura Inglesa, Rio de Janeiro, Brazil. *Language Teaching Research* 1 (1): 73–79.

American Council on Teaching Foreign Languages (ACTFL). 1986. *ACTFL proficiency guidelines.* Hastings-on-Hudson, NY: Author.

Apple, M. 1986. *Teachers and texts: A political economy of class and gender relations in education.* New York: Routledge.

Bailey, K. et al. 1996. The language learner's autobiography: Examining the "apprenticeship of observation." In Freeman, D. and J. C. Richards (eds.), *Teacher learning in language teaching.* New York: Cambridge University Press. 11-29.

Baumann, J. 1996. Conflict or compatibility in classroom inquiry: One teacher's struggle to balance teaching and research. *Educational Researcher* 25 (7): 29–36.

Bazerman, C. 1988. *Shaping written knowledge: The genre and activity of the experimental article in science.* Madison, WI: University of Wisconsin Press.

Ben-Peretz, M. 1995. *Learning from experience: Memory and the teacher's account of teaching.* Albany, NY: State University of New York Press.

Berliner, D. 1988. *The development of expertise in pedagogy.* Washington, DC: American Association of Colleges for Teacher Education.

Boas, Franz. 1943. Recent anthropology. *Science* 98: 311–314, 334–337.

Boles, K., and M. Anderson. 1996. "Spanning Boundaries." Paper given at the American Educational Research Association.

Bullough, R. 1989. *First-year teacher: A case study.* New York: Teachers College Press.

Burns, A., and S. Hood. 1995. *Teachers' voices: Exploring course design in a changing curriculum.* Sydney, Australia: National Centre for English Language Teaching and Research.

Calkins, L. M. 1986. *The art of teaching writing.* Portsmouth, NH: Heinemann.

Calkins, L. M. 1983. *Lessons from a child: On the teaching and learning of writing.* Portsmouth, NH: Heinemann.

Cambone, J. 1990. Tipping the balance. *Harvard Educational Review* 60 (2): 217–236.

Carini, P. 1979. *The art of seeing and the visibility of the person.* University of North Dakota Press.

Carter, K. 1993. The place of story in the study of teaching and teacher education. *Educational Researcher* 22 (1): 5–12, 18.

Cazden, C. 1988. *Classroom discourse: The language of teaching and learning.* Portsmouth, NH : Heinemann.

Clark, C., and P. Peterson. 1986. Teachers' thought processes. In M. Wittrock (ed.), *Handbook of research on teaching* (3rd ed.). New York: Macmillan Publishing. 255–297.

Cochran-Smith, M., and S. Lytle (eds.). 1993. *Inside-outside: Teacher research and knowledge*. New York: Teachers College Press.

Cohen, E. 1986. *Designing group work: Strategies for the heterogeneous classroom*. New York: Teachers College Press.

Cronbach, L. 1975. Beyond the two disciplines of scientific psychology. *American Psychologist* 30 (2).

Cronbach, L., and P. Suppes (eds.) 1969. *Research for tomorrow's schools: Disciplined inquiry in education*. New York: Macmillan.

Day, R. 1990. Teacher observation in second language teacher education. In Richards, J. and D. Nunan (eds.), *Second language teacher education*. New York: Cambridge University Press. 43-61.

Denzin, N. K. (ed.). 1978. *Sociological methods: a source book*. New York: McGraw Hill.

Dewey, J. 1933. *How we think*. Buffalo NY: Prometheus Books.

Duckworth, E. 1987. The virtues of not knowing. In *The having of wonderful ideas and other essays on teaching and learning*. New York: Teachers College Press. 64–69.

Eisner, E. 1997. The promise and the perils of alternative forms of data representation. *Educational Researcher* 26 (6): 4–9.

Elbaz, F. 1992. Hope, attentiveness, and caring for difference: The moral voice of teaching. *Teaching and teacher education* 8 (5/6): 421–432.

Fanselow, J. 1977. Beyond Rashomon: Conceptualizing and observing the teaching act. *TESOL Quarterly* 11 (1): 17–41.

Fine, M. 1996. *Talking across boundaries: Participatory evaluation research in an urban middle school*. New York: City University of New York Press.

Fine, M. 1994. Working the hyphens: Reinventing self and other in qualitative research. In Denzin, N. and Y. Lincoln (eds.), *Handbook of qualitative research*. Thousand Oaks, CA: Sage. 70–83.

Fishman, J. 1982. Whorfianism of the third kind: Ethnolinguistic diversity as a world-wide societal asset. *Language in society* 11: 1–4.

Fleischer, C. 1995. *Composing teacher-research: A prosaic history*. Albany, NY: State University of New York Press.

Freedman, S., J. Jackson, and K. Boles. 1983. Teaching: an imperiled "profession." In Shulman, L. and G. Sykes (eds.), *Handbook of teaching and policy*. New York: Longman. 261–299.

Freeman, D. 1996. Redefining the relationship between research and what teachers know. In Bailey, K. and D. Nunan (eds.), *Voices from the language classroom*. New York: Cambridge University Press. 88–115.

Freeman, D. 1994. Educational linguistics and the knowledge-base of language teaching. In J. E. Alatis (ed.), *Georgetown University Roundtable on Languages and Linguistics 1994*. Washington DC: Georgetown University. 180–196.

Freeman, D. 1992. Collaboration: Constructing shared understandings in a second language classroom. In D. Nunan (ed.), *Collaborative Language Learning and Teaching*. Cambridge: Cambridge University Press. 56–80.

Freeman, D., and J. C. Richards (eds.). 1996. *Teacher learning in language teaching*. New York: Cambridge University Press.

Freeman, D. and J. Richards. 1993. Conceptions of teaching and the education of second language teachers. *TESOL Quarterly* 27(2): 193–216.

Fryling, K. Chico's story. Unpublished research memo, School for International Training.

Gallas, K. 1994. *The languages of learning: How children talk, write, dance, draw and sing their understanding of the world.* New York: Teachers College Press.

Gandhi, M. 1957. *An autobiography: The story of my experiments with truth.* Boston: Beacon Press.

Gattegno, C. 1976. *The commonsense of teaching foreign languages.* New York: Educational Solutions.

Geertz, C. 1980. Blurred genres: The reconfiguration of social thought. *American Scholar* 49.

Geertz, C. 1977. *Interpretation of cultures.* New York: Basic Books.

Genburg, V. 1992. Patterns and organizing perspectives: A view of expertise. *Teaching and Teacher Education* 8 (5/6): 485–496.

Graves, K. (ed.). 1996. *Teachers as course developers.* New York: Cambridge University Press.

Grossman, P. 1990. *The making of a teacher: Teacher knowledge and teacher education.* New York: Teachers College Press.

Halliday, M. A. K., and R. Hasan. 1989. *Language, context, and text: Aspects of language in social-semiotic perspective* (2nd ed.). Oxford: Oxford University Press.

Halkes, R., and J. Olson. 1984. *Teacher thinking: A new perspective on persisting problems in education.* Lisse, Netherlands: Swets and Zeitlinger.

Hawkins, D. 1967. I-thou-it. In *The Informed Vision: Essays and Learning and Human Nature.* New Jersey: Agathon Press. 48–62.

Heath, S. B. 1983. *Ways with words: Language, life, and work in communities and classrooms.* New York: Cambridge University Press.

Hochschild, A. R. 1997. There's no place like work. *New York Times Magazine* 20 (April): 51–55, 81, 84.

Hoganson, A. 1996. What does "knowing Spanish" mean? Unpublished research memo, School for International Training.

Hopkins, D. 1995. *A teacher's guide to classroom research* (2nd ed.). Philadelphia: Open University Press.

Howe, F. R., and R. C. Dougherty. 1993. Ethics, institutional review boards, and the changing face of educational research. *Educational Researcher* 22 (9): 16–20.

Hubbard, R., and B. Power. 1993. *The art of classroom inquiry.* Portsmouth, NH: Heinemann.

Hyon, S. 1996. Genre in three traditions: Implications for ESL. *TESOL Quarterly* 30 (4): 693–722.

Jackson, P. 1968. *Life in classrooms.* New York: Teachers College Press.

Johnson, K. and G. Johnson. 1998. *TeacherSource: Teachers understanding teaching.* Boston: Heinle and Heinle.

Kemmis, S., and R. McTaggart. 1995. *The action research planner* (rev. ed.). Geelong, Australia: Deakin University Press.

Kennedy, M. 1990. *A survey of recent literature on teachers' subject matter knowledge.* East Lansing, MI: National Center for Research on Teacher Learning.

Kerlinger, F. 1986. *Foundations of behavioral research* (3rd ed.). New York: Holt, Rinehart, and Winston.

Kincheloe. J. 1991. *Teachers as researchers: Qualitative inquiry as a path to empowerment.* London: Falmer Press.

Kirk, J., and M. Miller. 1986. *Reliability and validity in qualitative research.* Newbury Park, CA: Sage.

Levine, M. 1997 *Making professional development schools work: Politics, policy and practice.* New York: Teachers College Press.

Lightfoot, S. L. 1983. *The good high school: Portraits in character and culture.* New York: Basic Books.

Lincoln, Y., and E. Guba. *Naturalistic inquiry.* Newbury Park, CA: Sage.

Lipsky. M. 1980. *Street-level bureaucracy: Dilemmas of the individual in public service.* New York: Russell Sage.

Lortie, D. 1975. *Schoolteacher: A sociological study.* Chicago: University of Chicago Press.

MacDonald, J. 1992. *Teaching: Making sense of an uncertain craft.* New York: Teachers College Press

Malinowski, B. 1960. *A scientific theory of culture and other essays.* New York: Oxford University Press.

Marshall, C., and G. Rossman. 1989. *Designing qualitative research.* New York: Cambridge University Press.

Martin, J., F. Christie, and J. Rothery. 1987. Social processes in education: A reply to Sawyer and Watson (and others). In I. Reid (ed.), *The place of genre in learning: Current debates.* Geelong, Australia: Deakin University Press. 46–57

Marton, F. 1981. Phenomenography: Describing conceptions of the world around us. *Instructional Science* 10: 177–200.

Marton, F., and S. Booth. 1996. *Learning and awareness.* Mahwah, NJ: Lawrence Erlbaum.

Mathes, D. Doing pair work in a sixth-grade class. Unpublished research memo, School for International Training.

Maxwell, J. 1996. *Qualitative research design: An interactive approach.* Thousand Oaks, CA: Sage.

McDonough, J., and S. McDonough. 1997. *Research methods for English language teachers.* London: Arnold.

McLaughlin, D. and W. Tierney. 1993. *Naming silenced lives: Personal narratives and processes of educational change.* New York: Routledge.

Miles. M., and M. Huberman. 1984. *Qualitative data analysis* (1st ed.). Newbury Park, CA: Sage.

Miller, C. 1984. Genre as social action. *Quarterly Journal of Speech* 70: 151–167.

Mishler. E. 1990. Validation in inquiry-guided research: The role of exemplars in narrative studies. *Harvard Educational Review* 60: 415–442.

Monk, M. 1997. Cunningham and the Freedom in Precision. *New York Times,* The New Season/Dance (Sept 7, 1997): 13, 35.

Morrison, T. 1994. *Nobel lecture on literature.* New York: Alfred Knopf.

Mortimer, K. 1996. Adolescents, anxiety, and second language learning. Unpublished research memo, School for International Training.

Moss, P. 1994. Can there be validity without reliability? *Educational Researcher* 23 (2): 5–12.

Neuman, L. 1991. *Social research methods.* Boston: Allyn and Bacon.

Nunan, D. 1992. *Research methods in language learning.* New York: Cambridge University Press.

Paley, V. 1986. On listening to what children say. *Harvard Educational Review* 56 (2): 122–131.

Paley, V. 1990. *The boy who would be a helicopter: The uses of storytelling in the classroom.* Cambridge: Harvard University Press.

Paley, V. 1986. *Mollie is three: Growing up in school.* Chicago: University of Chicago Press.

Paley, V. 1981. *Wally's stories.* Cambridge: Harvard University Press.

Patton, M.Q. 1990. *Qualitative evaluation and research methods* (2nd ed.). Newbury Park, CA: Sage.

Pearson. A. 1989. *The teacher: Theory and practice in teacher education.* New York: Routledge.

Pike. K. 1967. *Language in relation to a unified theory of the structure of the human behavior.* The Hague: Mouton.

Schon, D. 1983. *The reflective practitioner: How professionals think in action.* New York: Basic Books.

Selinger, H., and E. Shohamy. 1989. *Second language research methods.* Oxford: Oxford University Press.

Shanker, A. 1996. Where we stand: An important question. *New York Sunday Times,* September 1, 1996, p. 7.

Shulman. L. 1988. The disciplines of inquiry in education: an overview. In R. Jager (ed.), *Complementary methods of research in education.* Washington DC: American Educational Research Association. 3–18.

Shulman, L. 1987. Knowledge-base and teaching: Foundations of the new reform. *Harvard Educational Review* 57 (1): 1–22.

Sizer, T. 1992. *Horace's school: Redesigning the American high school.* Boston: Houghton Mifflin.

Sizer, T. 1983. *Horace's compromise: The dilemma of the American high school.* Boston: Houghton Mifflin.

Smith, M.L. and L. Shepard. 1987. What doesn't work: Explaining policies of retention in early grades. *Phi Delta Kappan,* 69 (October, 1987): 129-134.

Stern, H.H. 1983. *Fundamental concepts of language teaching.* Oxford: Oxford University Press.

Stevick, E. 1980. *Teaching languages: A way and ways.* Rowley, MA: Newbury House.

Strauss, A. 1987. *Qualitative analysis for social scientists.* New York: Cambridge University Press.

Stringer. E. 1996. *Action research: A handbook for practitioners.* Thousand Oaks, CA: Sage.

Suppes, P. (ed.). 1978. *Impact of research on education.* Washington DC: National Academy of Education.

Swales, J. 1990. *Genre analysis: English in academic and research settings.* New York: Cambridge University Press.

van Lier, L. 1994. Educational linguistics: Field and project. In J. E. Alatis (ed.), *Georgetown University Roundtable on Languages and Linguistics 1994.* Washington DC: Georgetown University. 197–209.

van Lier, L. 1988. *The classroom and the language learner.* London: Longman.

Wilson, S. 1995. Not tension but intention: A response to Wong's analysis of the researcher/teacher. *Educational Researcher* 24 (89): 19–22.

Wolcott, H. 1994. *Transforming qualitative data: Description, analysis, and interpretation.* Thousand Oaks, CA: Sage.

Wong, D. 1995. Challenges confronting the researcher/teacher: Conflicts of purpose and conduct. *Educational Researcher* 24 (3): 22–28.

Zeichner, K., and D. Liston. 1996. *Reflective teaching: An introduction.* Mahwah, NJ: Lawrence Erlbaum.